Advanced Information and Knowledge Processing

T0191838

K.C. Tan, E.F. Khor and T.H. Lee

Multiobjective Evolutionary Algorithms and Applications

With 183 Figures

 Springer

K.C. Tan, PhD, BEng
E.F. Khor, PhD, BEng
T.H. Lee, PhD, BEng

Department of Electrical and Computer Engineering,
National University of Singapore, Republic of Singapore

Series Editors
Xindong Wu
Lakhmi Jain

British Library Cataloguing in Publication Data
Tan, K. C.
  Multiobjective evolutionary algorithms and applications. –
  (Advanced information and knowledge processing)
  1. Computer algorithms 2. Evolutionary computing
  3. Mathematical optimization
  I. Title II. Khor, E. F. III. Lee, T. H.
  005.1

Library of Congress Cataloging-in-Publication Data
A catalog record for this book is available from the Library of Congress

AI&KP ISSN 1610-3947
ISBN 978-1-84996-935-2   e-ISBN 978-1-84628-132-7
Springer is a part of Springer Science+Business Media
springeronline.com

34/3830-543210 Printed on acid-free paper

Preface

Many real-world design tasks involve optimizing a vector of objective functions on a feasible decision variable space. These objective functions are often non-commensurable and in competition with each other, and cannot be simply aggregated into a scalar function for optimization. This type of problem is known as the multiobjective (MO) optimization problem, for which the solution is a family of points known as a Pareto optimal set, where each objective component of any member in the set can only be improved by degrading at least one of its other objective components.

The multiobjective problems are often difficult to solve without the aid of powerful and efficient optimization algorithms. To obtain a good solution via conventional multiobjective optimization techniques such as the methods of inequalities, goal attainment or weighted sum approach, a continuous cost function and/or a set of precise settings of weights or goals are required, which are usually not well manageable or understood. Moreover, these algorithms usually give only a single solution at the end of each run, instead of finding the entire Pareto optimal set for the multiobjective optimization.

Emulating the Darwinian–Wallace principle of "survival-of-the-fittest" in natural selection and adaptation, evolutionary algorithms evaluate performances of candidate solutions at multiple points simultaneously. Unlike conventional methods that often combine multiple attributes to form a composite scalar objective function, multiobjective evolutionary algorithms (MOEAs) incorporate the concept of Pareto's optimality or modified selection schemes to evolve a family of solutions at multiple points along the tradeoffs simultaneously. They have been found to be very efficient and effective in solving sophisticated multiobjective problems where conventional optimization tools fail to work well.

The purpose of this book is to provide a comprehensive treatment on the design and application of multiobjective evolutionary algorithms. It emphasizes both the theoretical developments and practical implementations of multiobjective evolutionary algorithms without the requirement of profound mathematical knowledge. The text has been written for a wide readership and can be read by engineers, researchers, senior undergraduates and graduate students who are interested in the field of evolutionary algorithms and multiobjective optimization. The assumed background for the book is some basic knowledge of evolutionary computation.

The book is organized into two parts. The first part, consisting of nine chapters, covers the theory and development of multiobjective evolutionary algorithms. The second part contains five chapters and provides a number of practical applications of evolutionary multiobjective optimization.

Chapter 1 gives the definition of multiobjective problem and the background of multiobjective optimization. Chapter 2 presents a survey and highlights the development trends of multiobjective evolutionary algorithms. Chapter 3 provides a conceptual framework for evolutionary multiobjective optimization and studies the effect of various distribution preservation mechanisms. Chapter 4 introduces a goal-sequence domination scheme that allows specifications such as hard/soft priorities and constraints to be incorporated for better decision support in multiobjective optimization. Besides, a few advanced features for multiobjective evolutionary algorithms are also presented in the chapter.

The concept of dynamic population size in multiobjective evolutionary algorithms is discussed in Chapter 5. Chapter 6 presents the idea of cooperative coevolution and distributed computing for multiobjective optimization. A new deductive approach of dynamic search space incorporating inductive learning for evolutionary multiobjective optimization is presented in Chapter 7. The performance comparisons of various multiobjective evolutionary algorithms are given in Chapter 8. Chapter 9 presents a graphical user interface-based multiobjective evolutionary algorithm toolbox for interactive computer-aided multiobjective optimization. A number of case studies including control system designs and vehicle routing problems are presented in Chapters 10 through 14, which illustrate the practical applications of multiobjective evolutionary algorithms.

Finally, we are very grateful to a number of current and former graduate students, especially Y.J. Yang, C.K. Goh, Y.H. Chew, and R. Sathikannan, for their contributions to this book.

National University of Singapore   K. C. Tan
National University of Singapore   E. F. Khor
National University of Singapore   T. H. Lee

July 2004

Contents

1
Introduction

Many real-world design tasks involve the search of a vector of optimal design variables to maximize/minimize certain design qualities based upon a scalar objective function. For instance, in control engineering, engineers are often involved in the task of finding the most suitable controller parameters in order to achieve the best performance in a control system. In some cases, however, the quality of the system performance may not be quantifiable as a simple objective function since the design quality may reflect different aspects of specifications that may be competing or noncommensurable to each other. To sustain the design quality, each objective function needs to be considered explicitly in the search of a set of optimal design variables.

For example, instead of concerning only one aspect of control performance such as tracking error of system responses, different aspects of performances reflecting the desired control quality can be considered. These specifications include fast system response, small steady-state error, good robustness, low implementation cost, and so on (Fonseca and Fleming 1994; Chipperfield and Fleming 1995; Tan and Li 1997; Liu and Mills 1998; Thompson and Fleming 1999). This type of problem is known as a multiobjective (MO) optimization problem. Instead of combining the various competing objective functions, each of the functions is treated separately in the optimization process, and the solution is a family of points known as the Pareto optimal set, where each objective component of any point along the Pareto front can only be improved by degrading at least one of its other objective components (Goldberg and Richardson 1987; Horn et al. 1994; Srinivas and Deb 1994).

1.1 Definition

The phrase "multiobjective optimization" is synonymous with "multivector optimization," "multicriteria optimization," or "multiperformance optimization" (Coello Coello 1998). Osyczka (1985) defines multiobjective optimization as a problem of finding:

A vector of decision variables which satisfies constraints and optimizes a vector function whose elements represent the objective functions. These functions form a mathematical description of performance criteria which are usually in conflict with each other. Hence, the term "optimize" means finding such a solution which would give the values of all the objective functions acceptable to the designer.

Consider a minimization problem; it tends to find a set of P for

$$\min_{P \in \Phi} F(P), \ P \in R^n, \tag{1.1}$$

where $P = \{p_1, p_2, \ldots, p_n\}$ is an n-dimensional vector having n decision variables or parameters and Φ defines a feasible set of P. $F = \{f_1, f_2, \ldots, f_m\}$ is an objective vector with m objective components to be minimized, which may be competing or noncommensurable to each other. For the performance comparisons among various algorithms, Keeney and Raiffa (1976) provide a number of desirable properties of the test functions. In short, the objective functions should be

1. Complete so that all pertinent aspects of the decision problem are presented.
2. Operational in that they can be used in a meaningful manner.
3. Decomposable if desegregation of objective functions is required or it is desirable.
4. Nonredundant so that no aspect of the decision problem is considered twice.
5. Minimal such that there is no other set of objective functions capable of representing the problem with a smaller number of elements.

Pareto Dominance

In the total absence of information regarding the preference of objectives, Pareto dominance can be used to assess the relative strength or fitness between any two candidate solutions in MO optimization (Steuer 1986; Fonseca and Fleming 1993). The concept has been widely adopted in the research of MO optimization since it was proposed by Pareto (1896). Without loss of generality, an objective vector F_a in a minimization problem is said to dominate another objective vector F_b, denoted by $F_a \prec F_b$, *iff*

$$f_{a,i} \leq f_{b,i} \ \forall \ i \in \{1, 2, \ldots, m\} \ \text{and} \ f_{a,j} < f_{b,j} \ \exists j \in \{1, 2, \ldots, m\}. \tag{1.2}$$

Local Pareto Optimal Set

If there exists no solution P_i in a set ψ, dominating any member P_j in a set Ω, where $\Omega \subseteq \psi \subseteq \Phi$, then Ω denotes a local Pareto optimal set. The symbol Ω refers to a Pareto optimal set found at each iteration or at the end of the optimization in a single run. The "Pareto optimal" solutions are also termed "noninferior," "admissible," or "efficient" solutions (Horn 1997). Their corresponding objective vectors are termed "nondominated" (Van Veldhuizen and Lamont 1999).

Global Pareto Optimal Set

If there exists no solution P_i in the feasible set Φ, dominating any member P_k in a set Γ, where $\Gamma \subseteq \Phi$, then Γ denotes the global Pareto optimal set. Since $\Omega \subseteq \Phi$, it is always true that there is no solution P_j in a local Pareto optimal set, Ω, dominating any solution P_k in the global Pareto optimal set, Γ. The symbol Γ refers to the actual Pareto optimal set for MO optimization. It can be obtained from the solutions of objective functions concerning the space of Φ or approximated through many repeated optimization runs.

Pareto Front and Its Structure

According to (Van Veldhuizen and Lamont 2000), for a given MO optimization function $F(P)$ and Pareto optimal set Ω, the Pareto front PF^* is defined as

$$PF^* = \{F(P) = (f_1(P), f_2(P), \cdots, f_m(P)) \mid P \in \Omega\}. \tag{1.3}$$

Concerning the structure of a Pareto front, Horn and Nafpliotis (1993) state that the Pareto front is an $(m - 1)$-dimension surface in an m-objective optimization problem. Van Veldhuizen and Lamont (1999) later point out that the Pareto front for MO optimization with the number of objectives $m = 2$ is at most a (restricted) curve and is at most a (restricted) $(m - 1)$-dimension surface when $m \geq 3$.

Totally Conflicting, Nonconflicting, and Partially Conflicting Objective Functions

For any MO optimization problem, the objective functions can be categorized as totally conflicting, nonconflicting, or partially conflicting. In a given solution set Φ, a vector of objective functions $F = \{f_1, f_2, \ldots, f_m\}$ is said to be totally conflicting if there exist no two solutions P_a and P_b in the set Φ such that $(F_a \prec F_b) \vee (F_b \prec F_a)$. No optimization is needed for this class of MO problems since the solution set Φ already represents the global Pareto optimal solutions, i.e., $\Gamma = \Phi$.

On the other hand, the objective functions are said to be nonconflicting if any two solutions P_a and P_b in a set Φ satisfy the condition of $(F_a \prec F_b) \vee (F_b \prec F_a)$. This class of MO problems can be easily converted into single-objective problems, either by arbitrarily considering only one of the objective components during the optimization or by combining the multiple objectives into a scalar function. Therefore, any improvement for one objective component will lead to the improvement of the remaining objective components, and vice versa. The size of the global or local Pareto optimal set is equal to one for this class of MO problems.

If an MO optimization problem belongs to neither the first class nor the second, then it belongs to the third class of partially conflicting objective functions. In this case, a vector of objective functions $F = \{f_1, f_2, \ldots, f_m\}$ is said to be partially conflicting if there exist nonempty sets P_a and P_b such that $(F_a \prec F_b) \vee (F_b \prec F_a)$. Note that many real-world design optimization tasks belong to this class of MO problems, where a set of Pareto optimal solutions representing the tradeoffs among the conflicting objectives are desired.

Example of an MO Problem

Consider a two-objective optimization problem FON (Fonseca and Fleming 1993), where the two functions, f_1 and f_2, to be minimized are given as

$$f_1(x_1,...,x_8) = 1 - \exp\left(-\sum_{i=1}^{8} \left(x_i - \frac{1}{\sqrt{8}} \right)^2 \right),$$ (1.4a)

$$f_2(x_1,...,x_8) = 1 - \exp\left(-\sum_{i=1}^{8} \left(x_i + \frac{1}{\sqrt{8}} \right)^2 \right),$$ (1.4b)

where $-2 \le x_i < 2$, $\forall\ i = 1,2,...,8$. According to (1.4), there are eight parameters, $x_1,...,x_8$, to be determined such that f_1 and f_2 are minimum.

The tradeoff curve is shown in Fig. 1.1, where the shaded area represents the infeasible region in the objective domain. As shown in the figure, the solutions A and B constitute the nondominated solutions. However, the solution C is a dominated solution since there exists a solution B that is better than C for both the objectives of f_1 and f_2.

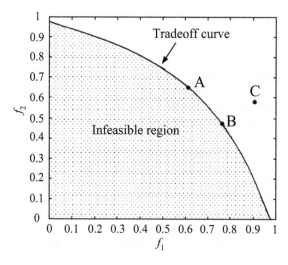

Fig. 1.1. Tradeoff curve in the objective domain.

1.2 Multiobjective Optimization

In MO optimization, a specific and compromised decision is often needed based upon the set of tradeoff solutions. The final solution for the MO optimization thus results from both the process of optimization and decision making, which can be defined as (Hwang and Masud 1979): (1) priori preference articulation: This method transforms the MO problem into a single-objective problem prior to the optimization; (2) progressive preference articulation: Decision and optimization are intertwined where partial preference information is provided upon which optimization occurs; (3) posteriori preference articulation: A set of efficient candidate solutions is found from a certain method and then a decision is made on the choice of the best solution.

The priori preference articulation transforms the MO problem into a single-objective problem. Certain knowledge of the problem at hand is often required in order to employ such a technique. Generally, single-objective optimization approaches can only provide, in the best case, a single Pareto optimal solution at the end of each simulation. A representative part of the Pareto set is then sampled by repeatedly running the algorithm with a different vector of weights each time (Lahanas et al. 2003). Such an optimization approach is often sensitive to the objective weights, and thus it is difficult to find a good approximation to the entire Pareto front efficiently. The single-objective, weighted-sum approach for a two-objective problem (Lahanas et al. 2003) is given as $y = w_1 f_1(x) + w_2 f_2(x)$, i.e. $f_2(x) = -(w_1 / w_2) f_1(x) + y / w_2$, where w_1 and w_2 are the weight values for f_1 and f_2, respectively. The minimization of the weighted sum can be interpreted as finding the value of y such that the line with a slope of $-w_1 / w_2$ touches the Pareto front as it proceeds outward from the origin. Therefore, this approach cannot find any tradeoff solutions that are located on the nonconvex part of the Pareto front (Coello Coello 1998; Deb 2001).

The use of multiobjective evolutionary algorithms (MOEAs) in posteriori preference articulation has been gaining significant attention over the years. This can be reflected by the significantly increased number of related publications in the literature as well as the success of the international conference series on evolutionary multicriterion optimization (EMO). As stated by Corne et al. (2003), single-objective approaches are almost invariably unwise simplifications of the real problem and fast and effective techniques are now available, capable of finding a well-distributed set of diverse tradeoff solutions, with little or no more effort than sophisticated single-objective optimizers would have taken to find a single one. The diversity of ideas resulting from evolutionary MO optimization gives the problem-solver a better view of the space of possible solutions, and consequently a better final solution to the problem at hand.

In the optimization process of posteriori preference articulation, the aim is to find as many Pareto optimal solutions as possible. Deb (2001) points out two important issues in MO optimization: (1) to find a set of solutions as close as possible to the Pareto front; (2) to find a set of solutions as diverse as possible. As stated by Zitzler and Thiele (1999), it is also important to maximize the spread of the obtained nondominated front in MO optimization, i.e., for each objective a wide range of values should be covered by the nondominated solutions.

A number of survey papers on MOEAs are available in the literature, such as Fonseca and Fleming (1995a); Coello Coello (1996, 1998); Bentley and Wakefield (1997); Horn (1997); Van Veldhuizen and Lamont (2000); Tan et al. (2002a). In particular, Coello Coello (1998) classifies the various techniques into three main groups based upon the different implementation strategies in cost assignment and selection method, and Tan et al. (2002a) discuss the algorithms in terms of the feature elements representing the basis of MO handling tools in evolutionary algorithms.

1.3 Preview of Chapters

The book is organized into two parts. The first part, comprising Chapters 1 through 9, covers the theory and development of multiobjective evolutionary algorithms. The second part, Chapters 10 through 14, provides a number of practical applications of evolutionary MO optimization.

Chapter 2 gives a survey and discusses the development trends of MOEAs. The general algorithm structures for various MOEAs are also described to provide a better insight of their implementations. Since most MOEAs exhibit common characteristics, a conceptual framework for evolutionary multiobjective optimization is presented in Chapter 3. The effects of different distribution preservation mechanisms in MOEAs are also examined in the chapter.

Chapter 4 presents a goal-sequence domination scheme for better decision support in MO optimization. Besides the usual goal and priority information, it allows the accommodation of advanced specifications, such as soft/hard constraints and multiple sets of goals and priorities. A few advanced features for MOEAs are also discussed in the chapter, including a dynamic sharing scheme that adapts the sharing radius according to the online population distribution, a switching preserved strategy that ensures the evolutionary search diversity and stability, and a convergence representation for MO optimization by means of population domination.

Chapter 5 studies the concept of dynamic population size that is computed adaptively according to the online discovered tradeoff surface and the desired population distribution density. Chapter 6 presents a cooperative coevolutionary algorithm (CCEA) for MO optimization, which evolves multiple solutions in the form of cooperative subpopulations. It applies an archive to store nondominated solutions and evaluates individuals in the subpopulations based on Pareto dominance. Since multiple subpopulations are evolved in CCEA simultaneously, a computing structure suitable for parallel processing where the computational workload of CCEA can be shared among multiple computers over the network is also presented in the chapter.

Without the requirement of fixing the range of parameter values in evolutionary algorithms, Chapter 7 presents a deductive approach of dynamic search space with inductive learning for MOEAs. Chapter 8 gives an extensive performance comparison of various MOEAs based upon 10 benchmark MO problems with different characteristics and challenges. Besides considering the usual two important aspects of MO performance, i.e., the spread across Pareto optimal front and the ability to attain the final tradeoffs, a few other measures are also adopted for the performance comparisons in the chapter.

Chapter 9 presents an interactive graphical user interface-based MOEA toolbox for computer-aided MO optimization. To use the toolbox, the problem-solver merely needs to provide a simple "model" file that specifies the objective function corresponding to his or her particular optimization problem. Other aspects such as decision variable settings, optimization process monitoring, or graphical results analysis can be performed easily via the embedded GUIs in the toolbox. Chapter 10 presents an evolutionary performance-prioritized computer-aided control system design (CACSD) methodology. Advantages of the evolutionary CACSD approach are illustrated upon an MIMO ill-conditioned distillation system, which offers a set of low-order Pareto optimal controllers satisfying all the conflicting performance requirements in the face of system constraints and uncertainties.

Chapter 11 presents an MOEA-based automated design methodology for quantitative feedback theory (QFT) control systems, which can evolve both the nominal controller and prefilter simultaneously to meet the usually conflicting performance requirements without going through the sequential and conservative design stages for each of the multivariable subsystems. It is shown that such an evolutionary design approach avoids the need of QFT bound computation as well as the usual trial-and-error loop-shaping design procedures in QFT.

Chapter 12 presents the evolutionary design and implementation of a robust two-degree-of-freedom servo system for physical 3.5-inch hard disk drive with a single voice-coil-motor actuator. Besides the simplicity in controller structure, such an evolutionary servo design approach is capable of meeting various performance specifications in both the time and frequency domains. It is shown that the servo system optimally moves the magnetic head onto the desired track with minimal control effort and keeps it on the track robustly against plant uncertainties or runout disturbances.

Chapter 13 presents the application of MOEAs in solving vehicle routing problem with time window constraints (VRPTW). The VRPTW is inherently a sequence-oriented MO problem that involves the optimization of routes for multiple vehicles in order to minimize a set of objectives like traveling distance and number of vehicles simultaneously. Chapter 14 studies the transportation problem of moving empty or laden containers for a logistic company. A mathematical model for such a truck and trailer vehicle routing problem (TTVRP) is constructed, and a hybrid MOEA is employed to minimize the routing distance and the number of trucks required, subject to a number of constraints such as time windows and availability of trailers.

2
Review of MOEAs

2.1 Introduction

In the early stage of MO optimization, multiple objectives are usually linearly combined into a scalar objective via a predetermined aggregating function to reflect the search for a particular solution on the tradeoff surface (Jakob et al. 1992; Wilson and Macleod 1993). The whole tradeoff is then discovered by repeating the process numerous times with different settings for the aggregating function. The drawback to this approach is that the weights are difficult to determine precisely, especially when there is insufficient information or knowledge concerning the optimization problem. Other objective reduction methods include the use of penalty functions (Adeli and Cheng 1994) and the reduction of MO into a single objective (Ritzel et al. 1994). As mentioned by Coello Coello (1996), these conventional MO optimization approaches often have the disadvantage of missing the concave portions of a tradeoff curve.

Unlike conventional methods, evolutionary algorithms evaluate performances of candidate solutions at multiple points simultaneously, which have been shown to be very suitable for solving MO optimization problems. The origins of evolutionary algorithms can be traced back to the late 1950s, and since the 1970s several evolutionary methodologies have been proposed. Schaffer (1985) proposed a vector evaluated genetic algorithm (VEGA) that treats the multiple objectives separately in the evolution in order to generate a set of nondominated solutions in a single run. Although this method is simple to implement, it only managed to find certain extreme solutions along the Pareto front. Moreover, the process of shuffling and merging of all subpopulations in the approach is similar to fitness averaging for each of the objective components (Richardson et al. 1989).

Extending from VEGA, Lis and Eiben (1997) proposed a multisexual genetic algorithm (MSGA) where each individual has an additional feature of sex or gender, and only one individual from each sex is used in the recombination. There are as many sexes as the optimization criteria, and each individual is evaluated according to the optimization criteria related to its sex. The method was generalized from Allenson (1992) where only male–female mating is allowed and such a gender is assigned randomly at birth. Another variant of VEGA includes the approach of randomizing weights, which applied a modified selection scheme to select individuals extended from a weighted sum of the MO functions (Hajela and Lin 1992; Fourman 1985). In such an approach, the weights attached to the MO functions are not constant but vary for each of the reproduction operations.

By using preference relationship, Fourman (1985) ranked each objective component according to its relative importance in the optimization problem. Another approach is based on the transformation of noncrisp (qualitative specifications) relationships among the objectives into quantitative attributes (number) for an appropriate weight of each objective in a way similar to the linguistic ranking methods (Chen et al. 1992; Cvetkovic and Parmee 1998). With certain similarity, Greenwood et al. (1996) propose a compromise between no preference information (in the case of pure Pareto ranking) and aggregation methods such as the weighted-sum approach. They extend the concept of Pareto dominance by elements of imprecisely specified multi-attribute value theory in order to incorporate preference in MO optimization. Goldberg (1989a) suggests the Pareto-based fitness assignment scheme as a means of assigning equal probability of reproduction to all nondominated individuals in a population. The approach has several variants, such as multiobjective genetic algorithm (MOGA) (Fonseca and Fleming 1993), nondominated sorting genetic algorithm (NSGA) (Srinivas and Deb 1994), niched Pareto genetic algorithm (NPGA) (Horn et al. 1994), nongenerational evolutionary algorithm (Valenzuela-Rendón and Uresti-Charre 1997), strength Pareto evolutionary algorithm (SPEA) (Zitzler and Thiele 1999), incrementing multiobjective evolutionary algorithm (IMOEA) (Tan et al. 2001c), and so on.

2.2 Survey of MOEAs

In this section, various MOEAs are reviewed based on different perspectives from the existing surveys in the literature. Instead of classifying the various approaches into different classes, Table 2.1 shows a list of MOEAs and their frequently used feature elements. The labels "1" in the table represent ownership of the corresponding elements (columnwise) under the corresponding techniques (row-wise). These feature elements are divided into two major groups according to their functionalities, i.e., MO handling elements and supporting elements. The first category contains elements that provide immediate usefulness for finding the nondominated set in MO optimization, including *Weights*, *Min-Max*, *Pareto*, *Goals*, *Pref*, *Gene*, *Sub-Pop*, *Fuzzy*, and *Others*. On the other hand, the second category of elements plays an indirect role of supporting the algorithms, including *Dist*, *Mat*, *Sub-Reg*, *Ext-Pop*, *Elitism*, and *A-Evo*. The description for these two categories of elements is given in Table 2.2 and Table 2.3, respectively.

It can be observed that some of the feature elements are common to a number of techniques, as shown in Table 2.1. At the same time, there exist several algorithms that apply more than one element of MO handling techniques and/or supporting operators. This suggests that it is not easy to classify MOEAs into different distinct classes, e.g., any attempts to do this may lead to an imprecise classification where the intersections among different classes are neglected. The

MOEAs are thus described here in terms of their feature elements representing the basis of MO handling tools as well as the way that these feature elements are integrated into the algorithms.

Table 2.1. Basic Elements in MOEAs (Continued on Next Page)

MOEAs	Weights	Min-Max	Pareto	Goals	Pref	Gene	Sub-Pop	Fuzzy	Others	Dist	Mat	Sub-Reg	Ext-Pop	Elitism	A-Evo
Charnes & Cooper (1961)				1											
Ijiri (1965)				1											
Jutler (1967)	1	1													
Solich (1969)	1	1													
Fourman (1985)					1										
Schaffer (1985): VEGA							1								
Goldberg & Richardson (1987)			1												
Allenson (1992)							1								
Chen et al. (1992)	1				1										
Hajela & Lin (1992): HLGA	1						1			1	1				
Jakob et al. (1992)	1														
Fonseca & Fleming (1993): MOGA			1	1	1					1	1				
Wilson & Macleod (1993)					1										
Adeli & Cheng (1994)	1														
Horn et al. (1994): NPGA			1							1					
Ritzel et al. (1994)	1								1						
Srinivas & Deb (1994): NSGA			1							1					
Sandgren (1994)					1										
Murata & Ishibuchi (1995): MIMOGA	1												1	1	
Vemuri & Cedeño (1995)	1														
Coello Coello (1996): Monte Carlo I	1	1										1			
Coello Coello (1996): Monte Carlo II		1	1							1					
Greenwood et al. (1996)			1		1					1					
Kita et al. (1996)			1												
Sakawa et al. (1996)				1				1							
Viennet et al. (1996)								1						1	
Bentley & Wakefield (1997): SWR	1														
Bentley & Wakefield (1997): SWGR	1														
Bentley & Wakefield (1997): WAR	1														
Lis & Eiben (1997): MSGA							1								
Marcu (1997)			1	1											
Fujita et al. (1998)			1							1	1				
Jaszkiewicz (1998)	1						1						1		
Laumanns et al. (1998)							1								
Voget & Kolonko (1998)			1					1							
Cvetkovic & Parmee (1999)	1				1										
Hiroyasu et al. (1999)			1	1			1			1					
Knowles & Corne (1999): PAES			1							1		1		1	
Romero & Manzanares (1999): MOAQ									1						
Sait et al. (1999)					1			1							
Tagami & Kawabe (1999)			1							1		1			
Tan et al. (1999b): MOEA			1		1					1				1	
Zitzler & Thiele (1999): SPEA			1							1				1	1

Table 2.1. (Continued) Basic Elements in MOEAs

MOEAs	Weights	Min-Max	Pareto	Goals	Pref	Gene	Sub-Pop	Fuzzy	Others	Dist	Mat	Sub-Reg	Ext-Pop	Elitism	A-Evo
Andrzej & Stanislaw (2000)		1													
Corne et al. (2000): PESA			1							1		1	1		
Khor et al. (2000): IMOEA			1	1	1					1				1	
Knowles & Corne (2000b): M-PAES			1									1	1	1	
Mariano & Morales (2000): MDQL			1						1						
Rekick et al. (2000)					1										
Sefrioui & Periaux (2000)									1						
Abbass et al. (2001): PDE			1							1				1	1
Coello Coello & Pulido (2001): μGA			1							1		1	1	1	1
Corne et al. (2001): PESA-II			1									1	1	1	
Jin et al. (2001): EDWA	1												1	1	
Khor et al. (2001b): EMOEA			1	1	1					1			1	1	
Mao et al. (2001)			1					1							
McMullen (2001)			1									1			
Molyneaux et al. (2001): CPEA			1							1					
Sakawa & Yauchi (2001)		1		1				1					1	1	
Sbalzarini et al. (2001)			1	1									1	1	
Thierens & Bosman (2001)			1							1					
Zhao et al. (2001): PESM			1											1	
Zitzler et al. (2001): SPEA2			1							1			1	1	
Abbass (2002): SPDE			1							1				1	1
Coello Coello & Cortés (2002): MISA			1									1	1		1
Coello Coello & Lechuga (2002)			1							1		1	1		
Cvetkovic & Parmee (2002)					1			1							
Deb et al. (2002a): NSGA-II			1							1				1	
Esquivel et al. (2002)	1						1								
Everson et al. (2002): ESPEA			1							1			1	1	
Kadrovach et al. (2002): MMOSGA									1	1	1				
Keerativuttiumrong et al. (2002)			1				1			1					1
Khan N et al. (2002): MBOA			1							1				1	
Khan JA et al. (2002): BLFSE	1						1								1
Lu & Yen (2002a): RDGA			1								1	1		1	
Lu & Yen (2002b): DMOEA			1							1	1				
Madavan (2002)			1							1				1	1
Socha & Kisiel-Dorohinicki (2002)			1							1					1
Coello Coello & Becerra (2003): CAEP			1									1	1	1	
Kiyota et al. (2003): TSMC		1		1			1			1				1	
Knowles & Corne (2003): AGA			1							1				1	
Li X (2003)							1								1
Luh et al. (2003): MOIA			1							1					1
Pulido & Coello Coello (2003): μGA2			1									1	1	1	
Schütze et al. (2003)			1							1				1	1
Number of Occurrences	18	6	45	14	11	3	7	8	6	34	6	12	17	27	12
Frequency (%)	8	2.6	20	6.2	4.9	1.3	3.1	3.5	2.7	15	2.7	5.3	7.5	12	5.3

Table 2.2. MO Handling Elements in MOEAs

Label	Description
Weights	Multiple objectives are combined into scalar objective via a weight vector. Weights may be assigned through direct assignment, eigenvector method, entropy method, minimal information method, randomly determined or adaptively determined. It is difficult to precisely predetermine the weights. If the objective functions are simply weighted and added to produce a single fitness, the function with the largest range would dominate the evolution. A poor input value for the objective with a larger range makes the overall value much worse than a poor value for the objective with a smaller range (Bentley and Wakefield 1997). It suffers the disadvantage of missing concave portions of the tradeoff curve (Coello Coello 1996).
Min-Max	It uses the distance between an efficient design and a predefined ideal design. It attempts to find from the feasible domain an efficient design that is nearest to the ideal design in terms of the "min-max." It is capable of discovering all efficient solutions for an MO problem regardless if the problem is convex or nonconvex.
Pareto	It uses Pareto dominance scheme defined in (1.2) for fitness assignment and comparison of individuals in a population. The fitness assignment and comparison results will influence the process of selection and reproduction in the evolution.
Goals	It requires a set of goal settings that indicates the objective values to be attained in the optimization. It adopts the decision rule that the best compromise design should be the one that minimizes the deviation from the set of goals.
Pref	It requires a set of preferences/priorities for the objectives. It adopts the decision-rule that objectives with a higher priority are given a higher privilege to be optimized than those with a lower priority.
Gene	Chromosome and genes not only store information of decision variables or parameter values, but also influence the way that the fitness/cost assignment is performed for each individual. The genes can be either altered stochastically through a normal/special evolution process or assigned through a deterministic rule.
Sub-Pop	The main population is divided into several subpopulations where each subpopulation is optimized based on similar/different selection criteria. If different selection criteria are applied, it may refer to either the different objective components or the utility function of the objectives. The process of shuffling and merging of all subpopulations in the approach is similar to fitness averaging for each of the objective components (Richardson et al. 1989). If gender is applied to classify the population, a relatively large population size with a substantial computational effort is required in order to maintain a reasonably diverse spread of genders across the entire population (Coello Ceollo 1998).
Fuzzy	Fuzzy rules and fuzzy membership functions are applied to combine the multiple objectives and to handle the vague terms of the user specifications. The resulting fuzzy reasoning process is then used in the selection process.
Others	Any MO handling elements that are different from the above approaches.

Table 2.3. Supporting Elements in MOEAs

Label	Description
Dist	It involves explicit operators to distribute individuals in the space of either phenotype or genotype. This includes fitness sharing (Deb and Goldberg 1989), niching (Beasley et al. 1993), crowding (De Jong 1975), clearing (Pétrowski 1996), clustering (Zitzler and Thiele 1999), and others.
Mat	The crossover is restricted between any two "similar" individuals (based on a certain metric or the Euclidean distance) in order to reduce the number of unfit offspring resulting from mating among any arbitrary pairs of individuals, which could highly decrease the Pareto optimal solutions.
Sub-Reg	The phenotype or genotype space is divided into predefined regions in order to keep track of the degree of crowding in the space.
Ext-Pop	Besides the evolving population, an external population is applied to store the nondominated solutions obtained along the evolution. It is also called archive in some literatures.
Elitism	The Pareto optimal solutions are preserved and updated at each generation. In some methods, the diversity and uniform distribution are also taken into consideration for updating the nondominated individuals.
A-Evo	Atypical evolution from the standard evolution process. For instance, co-evolution, differential evolution, immune system, simulated evolution, agent-based evolution, microGA, etc.

2.3 Development Trends

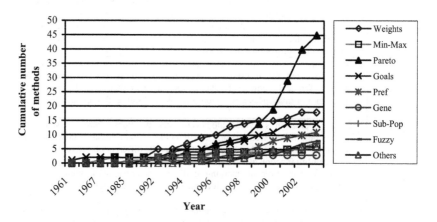

Fig. 2.1. Development trends of MO handling elements.

Based on the data in Table 2.1, Fig. 2.1 illustrates the development trends of MO handling elements over the years. The *y*-axis represents the cumulative number of methods applying the corresponding MO handling elements and the *x*-axis represents the year instances. As can be seen, the MO handling element of *goals* and *fuzzy* is among the earliest and the latest approaches, respectively. It can also be observed that the elements of *Min-Max, Gene, Sub-Pop, Fuzzy,* and *Others* have received less interest as compared to the elements of *Pareto, Weights, Goals,* and

Pref. Among the latter set of elements, *Weights* has attracted significant attention from 1985 to 1997, while the popularity of *Pareto* as an MO handling element continues to grow significantly over the years.

The development trends of supporting elements are depicted in Fig. 2.2. As can be seen, the supporting elements were developed more recently (since 1992) as compared to the MO handling elements (since 1961). Among the supporting elements, distribution operator (*Dist*) that helps to distribute individuals along the tradeoffs is the most popular element over the years, which is followed by the element of *Elitism* that assists to preserve good solutions at each generation.

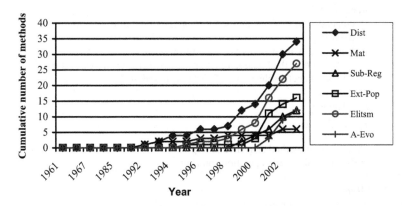

Fig. 2.2. Development trends of supporting elements.

2.4 Outline of Algorithms

In this section, eight popular MOEAs with various feature elements in handling MO optimization problems and maintaining population distribution on the tradeoff surface are described. The general structures for these algorithms are also presented to provide better insights on their implementations.

i. Vector Evaluated Genetic Algorithm (VEGA)

The vector evaluated genetic algorithm (VEGA) is proposed by Schaffer (1985). Based on the GENESIS program (Grefenstette 1984) as a simple genetic algorithm (SGA), Schaffer extends the way selections are performed to handle multiple objectives in a single run. The basic structure of VEGA is illustrated in Fig. 2.3, and the algorithm process flow is shown in Fig. 2.4. Given the number of optimization objectives as m and a fixed population size as P, m subpopulations each having P/m individuals are randomly formed from the population *Pop*. For $i = 1$ to m, each individual in subpopulation i is then evaluated based on the objective function i. The selected individuals from each subpopulation are shuffled and grouped together to form a new population of size P, which is followed by the genetic operations of crossover and mutation. The whole process is repeated in the next generation until a predetermined stopping criterion is met. This algorithm is among the first in the field that inspires researchers to explore the possibility of searching for multiple nondominated solutions in a single evolutionary process.

Initialize generation counter: $n = 0$.
Create a population, *Pop*.
Repeat while stopping criterion is not met.
    Initialize subpopulation counter: $i = 1$.
    Repeat while $i \le m$.
        Generate i th subpopulation, *SubPop*(i), by randomly selecting P/m individuals from *Pop*.
        Remove any individuals *SubPop*(i) from *Pop*.
        Generate the i th objective function values, $F(i)$, for individuals in *SubPop*(i).
        Perform genetic selection on *SubPop*(i) based on $F(i)$.
        $i = i + 1$.
    End Repeat
    $Pop = \bigcup_{i=1}^{m} SubPop(i)$.
    Shuffle the individual sequence in *Pop*.
    Perform usual genetic operations on *Pop*.
    $n = n + 1$.
End Repeat
Evaluate *Pop* for all objective function values, $F(\forall\ i)$.
Return (*Pop*, $F(\forall\ i)$, …).

Fig. 2.3. Main loop of VEGA.

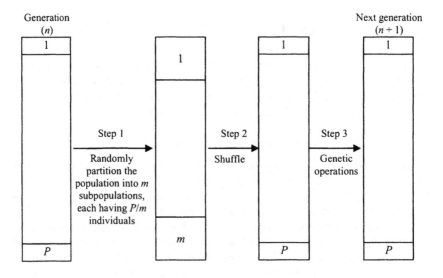

Fig. 2.4. Process flow of VEGA.

ii. Multiobjective Genetic Algorithm (MOGA)

Fonseca and Fleming (1993) propose the multiobjective genetic algorithm (MOGA) with a Pareto ranking scheme that assigns the same smallest rank value for all nondominated individuals, while the dominated individuals are ranked according to how many individuals in the population are dominating them. The rank of an individual i in a population is thus given as

$$\text{rank}(i) = 1 + q_i, \tag{2.1}$$

where q_i is the number of individuals that dominate individual i in the objective domain. Fonseca and Fleming (1998a) extend the domination scheme in MOGA to include goal and priority information for MO optimization. The underlying reason is that certain user knowledge may be available for an optimization problem, such as preference on certain objective components, optimization constraints, or approximated attainable regions of the tradeoffs. Subsequently the fitness of an individual i is computed by implementing a mapping inversely related to rank(i). Without loss of generality, let the fitness of individual i be

$$\text{fit}(i) = \text{inver}(\text{rank}(i)), \tag{2.2}$$

which should satisfy the following condition:

$$(\text{rank}(i) < \text{rank}(j)) \Leftrightarrow (\text{fit}(i) > \text{fit}(j)). \tag{2.3}$$

The obtained fitness value f will then be degraded based upon a sharing function (Goldberg 1989a; Fonseca and Fleming 1998a) according to the distribution density in the feature space in order to distribute the individuals in a population uniformly along the Pareto front. Consider a population containing P individuals, $X_1, X_2, ..., X_P, X_i \in U_1 \times U_2 \times ... \times U_m \, \forall \, i = 1, 2, ..., P$, in an m-dimensional feature space S (in the objective or parameter domain); the metric distance between any two individuals, i and j, is defined as

$$d(X_i, X_j) = \| X_i - X_j \|_2 , \tag{2.4}$$

where $\| \cdot \|_2$ implies the 2-norm. The amount of sharing contributed by each individual X_i into its neighboring individual X_j is determined by their proximity in the feature space based upon the distance $d(X_i, X_j)$ and the sharing distance σ_{share}, which is given as

$$SF(i, j) = \begin{cases} 1 - [d(X_i, X_j) / \sigma_{\text{share}}]^\alpha & \text{if } d(X_i, X_j) < \sigma_{\text{share}}, \\ 0 & \text{otherwise}, \end{cases} \tag{2.5}$$

where α is a parameter that regulates the shape of the sharing function (Goldberg 1989a). The sharing distance σ_{share} determines the extent of sharing allowed in terms of the radius distance. With the sharing information, the shared fitness of any individual i is given as

$$\text{fit}'(i) = \text{sharing}(\text{fit}(i), S) = \frac{\text{fit}(i)}{\sum_{j=1}^{P} \text{SF}(i, j)} \quad , \tag{2.6}$$

where S is the feature space for which the sharing is performed.

Figure 2.5 illustrates the basic algorithm structure of MOGA, which adopts the mechanism of ranking and fitness sharing as compared to SGA. Initially, a population of P new individuals is created and evaluated according to the multiple objective functions. This is followed by ranking the individuals, computing the fitness values, and performing fitness sharing to obtain the shared fitness values. Based upon the shared fitness values, a series of genetic operations, such as selection, crossover, and mutation, are applied to evolve for a new population. The whole process is repeated in the next generation until a predetermined stopping criterion is met.

```
Initialize generation counter: n = 0.
Create a population, Pop.
Repeat while stopping criterion is not met.
    Evaluate Pop for all objective function values, F.
    Based on (2.1), compute rank value rank(i) for each individual.
    Based on (2.2), compute fitness value fit(i) for each individual.
    Based on (2.6), compute shared fitness fit'(i) for each individual.
    Perform genetic selection on Pop based on the shared fitness.
    Perform genetic crossover and mutation on Pop with or without mating restriction.
    n = n + 1.
End Repeat
Evaluate Pop for all objective function values, F.
Based on (2.1), compute rank value rank(i) for each individual. Let rank = {rank(i): ∀
i = 1,...,P}.
Based on (2.2), compute fitness value fit(i) for each individual.
Based on (2.6), compute shared fitness fit'(i) for each individual.
Return (Pop, F, rank, ...).
```

Fig. 2.5. Main loop of MOGA.

In some applications, mating restriction (Deb and Goldberg 1989) is applied in MOGA (Fonseca and Fleming 1995b), where only pairs of individuals lie within a distance of σ_{mate} between each other in the feature space are allowed for mating. This is to reduce the number of unfit offspring resulting from the mating among any arbitrary pairs of individuals, which could highly decrease the Pareto optimal solutions. The MOGA has been widely cited and applied to solve a number of practical applications (Schroder et al. 1997; Fonseca and Fleming 1998b; Thompson et al. 1999).

iii. Aggregation by Variable Objective Weighting (HLGA)

This approach makes use of weighted-sum aggregation of the multiobjective functions to search for a set of nondominated solutions. It is labeled as HLGA (Hajela–

Lin genetic algorithm), which is proposed by Hajela and Lin (1992). Instead of Pareto ranking as applied in MOGA, the weighted-sum method is used for fitness assignment in this approach. Each objective is assigned a weight $w_j = [0,1]$ for the jth objective such that $\sum w_j = 1$, and the scalar fitness value fit(i) for an individual i is calculated by summing up the scaled weighted objective values as given below:

$$\text{fit}(i) = \sum_{j=1}^{m} w_j \cdot \frac{f_j(i)}{f_j^*}, \tag{2.7}$$

where f_j^* is a scaling parameter for the jth objective, which needs to be chosen properly for each objective f_j in order to cater for the difference in magnitudes for the various objective functions. To search for multiple solutions in parallel, the weights are not fixed but are encoded in the genotype and concatenated with the rest of the parameters to form a chromosome. The diversity of the weight combinations is subsequently promoted by a sharing function performed in the space S_w of the weighting variables. The shared fitness is given as

$$\text{fit}'(i) = \text{sharing}(\text{fit}(i), S_w) = \frac{\text{fit}(i)}{\sum_{j=1}^{P} \text{SF}(i,j)}. \tag{2.8}$$

The sharing function SF follows the definition of (2.5), where the metric distance is computed in the space S_w of the weighting variables. Let individual i be X_i = $[X_{W,i}, X_{1,i}, X_{2,i}, ..., X_{n,i}]$ and individual j be $X_j = [X_{W,j}, X_{1,j}, X_{2,j}, ..., X_{n,j}]$ for $(1+n)$ parameters. For each individual, the first parameter represents the weight combination and the rest contributes to the m objective values. For simplicity, X_W can be in the type of "integer" on a one-to-one mapping with different countable combination of weights w. For instance, given a two-objective optimization problem with 9 different weighting combinations $[w_1 = 0.1, w_2 = 0.9]$, $[w_1 = 0.2, w_2 = 0.8]$, ..., and $[w_1 = 0.9, w_2 = 0.1]$, the weighting variables can be defined as, X_W = $(1, 2, ..., 9) = ([0.1, 0.9], [0.2, 0.8], ..., [0.9, 0.1])$. The distance metric for a pair of individuals, i and j, is computed according to the variables representing the weight combinations,

$$d(X_i, X_j) = \| X_{W,i} - X_{W,j} \|_2. \tag{2.9}$$

With an appropriate setting of sharing distance σ_{share}, sharing can be applied to direct the genetic search toward finding the optimal individuals corresponding to the distributed weight combinations in order to obtain a set of dispersed individuals along the tradeoffs. Figure 2.6 depicts the basic algorithm structure of HLGA. It can be observed that the overall structure of HLGA is similar to MOGA, except for the part of computing the fitness value and the shared fitness. Unlike the approach of Pareto ranking in MOGA, a weighted-sum approach with sharing performed in the space of weighting variables is adopted in HLGA. The mating restriction, as explained in the approach of MOGA, can also be applied in HLGA for better stability in the genetic search.

Initialize generation counter: $n = 0$.
Create a population, *Pop*, with one additional parameter as a weighting variable for each individual.
Repeat while stopping criterion is not met.
　　Evaluate *Pop* for all objective function values, *F*.
　　Based on (2.7), compute fitness value fit(i) for each individual.
　　Based on (2.8), compute shared fitness fit'(i) for each individual.
　　Perform genetic selection on *Pop* based on the shared fitness.
　　Perform genetic crossover and mutation on *Pop* with or without mating restriction.
　　$n = n + 1$.
End Repeat
Evaluate *Pop* for all objective function values, *F*.
Based on (2.7), compute fitness value fit(i) for each individual.
Based on (2.8), compute shared fitness fit'(i) for each individual.
Return (*Pop*, *F*, fit($\forall$ i), …).

Fig. 2.6. Main loop of HLGA.

iv. Niched Pareto Genetic Algorithm (NPGA)

A salient feature of the niched Pareto genetic algorithm (NPGA) is the integration with a special tournament selection scheme based on Pareto dominance (Horn and Nafpliotis 1993). In general, tournament selection involves the process of randomly selecting a set of individuals from the population and choosing the best of the set for reproduction. To control the amount of selection pressure, and hence the convergence speed, the tournament size of the set can be adjusted. For example, a smaller tournament size often results in less selection pressure and thus a lower convergence speed. In order to search for the nondominated solutions and to maintain the distribution of individuals along the Pareto front, Horn and Nafpliotis (1993) modified the tournament selection by applying Pareto dominance and sharing (instead of fitness value) as the selection criterion. Since Pareto dominance is the key element in this type of selection, it is given the name of Pareto dominance tournaments.

Figure 2.7 illustrates the working process of the Pareto dominance tournaments. Given two candidate individuals *Ind1* and *Ind2*, and a comparison set *CompSet* of other t_{dom} individuals randomly selected from the population, the function "Pdom-Tour" of Pareto dominance tournaments returns a selected individual (either *Ind1* or *Ind2*) based on the Pareto dominance tournaments as proposed by Horn and Nafpliotis (1993). When both *Ind1* and *Ind2* are dominated or nondominated based on Pareto dominance in comparison to the *CompSet*, sharing is utilized to further differentiate the two individuals in order to prevent the effect of "genetic drift" that may cause individuals converging to only a portion of the tradeoff surface. Instead of two competing individuals, a number of other individuals or the comparison set are picked from the population at random for helping to determine the dominance of the individuals. Like the tournament size in a standard tournament selection scheme, t_{dom} can be adjusted to achieve a suitable dominance pressure (or selection pressure in a wider context).

Figure 2.8 illustrates the algorithm skeleton of NPGA that utilizes the routine of Pareto dominance tournaments (PdomTour). As can be seen, the structure of NPGA is rather similar to MOGA and NPGA, except for the way that individuals are selected for reproduction.

v. Nondominated Sorting Genetic Algorithm II (NSGA-II)

Deb et al. (2002a) propose the NSGA-II as an improved version of their previous NSGA (Srinivas and Deb 1994), which has a simpler computational complexity for nondominated sorting, elitism, and parameter setting requirement for maintaining the distribution of individuals. Two major subroutines have been proposed in NSGA-II, namely fast nondominated sorting for population sorting based on Pareto dominance and crowding distance assignment for calculating the density measure.

```
Function (SelInd) = PDomTour(Ind1, Ind2, CompSet)
    Ind1_dominated = FLASE.
    Ind2_dominated = FALSE.
    If Ind1 is dominated by any individual from CompSet, then
        Ind1_dominated = TRUE.
    Endif
    If Ind2 is dominated by any individual from CompSet, then
        Ind2_dominated = TRUE.
    Endif
    If Ind1_dominated == Ind2_dominated
        Based on (2.6), compute shared fitness fit'(Ind1) for individual Ind1.
        Based on (2.6), compute shared fitness fit'(Ind2) for individual Ind2.
        If fit'(Ind1) > fit'(Ind2)
            SelInd = Ind1.
        Else If fit'(Ind1) < fit'(Ind2)
            SelInd = Ind2.
        Else
            SelInd = [ ].
        End If
    Else
        If Ind1_dominated == FALSE
            SelInd = Ind1.
        Else
            SelInd = Ind2.
        End If
    End If
    Return (SelInd).
End Function
```

Fig. 2.7. Function of "PdomTour" for Pareto dominance tournaments.

Initialize generation counter: $n = 0$.
Create a population, *Pop*.
Repeat while stopping criterion is not met.
    Evaluate *Pop* for all objective function values, **F**.
    SelPop = [ ].
    Repeat while individuals in *SelPop* is not full.
        TempPop = Pop.
        *Ind*1 = a randomly selected individual from *TempPop*.
        Remove *Ind*1 from *TempPop*.
        *Ind*2 = a randomly selected individual from *TempPop*.
        Remove *Ind*2 from *TempPop*.
        CompSet = t_{dom} randomly selected individuals from *TempPop*.
        SelInd = PDomTour(*Ind*1, *Ind*2, *CompSet*).
        If *SelInd* is not [ ]
            Add individual *SelInd* to *SelPop*.
        End If
    End Repeat
    Pop = SelPop.
    Perform genetic crossover and mutation on *Pop*.
    $n = n + 1$.
End Repeat
Return (*Pop*, …).

Fig. 2.8. Main loop of NPGA.

Function (rank) = FNDomSort(*Pop*)
    Repeat for each solution *i* in *Pop*.
        n_i is the number of solutions dominating the individual *i*.
        S_i is a set of individuals dominated by individual *i*.
    End Repeat
    Q = set of individuals in *Pop* with $n_i = 0$.
    CurRank = 0.
    Repeat while Q is not [ ].
        R = [ ].
        CurRank = CurRank + 1.
        Repeat for each individual *i* in Q.
            rank(*i*) = *CurRank*.
            Repeat for each solution *j* in set S_i.
                $n_j = n_j - 1$.
                If $n_j == 0$
                    Put individual *j* in R.
                End If
            End Repeat
        End Repeat
        $Q = R$.
    End Repeat
    Return (rank).
End Function

Fig. 2.9. Function of "FNDomSort" for fast nondominated sorting.

a. Fast Nondominated Sorting

As shown in Fig. 2.9, fast nondominated sorting is generally a partial sorting approach to determine the rank value for each individual in the population. First, all individuals are compared with each other to obtain the information of n_i and S_i for each individual i in the population Pop. With this information, looping is performed for each level of nondominated front on which the nondominated individual i will possess n_i equal to 0 until no further individual for the following level is found. In terms of the number of dominance comparisons, this sorting approach was claimed to have the overall complexity of $O(MP^2)$, where M is the number of objective components and P is the population size.

b. Crowding Distance Assignment

The sharing function in NSGA was replaced by crowded distance assignment in NSGA-II to eliminate the difficulties of (1) sensitivity to the setting of σ_{share} value for maintaining the spread of solutions and (2) the overall complexity of $O(N^2)$ for the sharing scheme (Goldberg 1989a). Figure 2.10 depicts the routine of crowded distance assignment (CrwdDA), which returns a density estimate called the crowding distance ($CDtc$) for each individual in the interested population (Pop). The measure of crowding distance is generally based on the average distance of two individuals on either side of an individual along each of the objectives. In order to compute the value of crowding distance for crowded distance assignment, the population Pop is sorted according to each objective component in an ascending order.

Function $(CDtc)$ = CrwdDA(Pop)

$\quad F(i,j)$ = the normalized j^{th} objective function of individual i in population Pop.

$\quad f_j^{\max}$ = max($F(i,j)$: $\forall i = 1, 2, ..., P$).

$\quad f_j^{\min}$ = min($F(i,j)$: $\forall i = 1, 2, ..., P$).

$\quad P$ = number of individuals in Pop.

$\quad CDtc(i) = 0, \forall i = 1, 2, ..., P$.

$\quad$**Repeat** for each objective j.

$\qquad Idx$ = index vector based on the sorting of vector $[F(i,j)$: $\forall i = 1, 2, ..., P]$.

$\qquad CDtc(Idx(1)) = CDtc(Idx(P)) = \infty$.   % Boundary points are always selected

$\qquad$**Repeat** for each individual i from 2 to $(P - 1)$.

$\qquad\quad CDtc(Idx(i)) = CDtc(Idx(i)) +$

$\qquad\qquad [F(Idx(i + 1), j) - F(Idx(i - 1), j)]/(f_j^{\max} - f_j^{\min})$.

$\qquad$**End Repeat**

$\quad$**End Repeat**

$\quad$**Return** $(CDtc)$.

End Function

Fig. 2.10. Function of "CrwdDA" for crowding distance assignment.

For each objective component, the first and the last individual in the respective sorted list are assigned an infinite distance value. For the rest of individuals, the distance is equal to the normalized absolute difference of the objective function values between two adjacent individuals. This computation is repeated for other objective components, and the crowding distance is calculated as the sum of individual distance corresponding to each objective component. Obviously, an individual with a larger crowding distance is regarded as less crowded by other individuals. As the complexity of this crowded distance assignment is governed by the sorting algorithm, the distance assignment procedure has a computational complexity of $O(MP\log P)$.

Subsequently, the criterion of selecting an individual from two competing individuals is similar to NPGA (Horn and Nafpliotis 1993), except that crowding distance assignment is applied in NSGA-II instead of the sharing method. Here two individuals are first compared based on their rank values and the one with a smaller rank (more dominating capability) is preferred. If both form a tie, then the comparison will be based on the crowding distance and the one with a larger distance is preferred. This comparison scheme is called crowded comparison operator.

c. General Structure of NSGA-II

Initialize generation counter: $n = 0$.
Create a parent population, *Ppop* of size *P*.
Initialize offspring population as *Opop* = [ ]
Repeat while stopping criterion is not met.
    Cpop = *Ppop* $\cup$ *Opop*.
    rank = FNDomSort(*Cpop*).
    Ppop = [ ].
    rankP = the rank value of *P* th individual in *Cpop* sorted in ascending order of *rank*.
    Ppop = individuals from *Cpop* with the rank < *rankP*.
    PpopSize = number of individuals in *Ppop*.
    Tpop = individuals from *Cpop* with rank value of *rankP*.
    CDtc = CrwdDA(*Tpop*).
    Ppop = *Ppop* $\cup$ {(*P*-*PpopSize*) individuals with the largest *CDtc*}.
    Opop = genetic_operators(*Ppop*).
    $n = n + 1$.
End Repeat
Return (*Ppop*, *Opop*, …).

Fig. 2.11. Main loop of NSGA-II.

Figure 2.11 provides the overall structure of NSGA-II incorporating the fast nondominated sorting (FNDomSort) and crowding distance assignment (CrwdDA). First, the parent population *Ppop* (self-created in the first generation) is combined with offspring population *Opop* (empty in the first generation) to form *Cpop*, taking a population size of *P* in the first generation (since *Opop* is initially empty) and 2*P* in the next generation. Subsequently, *P* individuals are selected from *Cpop* according to the selection criteria used in the crowded comparison operator, and the selected individuals are pooled in *Ppop*. At this stage, the fast nondominated sorting and crowding distance assignment are used in the algorithm. Standard genetic operators, such as selection, crossover, and mutation, are then applied on *Ppop* to generate an offspring population *Opop*. The whole process is repeated in the next generation until a predetermined stopping criterion is met.

vi. Strength Pareto Evolutionary Algorithm 2 (SPEA2)

Zitzler et al. (2001) propose the SPEA2 to address the potential weaknesses of their previous SPEA (Zitzler and Thiele 1999). In SPEA, two population sizes with P for the population and P' for the archive are involved. At each generation, the nondominated individuals in P are copied to the archive and any dominated individuals in the archive are removed. If the individuals in the archive exceed a predefined threshold, the archive will be pruned by means of clustering. In SPEA, individuals in the archive are ranked with reference to the members of the population, while individuals in the population are evaluated with reference to the members of the archive. Fitness sharing is also included in SPEA where niches are not defined in terms of distance but are based on Pareto dominance.

The SPEA2 is an improved version of SPEA with the following changes: (1) a fitness assignment strategy that incorporates density information and considers for every individual regarding how many other individuals it dominates or dominated by; (2) a fixed archive size (in SPEA, the size of archive may vary over time), i.e., the archive is filled up with dominated individuals whenever the number of nondominated individuals is less than the predefined archive size; and (3) replacement of clustering with an alternative truncation method that has similar features but does not lose the boundary points.

The general structure of SPEA2 is depicted in Fig. 2.12. At each generation, fitness values are assigned to individuals in the population *Pop* and the archive *Arc* that is empty in the first generation. All the nondominated individuals in *Pop* and *Arc* are then stored in a temporary population (*TempArc*), which will be truncated if the number of nondominated individuals in the *TempArc* exceeds a predefined size of P'. However, if the size of *TempArc* is less then P', it will be filled up by dominated individuals with high fitness values from *Pop* and *Arc*. Subsequently, all the new archived individuals in *TempArc* will be stored in *Arc* and the genetic operations such as selection, recombination, and mutation will be applied on *Arc* to generate the offspring in *Pop*. When the stopping criterion is met, the evolution will be terminated and the latest individuals in the *Arc* will be returned.

In the fitness assignment, each individual i in the archive *Arc* and population *Pop* is assigned the value of $S(i)$ defined as

$$S(i) = |\{ j | j \in Arc \cup Pop \text{ and } i \text{ dominates } j \}|, \tag{2.10}$$

where $|\,.\,|$ denotes the cardinality of a set. Based on the S value, the raw fitness $R(i)$ of an individual i is defined by the strength of its dominators as given by

$$R(i) = \sum\nolimits_{j \in Arc \cup Pop, \; j \text{ dominates } i} S(j). \tag{2.11}$$

Subsequently, density estimation is applied to any individuals with identical raw fitness values. In SPEA2, the density estimation of an individual i is defined as

$$D(i) = \frac{1}{d_i^k + 2},$$
(2.12)

where d_i^k is the distance of individual i to its kth nearest neighbor. The summation of $D(i)$ and $R(i)$ gives the overall fitness of $F(i)$, which is used in the process of removing any extra individuals from the archive or filling up the archive with other individuals.

Initialize generation counter: $n = 0$.
P = size of internal population.
P' = size of archive.
Generate an initial population Pop of size P.
Generate an empty archive $Arc = [\ ]$.
Repeat while stopping criterion is not met.
    Calculate fitness values of individuals in Pop and Arc.
    $TempArc$ = {all nondominated individuals in $Arc \cup Pop$}.
    If size of $TempArc > P'$
        Truncate $TempArc$ to size P' based on fitness values.
    Else If size of $TempArc < P'$
        Fill the empty space in $TempArc$ with individuals in Arc and Pop based on fitness values.
    End If
    $Arc = TempArc$.
    If stopping criterion is not met
        Apply genetic operators on Arc and store the offspring in Pop.
        $n = n + 1$.
    End If
End Repeat
Return $(Arc, \ldots)$.

Fig. 2.12. Main loop of SPEA2.

vii. Pareto Archived Evolution Strategy (PAES)

The PAES is proposed as a local search approach for MO optimization of an off-line routing problem (Knowles and Corne 1999), which is later applied to solve a broad range of problems (Knowles and Corne 2000a). Figure 2.13 provides the general structure of a (1+1)-PAES. As can be seen, the algorithm is composed of three elements, i.e., the candidate individual (C) generator, the candidate individual acceptance function, and the archive (Arc). The function of candidate individual C generator is similar to a simple mutation or hill climbing for the current individual, while the Arc is applied as a pool to explicitly store good individuals in order to maintain the spread of the Pareto front. Figure 2.14 illustrates the heuristic reasoning of function test(C, M, Arc), which is applied to accept or reject the mutant individual M as well as to decide if the individual should be archived. The idea is to check the attribute of Pareto dominance and/or the degree of crowding of the mutant individual M in comparison with the current individual C and the archive Arc before the C and Arc are updated.

Initialize iteration counter: $n = 0$.
Generate an empty archive $Arc = [\ ]$.
Generate an initial current individual C.
$Arc = Arc \cup \{C\}$.
Repeat while stopping criterion is not met.
    Mutate C to produce an offspring M.
    If C dominates M
        Discard M.
    Else If M dominates C
        Replace $C = M$.
        $Arc = Arc \cup \{M\}$.
    Else If M is dominated by any individual in Arc
        Discard M.
    Else
        $(C, M, Arc) = \text{test}(C, M, Arc)$.
    End If
    $n = n + 1$.
End Repeat
Return $(Arc, \ldots)$.

Fig. 2.13. Main loop of (1+1)-PAES.

Function $(C, M, Arc) = \text{test}(C, M, Arc)$.
    If Arc is not full
        $Arc = Arc \cup \{M\}$.
        If M is in a less crowded region of Arc than C
            $C = M$.
        End If
    Else
        If M is in a less crowded region of Arc than X for some members in Arc
            $Arc = Arc\ /\ \{\text{a member of } Arc \text{ from the most crowded region}\}$.
            $Arc = Arc \cup \{M\}$.
            If M is in a less crowded region of Arc than C
                $C = M$.
            End If
        Else
            If M is in a less crowded region of Arc than C
                $C = M$.
            End If
        End If
    End If
    Return (C, M, Arc).
End Function

Fig. 2.14. Heuristic reasoning in test(C, M, Arc).

To compare the degree of crowding in any interested regions, a crowding procedure that recursively divides the m-dimension objective space is adopted in PAES. In this procedure, the grid location for each generated individual is determined in the objective space. A map of the grid is also maintained in order to indicate the number of individuals residing at each grid location. With the aid of the map, individual A is said to be in a less crowded region than B if A's grid location has a smaller number of individuals than that of B's grid location. The (1+1)-PAES was later generalized to $(\mu+\lambda)$-PAES having μ current individuals and λ mutants (Knowles and Corne 2000a), i.e., λ mutants are generated by mutating current individuals chosen via tournament selection.

viii. Pareto Envelope-based Selection Algorithm (PESA)

Initialize generation counter: $n = 0$.
P = size of internal population $Ipop$.
P' = size of archive Arc.
Generate an initial $Ipop$ of size P.
Generate an empty archive Arc = [ ].
Repeat while stopping criterion is not met.
    Arc = {all nondominated individuals in $Arc \cup Ipop$}.
    If size of $Arc > P$'
        Truncate Arc to size P' based on squeeze factor in crowding strategy.
    End If
    If stopping criterion is not met
        $Ipop$ = [ ].
        Repeat until $Ipop$ reaches the size of P.
            With probability p_c, select two parents from Arc based on squeeze factor in crowding strategy, which is followed by crossover and mutation to reproduce an offspring for $Ipop$.
            With probability $(1 - p_c)$, select one parent from Arc based on squeeze factor in crowding strategy and mutate it to reproduce an offspring for $Ipop$.
        End Repeat
        $n = n + 1$.
    End If
End Repeat
Return $(Arc, \ldots)$.

Fig. 2.15. Main loop of PESA.

Corne et al. (2000) propose the PESA by incorporating ideas from both SPEA and PAES. The outline of the PESA is given in Fig. 2.15. Similar to SPEA, the PESA has two populations consisting of an internal population $Ipop$ (labeled as IP in the original literature) and an external population or archive Arc (labeled as EP in the original literature). Like PAES, the PESA uses a hypergrid division in the objective space to keep track of the degree of crowding (or squeeze factor), which is simply the number of individuals at different hypergrid locations of the archive Arc. The attribute of the squeeze factor is then utilized to select individuals from the *Arc* for maintaining population diversity in the objective domain. The squeeze factor is also applied to remove any extra nondominated individuals in the *Arc*.

2.5 Conclusions

This chapter has presented an introduction to the historical developments of MOEAs, with a comprehensive review based on different perspectives from the existing surveys in literature. Instead of classifying the MOEAs into different classes, the algorithms have been discussed in terms of their feature elements representing the basis of MO handling tools as well as the way that these feature elements have been integrated. Subsequently, the development trends of various feature elements in MOEAs over the years have been shown, including the MO handling elements and supporting elements. The trends have revealed that the *Pareto* has achieved the highest growth among the various MO handling elements since 1999, while the distribution operator (*Dist*) for distributing individuals along the tradeoffs has been the most popular supporting element over the years. Finally, eight popular MOEAs have been described and the general structures of these algorithms have been presented to provide better insights on their implementations.

3
Conceptual Framework and Distribution Preservation Mechanisms for MOEAs

3.1 Introduction

Many variants of MOEAs have been proposed and implemented in the literature. For example, VEGA (Schaffer 1985), MOGA (Fonseca and Fleming 1993), HLGA (Hajela and Lin 1992), NPGA (Horn et al. 1994), MOEA (Tan et al. 2001a), and so forth, work on a single population, while SPEA (Zitzler and Thiele 1999), SPEA-2 (Zitzler et al. 2001), PAES (Knowles and Corne 2000a) and so on, involve an external population or memory for storing the nondominated individuals. Nevertheless, most of the evolutionary techniques for MO optimization exhibit common characteristics that can be represented in a framework, as will be presented in this chapter. The chapter also studies the characteristics of various distribution preservation mechanisms in MOEAs, which are an important feature for distributing nondominated individuals on the discovered tradeoff surface.

3.2 A Conceptual Framework

A conceptual framework for MOEAs is shown in Fig. 3.1. The MOEAs were originated from single-objective evolutionary algorithms (Goldberg 1989a) in the sense that both approaches involved the iterative updating of a set of individuals until a prespecified optimization goal or stopping criterion is met. A series of processes including individual assessment and genetic operations are performed at each generation in order to improve adaptability of population in the given test environment. In many evolutionary algorithms, elitism is applied to preserve the best individuals at each generation for good convergence. Besides, archiving is also incorporated in some MOEAs to keep the best individuals at each generation, but without involving them in generating the offspring as in the approach of elitism. Overall the MOEAs differ from single-objective evolutionary algorithms mainly in the process of individual assessment and elitism/archiving. Since archiving is a subfunction of elitism (as it applies the same concept of elitism to preserve the best individuals but without involving these individuals for reproduction), only the individual assessment and elitism are further discussed in the following subsections.

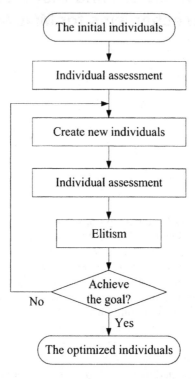

Fig. 3.1. The framework of MO evolutionary algorithms.

3.2.1 Individual Assessment

In order to evolve the population toward the global tradeoff as well as to diversify the individuals uniformly on the discovered tradeoff surface, the individual assessment scheme in MOEAs should be designed in such a way that a pressure (denoted as $\bar{P}_n$ in Fig. 3.2) is exerted to promote the individuals in a direction normal to the tradeoff region and another pressure (denoted as $\bar{P}_t$ in Fig. 3.2) tangentially to that region is induced at the same time. These two pressures, which are normally orthogonal to each other, give a unified pressure for the assessment (denoted as $\bar{P}_u$ in Fig. 3.2) that directs the evolutionary search in the context of MO optimization. A number of MOEAs such as MIMOGA (Murata and Ishibuchi 1995), MSGA (Lis and Eiben 1997), and VEGA (Schaffer 1985), implement the $\bar{P}_u$ directly in the assessment. For example, MIMOGA applies the random assignment of weights on each individual to exert the $\bar{P}_u$ that is varied for each individual. Although these approaches are simple, they usually do not allow good control on the direction of the exerted $\bar{P}_u$. For other MOEAs, the $\bar{P}_n$ and $\bar{P}_t$ are often implemented explicitly in different feature elements, and one of the widely used MO assessment techniques for exerting the $\bar{P}_n$ is Pareto dominance (Goldberg and Richardson 1987).

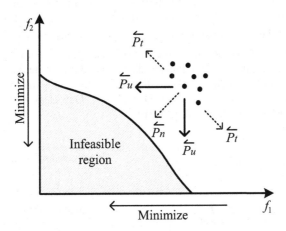

Fig. 3.2. The improvement pressures in MO optimization.

Although the use of Pareto dominance has shown its effectiveness for attaining the final tradeoffs in MO optimization (Fonseca and Fleming 1993; Horn et al. 1994; Srinivas and Deb 1994), it does not encourage distribution of individuals on the discovered tradeoff surface. As shown by Fonseca and Fleming (1995b), individuals in a population tend to converge to arbitrary portions of the discovered tradeoff surface instead of distributing themselves on the entire surface. Hence MO assessment alone is not sufficient for maintaining the population distribution, since it fails to induce the $\bar{P}_t$ for the tangential effect in MO optimization. To address the issue, density assessment is needed for MOEAs to induce the $\bar{P}_t$ and to help in assessing the distribution density at the inhabited subdivisions in the feature space, where subsequent decisions could be made to balance the distribution density among all subdivisions.

Many approaches for individual assessment have been proposed and integrated into MOEAs in different ways. As shown in Fig. 3.3, these methods can be categorized into aggregated and comparative approaches. In the aggregated approach, the results from MO and density assessments are aggregated to unify the decision of individual assessment. The aggregation function applied can be either linear as in the nongenerational GA (Valenzuela-Rendón and Uresti-Charre 1997) or nonlinear as in the MOGA (Fonseca and Fleming 1993). In this approach, the effects of $\bar{P}_n$ and $\bar{P}_t$ on the resulting $\bar{P}_u$ highly rely on the use of aggregation function, which needs to be constructed carefully in order to keep a balance between the $\bar{P}_n$ and $\bar{P}_t$.

In the comparative approach, only individuals that are equally fit after the fitness comparisons in MO assessment will be further evaluated via the density assessment. The fitness comparison among individuals can be performed either pairwise (where only two individuals are compared at a time) or teamwise (where more than two individuals are compared at a time). Such an approach indirectly assigns a priority, where a decision made from the MO assessment is more important than that of the density assessment. This leads to a larger effect of $\bar{P}_n$ on $\bar{P}_u$ at the initial stage of evolution. As the individuals begin to converge to the final tradeoffs, the density assessment helps to disperse and distribute the individuals on the tradeoff surface. Existing MOEAs that adopt the comparative approach include Horn et al. (1994), Srinivas and Deb (1994), Deb et al. (2002a), Knowles and Corne (2000a), and Khor et al. (2001b).

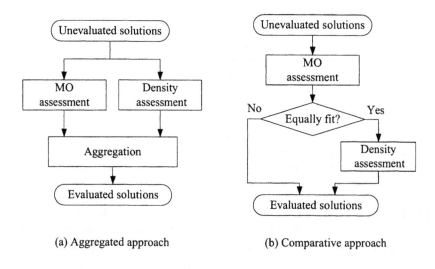

(a) Aggregated approach   (b) Comparative approach

Fig. 3.3. Generalized MO evaluation approaches.

3.2.2 Elitism

The purpose of incorporating elitism in MOEAs is to keep record of a set of the best-found nondominated individuals (elitist individuals) in the evolution in order to achieve a better convergence. Existing MOEAs that adopt the feature of elitism include Zitzler and Thiele (1999), Tan et al. (2001c), Deb et al. (2002a), Coello Coello and Pulido (2001), and Khor et al. (2001b). Due to the limited computing and memory resources in implementation, the number of elitist individuals is often bounded. A pruning process is performed if the size of the elitist individuals exceeds a predefined limit.

As shown in Fig. 3.4, there are two different approaches of pruning, e.g., batch mode and recurrence mode. Let X denote an individual set that consists of the current elitist individuals and the promising individuals from genetic reproduction, which exceeds the allowable size of elitist individuals X'. In the batch-mode pruning process, all individuals from X undergo the MO assessment (as discussed in Section 3.2.1) and the results are applied to prune X to X'. In the recurrence mode, for a given population X, a group of the least promising individuals according to MO assessment is removed to complete a cycle. This process is repeated to further remove another set of the least promising individuals from the remaining individuals until a desired size is reached. Although the recurrence mode of pruning has a higher tendency of avoiding the extinction of local individuals leading to the discontinuity of Pareto front, it often requires more computational effort as compared to the batch-mode pruning due to its recurrent process of pruning.

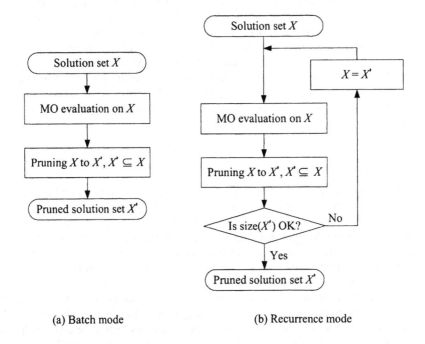

(a) Batch mode   (b) Recurrence mode

Fig. 3.4. Two modes of pruning process for elitism in MOEAs.

Generally, the elitist set X' can be either stored externally, which is often identified as the second or external population (Zitzler and Thiele 1999; Borges and Barbosa 2000; Knowles and Corne 2000a; Coello Coello and Pulido 2001), or given a surviving probability of 1. If the former case is employed, the elitist set X'

can optionally take part in the reproduction process for faster convergence. However, this approach should be implemented carefully in order to avoid premature convergence due to overinfluence by the elitist set.

3.2.3 Density Assessment

Density assessment is incorporated in MOEAs to encourage divergence in the tangential direction of the discovered tradeoff surface by giving biased selection probability at the less crowded region. Many density assessment techniques have been proposed for MOEAs over the years, which include sharing (Goldberg 1989a), grid mapping (Knowles and Corne 2000a; Coello Coello and Pulido 2001), clustering (Zitzler and Thiele 1999), crowding (Deb et al. 2002a), and lateral interference (Khor et al. 2001b).

i. Sharing (Sha)

Sharing was originally proposed by Goldberg (1989a) to search for multiple solutions in a single-objective problem with more than one equal or unequal peak. The concept was later applied to distribute nondominated individuals along the Pareto front for MO optimization, including multiobjective genetic algorithm (MOGA) (Fonseca and Fleming 1993), niched Pareto genetic algorithm (NPGA) (Horn and Nafpliotis 1993), nondominated sorting genetic algorithm (NSGA) (Srinivas and Deb 1994), multiobjective messy genetic algorithm (MOMGA) (David and Gary 2000), and nongenerational genetic algorithm (Borges and Barbosa 2000). A detailed description of the sharing approach can be found in the section on MOGA in Chapter 2.

ii. Grid Mapping (Gri)

In grid mapping (Knowles and Corne 2000a; Coello Coello and Pulido 2001), distribution density at a particular grid location in the feature space has direct relation to the number of individuals residing within that grid location. To keep track of the degree of crowding at different regions of the space, an m-dimensional grid is used, where m is the dimension of the feature space. When a new individual is generated, its grid location will be found and a map of the grid is maintained to indicate how many and which individuals in the population are residing at each grid location. To maintain the uniformity of distribution, individuals with a higher grid-location count are given less sampling probability in the selection process than those with a lower grid-location count. Since this technique depends heavily on the mapping of grids in the feature space of the population, it works well if any geometry knowledge of the best compromise is known a priori. The grid mapping has been applied in Pareto archived evolutionary strategy (PAES) (Knowles and Corne 2000a) and microgenetic algorithm (Coello Coello and Pulido 2001).

iii. Crowding (Cro)

Crowding is proposed by Deb et al. (2002a) in nondominated sorting genetic algorithm II (NSGA-II) and is used to obtain an estimate of the density of individuals surrounding a particular point in the population. It is generally based upon the average distance of two points on either side of the current point along each dimension of the feature space. Each of the dimensions then corresponds to an objective or parameter depending on the domain for which the crowding is applied. The detailed computation of crowding distance for each individual can be found in the section of NSGA-II in Chapter 2.

iv. Clustering (Clu)

Zitzler and Thiele (1999) apply the clustering (Morse 1980) in their strength Pareto evolutionary algorithm (SPEA). Initially, there is a distinct group or cluster for each external nondominated individual, and the distance d between all cluster pairs is calculated. The distance $d(c_1, c_2)$ between any two clusters, c_1 and c_2, is given as the average of all Euclidean distances $d(i, j)$, where i is an element in c_1 and j is an element in c_2. After all the cluster distances are calculated, the two clusters with a minimal d are combined to form a bigger cluster. Thereafter, the process of cluster distance calculation and clusters combination is continued until the number of clusters is reduced to the population size P. In general, it partitions a collection of P elements into n groups of relatively homogeneous elements, where $n < P$, based on the following procedures (Zitzler and Thiele 1999):

Step 1. Cluster set C is initialized; each external nondominated point $i \in P$ constitutes a distinct cluster: $C = \bigcup_{i} \{\{i\}\}$.

Step 2. If $|C| < n$, go to step 5, else go to step 3.

Step 3. The distance d of two clusters c_1 and c_2 ($\in C$), given as the average distance between pairs of individuals across the two clusters, is calculated.

Step 4. The two clusters c_1 and c_2 with the minimal distance d are determined; the chosen clusters are amalgamated into a larger cluster: $C = C \setminus \{c_1, c_2\} \cup \{c_1 \cup c_2\}$. Go to step 2.

Step 5. The nondominated set is reduced by selecting a representative individual per cluster. For this, the centroid is considered as a representative individual.

v. Lateral Interference (LI)

This lateral interference is proposed by Khor et al. (2001b), which works on the principle of interference competition. Consider a population X containing N individual points in an m-dimensional observed feature space S in the objective or parameter domain. The interference severity as a measure of distribution density of an individual j, denoted as $H_s(j)$, being interfered by others can be measured by the number of times that it has been interfered, which is equal to the number of territories T_i (Khor et al. 2001b) in which it is residing, i.e.

$$H_s(j) = \sum_{i=1, i \neq j}^{N} I_s(i, j),$$

(3.1a)

where

$$I_s(i,j) = \begin{cases} 1 & \text{if } x_j \in T_i, \\ 0 & \text{otherwise.} \end{cases} \tag{3.1b}$$

The territory of individual i, denoted as T_i, is the area where any other individuals are interfered with and inhibited by individual i from getting the resources. The sufficiency condition for a given point x_j to be within the territory T_i of an individual i, or mathematically $x_j \in T_i$ provided that $j \neq i$, is $\overline{d}(x_j, x_{s(i)}) \leq \lambda_i$, where $\overline{d}$ is the normalized metric distance, $s(i)$ is the index of the individual that is the closest to individual i, and λ_i is the influence distance of individual i given as

$$\lambda_i = \overline{d}(x_i, x_{s(i)}). \tag{3.1c}$$

Unlike the sharing method that applies a constant sharing distance among all individuals in the population, the lateral interference involves an influence distance (rather than sharing distance) that is adaptive to each individual, depending on the strength and area of territory of the individual, e.g., the larger the value of λ_i, the stronger the individual i is to interfere with its nearby individuals.

3.3 Distribution Preservation Mechanisms

As discussed in Chapter 2, the aim of evolutionary MO optimization is to distribute nondominated individuals uniformly on the discovered Pareto front as diversely as possible. For this purpose, various distribution preservation mechanisms have been proposed for MOEAs (Fonseca and Fleming 1993; Zitzler and Thiele 1999; Deb 2001; Knowles and Corne 2000a; Coello Coello et al. 2002; Khor et al. 2001b). Although these distribution preservation strategies have been implemented in different ways, they shared a common feature called density assessment that evaluates the density at different subdivisions of feature space in the parameter or objective domain. The effectiveness of a distribution preservation mechanism thus relies heavily on the adopted assessment technique, since different techniques will lead to different measure of distribution density. In this section, simulation studies for different distribution preservation mechanisms are presented over 15 representative distribution samples and the results are compared based upon 2 distribution metrics.

3.3.1 Performance Metrics on Distribution Quality

An important measure of distribution quality in MO optimization is the uniformity of the distributed individuals in a population. For this, uniform distribution (UD) can be used to reflect the degree of uniformity on a given distribution. To examine the UD of a population, the feature space S can be decomposed into a finite number of subdivisions. At each subdivision, the difference between the actual and desired niche count is recorded. The sum of these differences over all the subdivisions reflects inversely the measure of UD. Mathematically, the $UD(X)$ for a given population X (in general) is defined as

$$UD(X) = \frac{1}{1 + S_{nc}},$$ (3.2)

where S_{nc} is the standard deviation (Mason et al. 1988) of the niche count for the population X, which is given as

$$S_{nc} = \sqrt{\frac{\sum_{i}^{N} \left(n_c(i) - \breve{n}_c(i) \right)^2}{N - 1}},$$ (3.3)

where N is the number of subdivisions; $n_c(i)$ is the actual niche count at the ith region, and $\breve{n}_c$ is the desired niche count. There are two approaches for creating the subdivisions in the feature space, e.g., grid mapping and neighborhood mapping, as described below.

i. Uniform Distribution – Grid Mapping (UD-G)

In this approach, an m-dimensional grid is mapped onto the feature space that is divided in a way that each subdivision is equivalent to one grid location. Then the values of $\breve{n}_c(i)$ and $n_c(i)$ are equal to the niche count for the respective model and actual population at the ith grid location. This approach requires the definition of a model distribution in order to reflect the ideal case of population distribution. Such a requirement may be hard to satisfy in practice, since it needs to predefine the value of $\breve{n}_c(i)$ at each grid location i based on a model population distribution.

The computational effort for this approach also grows significantly as the dimension of the feature space is increased. Nevertheless, this approach provides an accurate measure if the user knows exactly how the individuals should be distributed in the feature space. Note that the measurement results from grid mapping often rely on the grid size, e.g., too small a grid size will lead to an overjudgment as more empty grid locations will emerge among the gaps of points. On the other hand, if the grid size is too large, the original shape of the distribution may not be well preserved because of the grid quantization error.

ii. Uniform Distribution – Neighborhood Mapping (UD-N)

This approach defines subdivision in the sense of neighborhood region with circular shape centered at different distribution points, for which the number of subdivisions is equal to the number of sample points. The neighborhood of a point is defined as the area within a predefined distance from the point, which is usually represented as r_n. The niche count $n_c(i)$ at the subdivision i is then equal to the number of points within the neighborhood of individual i,

$$n_c(i) = \sum_{j, j \neq i}^{N} f(i, j), \quad \text{where } f(i, j) = \begin{cases} 1 & \text{dist}(i, j) < r_n, \\ 0 & \text{else.} \end{cases}$$ (3.4)

where dist(i, j) is the distance between individuals i and j in the objective domain. Subsequently $\tilde{n}_c$ is computed as the average of $n_c(i)$ for all i. As compared to grid mapping, this approach is more flexible for different types of distributions, since it does not require any a prior knowledge regarding the desired population distribution. However, overlaps among subdivisions may exist in the neighborhood approach, which subsequently result in the emphasis of more crowded area than the less crowded one, e.g., different weights are implicitly imposed on different regions where a higher weight is given for a higher distribution density. Similar to the grid mapping that requires a predefined grid size, the neighborhood mapping also requires the setting of neighborhood size in terms of neighborhood radius r_n.

Figures 3.5 to 3.7 illustrate a few samples of convex, nonconvex, and line distributions with their respective measures of *UD-G* and *UD-N*. Unlike the convex distribution, the nonconvex and line distributions may impose additional difficulty for the measures of *UD-G* and *UD-N* in tracing the nonconvex portion if the grid size (for *UD-G*) and neighborhood size (for *UD-N*) are too large, as stated previously. By visual inspection, it can be seen that a more uniform distribution generally results in a higher value of *UD-G* and *UD-N*. For example, (i) the distribution in Fig. 3.5c has a higher *UD-G* and *UD-N* than that in Figs. 3.5a and 3.5b, (ii) the distribution in Fig. 3.6c has a higher *UD-G* and *UD-N* than that in Figs. 3.6a and 3.6b. In some cases, it can be observed that the larger the value of *UD-G*, the higher is the value of *UD-N* (cf. Figs. 3.5 and 3.7). However, in other cases, only a small difference is observed between the measures of *UD-G* and *UD-N* (cf. Figs. 3.6a and 3.6b). Further studies concerning this behavior are carried out and discussed below.

One of the simple yet representative illustrations for comparisons between *UD-G* and *UD-N* is given in Fig. 3.8, where sets of dots represent the point distribution, dotted lines represent the grid, and dotted circles represent the neighborhood boundaries of the points. It can be observed that the two different distributions give the same *UD-G* (0.3874) but a different *UD-N*, e.g., both distributions provide the same points count at each grid location. In terms of *UD-N*, the distribution in Fig. 3.8a is more uniform than that in Fig 3.8b, since the variance of neighborhood overlapping density over the distribution in Fig 3.8b is larger than that in Fig 3.8a.

On the other hand, distributions with the same *UD-N* may give a different *UD-G*. As illustrated in Fig. 3.9a, each point is located at one grid location, and thus an *UD-G* value of 1 is given. Since the overlapping density of the neighborhood of points is not uniform, an *UD-N* value lower than 1 (0.7101) is obtained. When the grid is offset to the left by half of the grain size as shown in Fig. 3.9b, a different value of *UD-G* is observed. This is because the points are not equally distributed over the grid although the same distribution is applied. This indicates that, besides grid size, any offset of the grid location will also affect the value of *UD-G*. Intuitively, the measurement result of *UD-N* is unique to the distribution for a fixed r_n, since the neighborhoods are mapped onto the distribution points instead of the feature space.

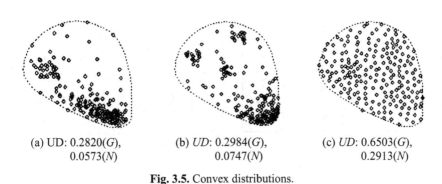

(a) UD: 0.2820(*G*),
0.0573(*N*)

(b) *UD*: 0.2984(*G*),
0.0747(*N*)

(c) *UD*: 0.6503(*G*),
0.2913(*N*)

Fig. 3.5. Convex distributions.

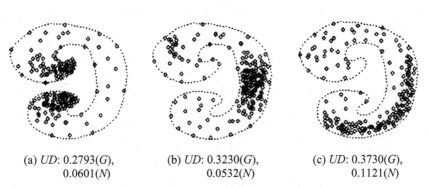

(a) *UD*: 0.2793(*G*),
0.0601(*N*)

(b) *UD*: 0.3230(*G*),
0.0532(*N*)

(c) *UD*: 0.3730(*G*),
0.1121(*N*)

Fig. 3.6. Nonconvex distributions.

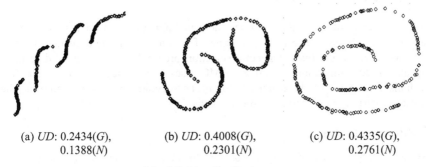

(a) *UD*: 0.2434(*G*),
0.1388(*N*)

(b) *UD*: 0.4008(*G*),
0.2301(*N*)

(c) *UD*: 0.4335(*G*),
0.2761(*N*)

Fig. 3.7. Line distributions.

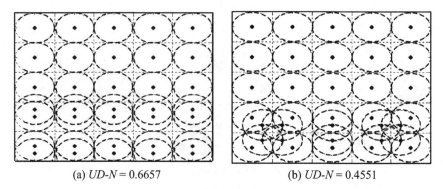

(a) $UD\text{-}N = 0.6657$ (b) $UD\text{-}N = 0.4551$

Fig. 3.8. Two distributions with $UD\text{-}G = 0.3874$.

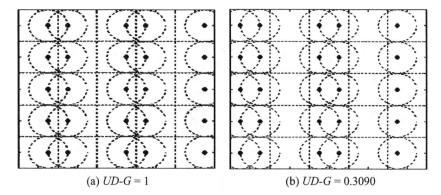

(a) $UD\text{-}G = 1$ (b) $UD\text{-}G = 0.3090$

Fig. 3.9. Two distributions with $UD\text{-}N = 0.7101$.

3.3.2 Evaluation and Comparison

This section studies the density assessment in MOEAs based upon two different aspects, i.e., the influence on the pruning of solution set in the elitism as well as the influence on the bias of genetic selection probability for the candidate individuals. In the simulation, the effect of MO assessment is neglected (e.g., all individuals are regarded to be equally fit) in order to avoid any bias in examining the various distribution preservation mechanisms.

i. Effects on Elitism

Here the influences of density assessment techniques in identifying and pruning individuals for better uniformity and distribution are studied. Three different types of point distributions are considered, e.g., convex, nonconvex, and line distributions. For each type, five (where three from each type have been shown in Figs.

3.5, 3.6, and 3.7) different point distributions, each consisting of 200 points, are applied and considered as the population X in Fig. 3.4. Different density assessment techniques are applied to prune the population to 100 points, including the methods of sharing (*Sha*) with $\sigma_{share} = 0.1$ in the normalized feature space, grid mapping (*Gri*) with grid size equal to the defined neighborhood size as adopted in sharing, crowding (*Cro*), clustering (*Clu*), and lateral interference (*LI*). Except clustering, these schemes are implemented in both the batch (*-B*) and recurrence (*-R*) modes of pruning process, which result in a total of 9 different pruning approaches. Generally, the clustering technique is implemented in recurrence mode where the number of clusters is reduced until the desired population size is reached. To compare uniformity of the output populations, the two different measures of *UD-G* and *UD-N* are used in the simulation.

Figure 3.10 summarizes the simulation results for the *UD* performances (*UD-G* and *UD-N*) on each pruning process. The statistical results over five distribution samples for each type are visualized in box plot format (Chambers et al. 1983). In each graph, the sequence of box plots from the left to right is based upon the sequence of pruning process given as follows: (i) *Ori*, (ii) *Sha-B*, (iii) *Sha-R*, (iv) *Gri-B*, (v) *Gri-R*, (vi) *Cro-B*, (vii) *Cro-R*, (viii) *Clu-R*, (ix) *LI-B*, and (x) *LI-R*. The *Ori* denotes the original population distribution before pruning. For all types of point distributions, the values of *UD-G* and *UD-N* for all techniques (indexes from 2 to 10) are larger than that of *Ori*. This shows that all the techniques have provided an improved distribution in terms of uniformity as compared to the original population. Among the techniques, the recurrence-mode grid mapping (*Gri-R*) performs the best based on the measure of *UD-G*, while the recurrence-mode sharing (*Sha-R*) distinguishes from others according to the measure of *UD-N*. This implies that the *UD-G* and *UD-N* are in favor of *Gri-R* and *Sha-R*, respectively. Concerning the modes of selection, the recurrence-mode (*-R*) is shown to match better with sharing (*Sha*) for all classes of distributions according to both the measures of *UD-G* and *UD-N*. It can also be observed that the recurrence mode performs better with grid mapping (*Gri*) based on the measure of *UD-G* for all classes of distributions. For the rest of the techniques, no clear evidence is observed.

To examine the results quantitatively, a number of distribution samples for the pruned populations according to various pruning processes are illustrated in Figs. 3.11 and 3.12. The original populations without density-based selection for the results in Figs. 3.11 and 3.12 are shown in Figs. 3.5b and 3.7b, respectively. As illustrated in Figs. 3.11 and 3.12, all techniques have generally removed the points in the crowded region, resulting in a more uniform distribution. For those with similar density assessment techniques, niches of extremely crowded points will extinct locally after the batch-mode pruning. This phenomenon is called "niche extinction," where individuals are disappeared or extinct locally, leading to discontinuity or gaps on the discovered tradeoff surface. It can be observed that the phenomenon of niche extinction is obvious for *Sha* (Figs. 3.11a and 3.11b; 3.12a and 3.12b) and *Gri* (Figs. 3.11c and 3.11d; 3.12c and 3.12d) and is less apparent for *Cro* (Figs. 3.11e and 3.11f; 3.12e and 3.12f) and *LI* (Figs. 3.11h and 3.11i; 3.12h and 3.12i). Concerning the clustering (*Clu-R*) technique, it gives better results for the line-type distribution as compared to the convex-type distribution.

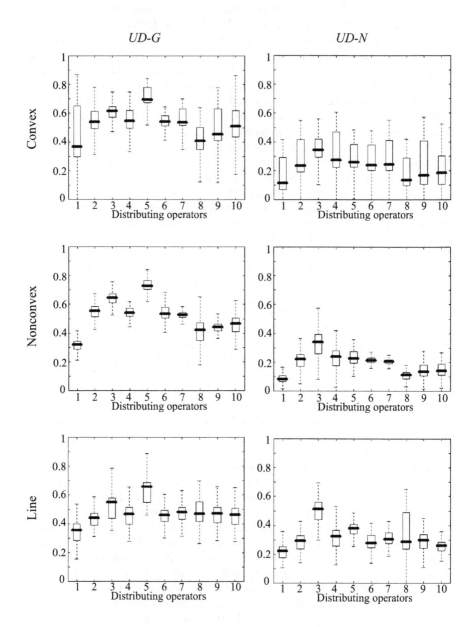

Fig. 3.10. Box plots of *UD* measure on various distributions.

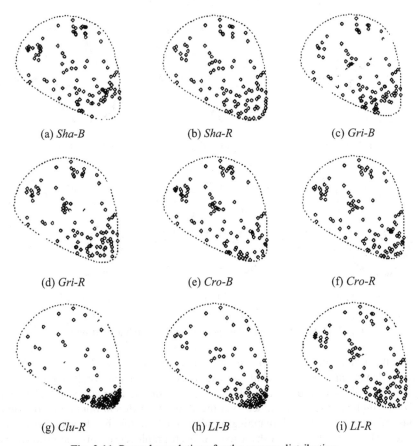

(a) *Sha-B*   (b) *Sha-R*   (c) *Gri-B*

(d) *Gri-R*   (e) *Cro-B*   (f) *Cro-R*

(g) *Clu-R*   (h) *LI-B*   (i) *LI-R*

Fig. 3.11. Pruned populations for the convex distribution.

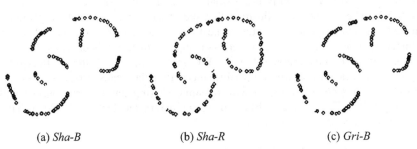

(a) *Sha-B*   (b) *Sha-R*   (c) *Gri-B*

Fig. 3.12. Pruned populations for the line distribution (continued on next page).

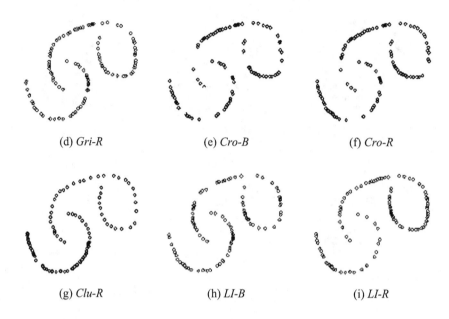

(d) *Gri-R*   (e) *Cro-B*   (f) *Cro-R*

(g) *Clu-R*   (h) *LI-B*   (i) *LI-R*

Fig. 3.12. (Continued) Pruned populations for the line distribution.

Unlike other approaches, the performance of sharing and grid mapping is highly dependent on the size of the examined subdivisions (called grain size). Figure 3.13 illustrates the effect of grain size on the performances of *UD-G* and *UD-N*, which are the mean values over the above 15 different population distributions of sharing and grid mapping implemented in the batch and recurrence modes. The "granularity" on the *x*-axis of each graph represents the ratio of the grain size over the whole feature space, where "0" indicates zero grain size and "1" denotes the entire feature space. It can be observed that a high performance of *UD* for *Sha* and *Gri* generally has a small value of granularity, except for *Sha-R* on *UD-N*. The results also illustrate that the sharing and grid mapping implemented in batch mode achieved the highest performance of *UD-G* and *UD-N* at a granularity index similar to each other. As compared to *Sha*, it is observed that *Gri* is more sensitive to the granularity index for most cases, which can be reflected by the more significant drop of *Gri* performances after the peaks. Besides these approaches, a number of schemes with dynamic sharing parameter (Fonseca and Fleming 1998b; Tan et al. 2003b) or no sharing parameter (Deb et al. 2002a) have also been proposed in the literature.

ii. Effects on Genetic Selection

Here the influences of density assessment techniques in biasing the sampling rate of genetic selection for evolving individuals in the feature space uniformly are studied. The program illustrated in Fig 3.1, excluding the feature of elitism to avoid unnecessary influence to the overall results, is adopted. The aim is to distribute the individuals uniformly in the entire 2-dimension parameter space with a range of [0, 1]. The population size is set as 100 and the simulation adopts a 5-digit decimal-coded chromosome representation (Tan et al. 2001e), 2-point crossover at a probability of 0.7, and standard mutation at a probability of 0.01.

The examined density assessment techniques are sharing (*Sha*) with $\sigma_{share} = 0.1$ in the normalized feature space, grid mapping (*Gri*) with grid size equal to the defined neighborhood size as adopted in sharing, crowding (*Cro*), and lateral interference (*LI*). The adopted genetic selection schemes are tournament (*TS*) (with tournament size of 2) and roulette wheel (*RwS*). The clustering method is excluded here since it cannot be directly applied to bias the probability of genetic selection. To avoid inappropriate parameter settings for *Sha* and *Gri*, the *Sha-r* and *Gri-r* with randomly assigned parameters are introduced to gauge the performance and to simulate the consequence when nondeterministically determined parameters for *Sha* and *Gri* are applied. Besides, the simulation results without any density assessment techniques (labeled as "*NIL*") are also included to evaluate the effects of distribution when no bias (e.g., all individuals are assigned an equal fitness) is applied to the genetic selection.

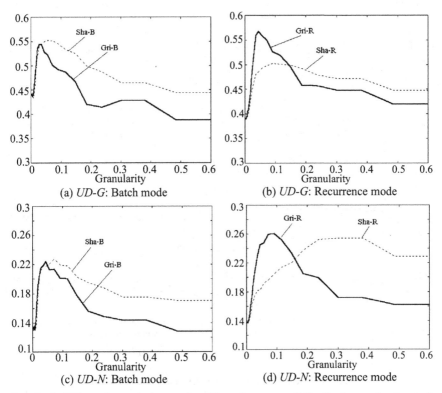

Fig. 3.13. Effect of granularity on the *UD* performance of distribution evaluation techniques.

Figure 3.14 illustrates the average trace of *UD-G* and *UD-N* over 30 simulation runs for various density assessments with *TS*. The *x*-axis denotes the number of evaluations or the number of individuals evaluated under the density assessment scheme. Generally, all techniques have improved the population distribution with a higher value of *UD-G* and *UD-N* than that of *NIL* along the evolution. It can be observed that grid mapping and sharing perform excellently if the parameters are chosen properly; otherwise the performance will degrade significantly (see *Gri-r* and *Sha-r*). As shown in the figures, crowding gives good results when it is incorporated with *TS* (rather than *RwS*). Since *RwS* is generally more sensitive to the measurement results of density assessment, a proper scaling of the crowding distance is essential for good performance of the crowding approach. It can also be observed that *LI* gives an average performance for all cases, showing its flexibility in working with both the approaches of *TS* and *RwS*.

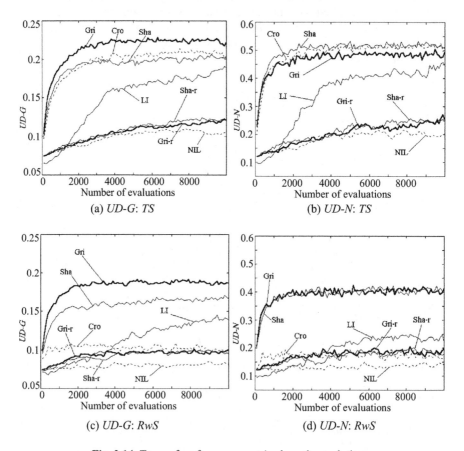

(a) *UD-G*: *TS*

(b) *UD-N*: *TS*

(c) *UD-G*: *RwS*

(d) *UD-N*: *RwS*

Fig. 3.14. Trace of performance metric along the evolution.

3.4 Conclusions

This chapter has reviewed a number of distribution preservation mechanisms for MOEAs and examined their characteristics and effectiveness. A conceptual framework consists of solution assessment and elitism has also been presented in the chapter. Simulation studies among different distribution preservation techniques have been performed over 15 representative distribution samples and the performances have been compared based upon two distribution metrics. It has been shown that all techniques examined are capable of improving population distributions in terms of uniformity. The results also unveiled that interactions between density assessment and genetic selection cannot be neglected, and the different distribution preservation mechanisms could be implemented in a modular fashion to achieve a better performance for MOEAs.

4
Decision Supports and Advanced Features for MOEAs

4.1 Introduction

This chapter presents an evolutionary algorithm with a goal-sequence domination scheme for better decision support in MO optimization. It allows the inclusion of advanced hard/soft priority and constraint information on each objective component and is capable of incorporating multiple specifications with overlapping or nonoverlapping objective functions via logical "OR" and "AND" connectives to drive the search toward multiple regions of the tradeoff surface. A few advanced features for MOEAs will also be presented in this chapter. These include a dynamic sharing scheme that is simple and adaptively estimated according to the online population distribution without needing any a priori parameter setting; a switching preserved strategy for stability and diversity of the Pareto front; and an MO convergence representation to provide useful information on convergence dynamics and stopping criterion for MO optimization. The advantages of these features are illustrated upon a benchmark MO optimization problem.

4.2 Domination Scheme

For an MO optimization problem with simple goal or priority specification on each objective function, the domination comparison scheme that directly utilizes the concept of Pareto dominance in (1.2) is not sufficient. The decision-maker may have in his or her mind the goals (desired target to attain), priorities (relative importance), and constraints (restriction on the feasibility of a solution) on some of the objective functions. Moreover, the optimization problem may be complex or involves optimizing a logical statement consists of "AND" and/or "OR" relations among the multiple set of specifications. In this section, the domination comparison scheme is reformulated to allow the decision-maker to provide, although not compulsory, more information for better decision supports in MO optimization.

4.2.1 Pareto-based Domination with Goal Information

This section is about a two-stage Pareto-based domination scheme for MO optimization, which is then extended to incorporate advanced soft/hard goal and priority specifications. Adopting the principle of Pareto dominance in (1.2), the first stage in the domination approach ranks all individuals that satisfy the goal setting to minimize the objective functions as much as possible. It assigns the same smallest cost for all nondominated individuals, while the dominated individuals are ranked according to how many individuals in the population dominate them. The second stage ranks the remaining individuals that do not meet the goal setting based upon the following extended domination scheme.

Let $F_a^{\hat{a}}$ and $F_b^{\hat{a}}$ denote the components of objective vectors F_a and F_b, respectively, which do not meet the goal vector G. Then for both F_a and F_b that do not totally satisfy G, the vector F_a is said to dominate vector F_b (denoted by $F_a \underset{G}{\prec} F_b$) iff

$$(F_a^{\hat{a}} \prec F_b^{\hat{a}}) \text{ or } (abs(F_a - G) \prec abs(F_b - G)), \tag{4.1}$$

where $abs(F) = \{|f_1|, |f_2|, ..., |f_m|\}$. For this, the rank begins from one increment of the maximum rank value obtained in the first stage of the cost assignment. Therefore, individuals that do not meet the goal will be directed toward the goal and the infinum in the objective domain, while those that have satisfied the goal will only be directed further toward the infinum. Note that $F_a^{\hat{a}}$ and $F_b^{\hat{a}}$ are incomparable if they are different in the dimension and/or the objective function corresponding to each component. Figure 4.1 shows an optimization problem with two objectives f_1 and f_2 to be minimized. The arrows in Fig. 4.1 indicate the transformation according to $F' = abs(F - G) + G$ of the objective function F to F' for individuals that do not satisfy the goal, with the goal as the new reference point in the transformed objective domain. It is obvious that the domination scheme is simple for comparing the strengths among partially or totally unsatisfactory individuals in a population. For comparisons among totally satisfactory individuals, the basic Pareto dominance is sufficient.

To study the computational efficiency in the approach, the population is divided into two separate groups by the goal satisfaction, and the domination comparison is performed separately in each group of individuals. The total number of domination comparisons for the two-stage domination scheme is $N_c = [n_{\hat{G}}(n_{\hat{G}}-1)+n_{\bar{G}}(n_{\bar{G}}-1)]$, where $n_{\hat{G}}$ is the number of individuals that completely satisfy the goal G and $n_{\bar{G}}$ is the number of individuals that partially satisfy or completely do not satisfy the goal G. Note that $n_{\hat{G}} + n_{\bar{G}} = N$ for a population size of N. Hence, in any generation, N_c is always not more than the total number of domination comparisons among all individuals in a population, where each individual in the population is compared with $(N-1)$ individuals, i.e., $N_c \leq N_{nc} = N(N-1)$. In the next section, the two-stage Pareto-based domination scheme will

be extended to incorporate soft/hard priority specifications for advanced MO optimization.

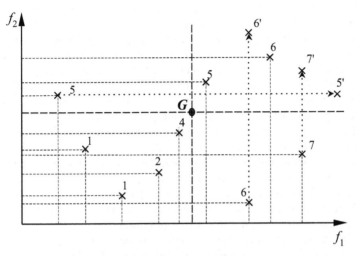

Fig. 4.1. Two-stage Pareto domination scheme with goal information.

4.2.2 Goal-Sequence Domination Scheme with Soft/Hard Priority Specifications

One of the advanced capabilities in evolutionary MO optimization is to incorporate cognitive specification, such as priority information that indicates the relative
importance of the multiple tasks to provide useful guidance in the optimization.
Consider a problem with multiple noncommensurable tasks, where each task is assigned a qualitative form of priority indicating its relative importance. In general,
there exist two alternatives to accomplish these tasks, i.e., to consider one task at a
time in a sequence according to the task priority or to accomplish all tasks at once
before considering any individual task according to the task priority. Intuitively,
the former approach provides good optimization performance for tasks with
higher-priority and may result in relatively poor performance for others. This is
due to the fact that optimizing the higher-priority tasks may be at the performance
expense of the lower-priority tasks. This definition of priority is denoted as "hard"
priority in this paper. On the other hand, the latter approach provides a distributed
approach in which all tasks aim at a compromise solution before the importance or
priority of individual task is considered. This is defined as "soft" priority. Similarly, priorities for different objective components in MO optimization can be
classified as "hard" or "soft" priority. With hard priorities, goal settings (if applicable) for higher-priority objective components must be satisfied first before attaining goals with lower priority. In contrast, soft priorities will first optimize the

overall performance of all objective components, as much as possible, before attaining any goal setting of an individual objective component in a sequence according to the priority vector. This addresses the difficulty of implementing soft priority in the function aggregating method (Bentley and Wakefield 1997).

To achieve greater flexibility in MO optimization, the two-stage Pareto domination scheme is further extended to incorporate both soft and hard priority specifications with or without goal information by means of goal-sequence domination (Tan et al. 2003b). Here, instead of having one priority vector to indicate priorities among the objective components (Fonseca and Fleming 1998a), two kinds of priority vectors are used to accommodate the soft/hard priority information. Consider an objective priority vector, $P_f \in N^{1 \times m}$ and a goal priority vector, $P_g \in N^{1 \times m}$, where $P_f(i)$ represents the priority for the ith objective component $F(i)$ that is to be minimized; $P_g(i)$ denotes the priority for the ith goal component $G(i)$ that is to be attained; m is the number of objectives to be minimized; and N denotes the natural numbers. The elements of the vector P_f and P_g can take any value in the natural numbers, with a lower number representing a higher priority and zero representing a "don't care" priority assignment. Note that repeated values among the elements in P_f and P_g can be used to indicate equal priority provided that $P_f(i) \neq P_g(i) \; \forall \; i \in \{1, 2, ..., m\}$, avoiding contradiction of the priority assignment.

With the combination of an objective priority vector P_f and a goal priority vector P_g, soft and hard priorities can be defined provided that there is more than one preference among the objective components as given by

$$\{(P_f : P_f(j) > 1) \;\; \vee \;\; (P_g : P_g(j) > 1)\} \; \exists \, j \in \{1, 2, ..., m\}. \tag{4.2}$$

Based on this, a priority setting is regarded as "soft" *iff*

$$\{(P_f : P_f(i) = 1) \;\; \vee \;\; (P_g : P_g(i) = 1)\} \; \forall \, i \in \{1, 2, ..., m\}; \tag{4.3}$$

else, the priority is denoted as "hard."

For example, the setting of $P_f = [1, 1, 2, 2]$ and $P_g = [0, 0, 0, 0]$ for a 4-objective optimization problem indicates that the first and second objective components are given top priority to be minimized, as much as possible, before considering minimization of the third and fourth objective components. Since all elements in P_g are zeros (don't care), no goal components will be considered in the minimization in this case. On the other hand, the setting of $P_f = [0, 0, 0, 0]$ and $P_g = [1, 1, 2, 2]$ implies that the first and second objective components are given the first priority to meet their respective goal components before considering the goal attainment for the third and fourth objective components. The above two different priority settings are all categorized as hard priorities since in both cases, objective components with higher priority are minimized before considering objective components with lower priority. For soft priority as defined in (4.3), the objective priority vector and goal priority vector can be set as $P_g = [1, 1, 1, 1]$ and $P_f = [2, 2, 3, 3]$, respectively. This implies that the evolution is directed toward pushing all objective components to the goal region before any attempt to minimize the higher-priority objective components in a sequence defined by the objective priority vector. The configuration of $P_g = [2, 2, 3, 3]$ and $P_f = [1, 1, 1, 1]$ is also considered as soft priority since it is aimed to minimize all objective components in the highest priority before further consideration of goals in the lower-priority level. It differs from the above in the sense that goal information in the highest priority is not considered (since P_f is used in the highest priority).

To systematically rank all individuals in a population to incorporate the soft/hard priority specifications, a sequence of goals corresponding to the priority information can be generated and represented by a goal-sequence matrix G' where the kth row in the matrix represents the goal vector for the corresponding kth priority. The number of goal vectors to be generated depends on the last level of priority z, where z is the maximum value of elements of P_g and P_f as given by

$$z = \max[P_g(i), P_f(j)] \quad \forall\ i, j \in \{1, 2, ..., m\}. \tag{4.4}$$

For this, the goal vector with the kth priority in the goal-sequence matrix, G'_k is defined as

$$\forall i = 1, ..., m, \quad G'_k(i) = \begin{cases} G(i) & \text{if } P_g(i) = k, \\ \min[F_{j=1,...,N}(i)] & \text{if } P_f(i) = k, \\ \max[F_{j=1,...,N}(i)] & \text{otherwise}, \end{cases} \tag{4.5}$$

where $k = 1, 2, ..., z$; N denotes the population size; $\min[F_{j=1,...,N}(i)]$ and $\max[F_{j=1,...,N}(i)]$ represent the minimum and maximum value of the ith objective function from the online population distribution, respectively. In (4.5), for any ith objective component of the kth priority level, the reason for assigning $G'_k(i)$ with $G(i)$ is to guide the individuals toward the goal regions; $\min[F_{j=1,...,N}(i)]$ is to minimize the corresponding objective component as much as possible; and $\max[F_{j=1,...,N}(i)]$ is to relax the requirements on the individuals to give other objective components more room for improvement. According to (4.5), the goal-sequence matrix G' is dynamic at each generation, as the values of $\min[F_{j=1,...,N}(i)]$ and $\max[F_{j=1,...,N}(i)]$ are dynamically computed on the online population distribution. After computing the sequence of goal vectors $G'_k \ \forall\ k \in \{1, 2, ..., z\}$, the individuals are first ranked according to the computed goal vector G'_1 for the first priority. Then each group of individuals that have the same rank value will be further compared and ranked according to the next goal vector G'_2 for the second priority to further evaluate the individual's domination in a population. In general, this ranking process continues until there is no individual with the same rank value or after ranking the goal G'_z that has the lowest priority in the goal-sequence matrix. Note that individuals with the same rank value will not be further evaluated for those components with "don't care" assignment.

With the goal-sequence domination scheme as given in (4.5), both hard and soft priority specifications can be incorporated in MO optimization. Without loss of generality, consider a two-objective optimization problem, with f_1 having a higher priority than f_2, as well as a goal setting of $G = [g_1, g_2]$. For soft priority optimization as defined in (4.3), the goal priority vector and objective priority vector can be set as $P_g = [1, 1]$ and $P_f = [2, 0]$, respectively. Let $\min[F(i)]$ and $\max[F(i)]$ denote the minimum and maximum value of the ith component of F in a population, respectively. The relevant goals in the goal-sequence matrix for each priority level as defined in (4.5) are then given as $G'_1 = G$ for the first priority and $G'_2 = \{\min[F(1)], \max[F(2)]\}$ for the second priority. The goal-sequence domination scheme for the two-objective minimization problem is illustrated in Fig. 4.2. Here, the rank value of each individual is denoted by $r_1 \rightarrow r_2$, where r_1 and r_2 are the rank values after the goal-sequence ranking of the first and second priority, respectively. The preference setting indicates that both g_1 and g_2 are given the same priority to be attained in the optimization before individuals are further ranked according to the higher priority of f_1. This is illustrated in Fig. 4.3a, which shows the location of the desired Pareto front (represented by the dark region) and the expected evolution direction (represented by the curved arrow) in the objective domain for an example with an infeasible goal setting G.

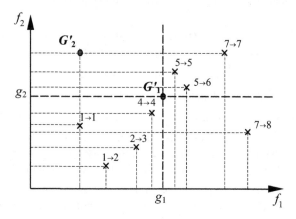

Fig. 4.2. Goal-sequence cost assignment with goal $G = \{g_1, g_2\}$, priority $P_g = [1, 1]$, and $P_f = [2, 0]$.

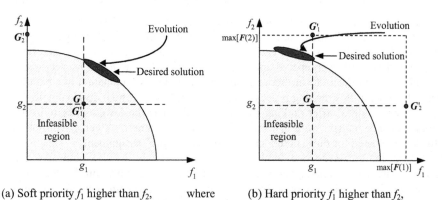

(a) Soft priority f_1 higher than f_2,   where   (b) Hard priority f_1 higher than f_2,
$P_g = [1, 1]$ and $P_f = [2, 0]$.   where $P_g = [1, 2]$ and $P_f = [0, 0]$.

Fig. 4.3. Illustration of soft and hard priority with infeasible goal setting.

For hard priority optimization as defined in (4.2) and (4.3), the goal priority vector and objective priority vector can be set as $P_g = [1, 2]$ and $P_f = [0, 0]$, respectively. According to (4.5), this gives a goal sequence of $G'_1 = [g_1, \max[F(2)]$ and $G'_2 = [\max[F(1)], g_2]$ for the first and second priority, respectively. It implies that g_1 is given higher priority than g_2 to be attained in the optimization. Figure 4.3b shows the location of the desired Pareto front (represented by the dark region) and the expected evolution direction (represented by curved arrow) in the objective domain. As compared to the solutions obtained in soft priority optimization, hard priority optimization attempts to attain the first goal component and leads to the solutions with better f_1 (higher priority) but worse f_2 (lower priority). It should be mentioned that the setting of soft/hard priority might be subjective or problem-dependent in practice. In general, the hard priority optimization may be appropriate for problems with well-defined goals in order to avoid stagnation with infeasible goal settings. Soft priority optimization is more suitable for applications where moderate performance among various objective components is desired. Besides soft/hard priority information, there may be additional specifications such as optimization constraints that are required to be satisfied in the optimization. These specifications could be incorporated in MO optimization by formulating the constraints as additional objective components to be optimized (Fonseca and Fleming 1998a). This will be discussed in the next section.

4.2.3 Optimization with Soft/Hard Constraints

Constraints often exist in practical optimization problems (Luus et al. 1995; Michalewicz and Schoenauer 1996; Fonseca and Fleming 1998a; Tan et al. 1999a). These constraints can be incorporated in the MO optimization function as objective components to be optimized. It could be in the form of a "hard" constraint where the optimization is directed toward attaining a threshold or goal, and further optimization is meaningless or not desirable whenever the goal has been satisfied. In contrast, a "soft" constraint requires that the value of the objective component corresponding to the constraint is optimized as much as possible. An easy approach to deal with both hard and soft constraints concurrently in evolutionary MO optimization is presented here (Tan et al. 2003b). At each generation, an updated objective function $F_x^{\#}$ concerning both hard and soft constraints for an individual x with its objective function F_x can be computed before the goal-sequence domination scheme as given by

$$F_x^{\#}(i) = \begin{cases} G(i) & \text{if } [G(i) \text{ is hard}] \wedge [F_x(i) < G(i)], \\ F_x(i) & \text{otherwise,} \end{cases} \quad \forall i = \{1,...,m\}. \quad (4.6)$$

In (4.6), the ith objective component that corresponds to a hard constraint is assigned to the value of $G(i)$ whenever the hard constraint has been satisfied. The underlying reason is that there is no ranking preference for any particular objective component that has the same value in an evolutionary optimization process, and thus the evolution will only be directed toward optimizing soft constraints and any unattained hard constraints, as desired.

4.2.4 Logical Connectives Among Goal and Priority Specifications

For MO optimization problems with a single goal or priority specification, the decision-maker often needs to "guess" an appropriate initial goal or priority vector and then manually observe the optimization progress. If any of the goal components is too stringent or too generous, the goal setting will have to be adjusted accordingly until a satisfactory solution can be obtained. This approach obviously requires extensive human observation and intervention, which can be tedious or inefficient in practice. Marcu (1997) proposed a method of adapting the goal values based upon the online population distribution at every generation. However, the adaptation of goal values is formulated in such a way that the search is always uniformly directed toward the middle region of the tradeoffs. This restriction may be undesirable for many applications, where the tradeoff surface is unknown or the search needs to be directed in any direction other than the middle region of the tradeoff surface. To reduce human interaction and to allow multiple sets of goal and priority specifications that direct the evolutionary search toward a different portion of the tradeoff surface in a single run, the goal-sequence domination scheme is extended here to enable logical statements such as "OR" ($\cup$) and "AND" ($\cap$) operations among multiple goal and priority specifications.

These logical operations can be built on top of the goal-sequence domination procedure for each specification. By doing this, the unified rank value for each individual can be determined and taken into effect immediately in the evolution toward the regions concerned. Consider ranking an objective vector F_x by comparing it to the rest of the individuals in a population with reference to two different specification settings of S_i and S_j, where S_i and S_j are the specifications concerning any set of objective functions with or without goals and priorities. Let these ranks be denoted by $rank(F_x, S_i)$ and $rank(F_x, S_j)$, respectively. The "OR" and "AND" operations for the two goal settings are then defined as

$$rank(F_x, S_i \cup S_j) = \min\left\{rank(F_x, S_i), rank(F_x, S_j)\right\}, \qquad (4.7a)$$

$$rank(F_x, S_i \cap S_j) = \max\left\{rank(F_x, S_i), rank(F_x, S_j)\right\}, \qquad (4.7b)$$

According to (4.7), the rank value of vector F_x for an "OR" operation between any two specifications S_i and S_j takes the minimum rank value with respect to the two specification settings. This is in order to evolve the population toward one of the specifications in which the objective vector is less strongly violated. In contrast, an "AND" operation takes the maximum rank value in order to direct the evolutionary search toward minimizing the amount of violation from both of the specifications concurrently. Clearly, the "AND" and "OR" operations in (4.7) can be easily extended to include general logical specifications with more complex connectives, such as "(S_i OR S_j) AND (S_k OR S_l)," if desired.

4.3 A Multiobjective Evolutionary Algorithm

4.3.1 Dynamic Sharing Distance

In order to evolve an evenly distributed population along the Pareto front or to distribute the population at multiple optima in the search space, many methods have been proposed, including fitness sharing (Deb and Goldberg 1989), fitness scaling (Goldberg 1989a), sequential niching (Beasley et al. 1993), dynamic niching (Miller and Shaw 1996), immune system (Forrest et al. 1993), ecological GAs (Davidor 1991; Mahfoud 1995), standard crowding (De Jong 1975), deterministic crowding (Mahfoud 1995), restricted tournament selection (Harik 1995), and clearing (Pétrowski 1996). Among these methods, the "niche induction" technique by means of a sharing function (Goldberg 1989a) is the most popular approach for evolving an evenly distributed population along the Pareto front for MO optimization. The amount of sharing contributed by each individual i into its neighboring individual j is determined by their proximity in the feature space based on the distance $d(i, j)$ and sharing distance σ_{share} as given by

$$SF(i, j) = \begin{cases} 1 - [d(i, j) / \sigma_{\text{share}}]^{\alpha} & \text{if } d(i, j) < \sigma_{\text{share}}, \\ 0 & \text{otherwise}, \end{cases} \quad (4.8)$$

where α is a parameter that regulates the shape of the sharing function and is commonly set to one (Goldberg 1989a). The sharing function in (4.8) requires a good setting of sharing distance σ_{share} to be estimated upon the tradeoff surface, which is usually unknown in many optimization problems (Coello Coello 1998). Moreover, the size of objective space usually cannot be predefined, as the exact bounds of the objective space are often undetermined. Fonseca and Fleming (1993) propose the method of Kernel density estimation to determine an appropriate sharing distance for MO optimization. However, the sharing process is performed in the "sphere" space, which may not reflect the actual objective space where the population is expected to be uniformly distributed. Miller and Shaw (1996) propose a dynamic sharing method where the peaks in the parameter domain are "dynamically" detected and recalculated at every generation while the sharing distance remains predefined. However, the approach is made on the assumption that the number of niche peaks can be estimated and the peaks are all at the minimum distance of $2\sigma_{\text{share}}$ from each other. Moreover, their formulation is defined in the parameter space to handle multimodal function optimization, which may not be appropriate for distributing the population uniformly along the Pareto optimal front in the objective domain.

In this section, a dynamic sharing method that adaptively computes the sharing distance σ_{share} to uniformly distribute all individuals along the Pareto optimal front at each generation is presented. This requires no prior knowledge of the tradeoff surface. Intuitively, the tradeoffs for an m-objective optimization problem are in the form of an $(m - 1)$-dimension hypersphere (Horn and Nafpliotis 1993; Tan et al. 1999a), whose volume can be approximated by the hypervolume $V_{pop}^{(n)}$ of a hypersphere as given by

$$V_{pop}^{(n)} = \frac{\pi^{(m-1)/2}}{\left(\dfrac{m-1}{2}\right)!} \times \left(\frac{d^{(n)}}{2}\right)^{m-1}, \qquad (4.9)$$

where $d^{(n)}$ is the diameter of the hypersphere at generation n. Note that computation of the diameter $d^{(n)}$ depends on the curvature of the tradeoff curve formed by the nondominated individuals in the objective space. For a two-objective optimization problem, the diameter $d^{(n)}$ is equal to the interpolated distance of the tradeoff curve covered by the nondominated individuals as shown in Fig. 4.4.

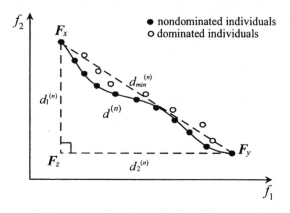

Fig. 4.4. The diameter $d^{(n)}$ of a tradeoff curve.

Although computation of $d^{(n)}$ that accurately represents the interpolated curvature of the nondominated individuals distribution is complex, it can be estimated by the average distance between the shortest and the longest possible diameter given by $d_{min}^{(n)}$ and $d_{max}^{(n)}$, respectively (Tan et al. 1999b, 2003b). Let F_x and F_y denote the objective vectors of the two farthest individuals in a population at generation n,

$$\left|F_x^{(n)} - F_y^{(n)}\right| = \max\left\{\ \left|F_i^{(n)} - F_j^{(n)}\right|,\ \forall i, j \in \{1, 2, ..., m\}\ \text{and}\ i \neq j\ \right\}. \qquad (4.10)$$

Note that $d_{max}^{(n)}$ can be computed as

$$d_{max}^{(n)} = d_1^{(n)} + d_2^{(n)}, \qquad (4.11)$$

where

$$F_z^{(n)}(i) = \min\left\{F_x^{(n)}(i), F_y^{(n)}(i)\right\},\ \forall\ i \in \{1, 2, ..., m\}\ , \qquad (4.12)$$

$$d_1^{(n)} = \left|F_x^{(n)} - F_z^{(n)}\right|, \qquad (4.13a)$$

$$d_2^{(n)} = \left| F_y^{(n)} - F_z^{(n)} \right|, \tag{4.13b}$$

and $d_{\min}^{(n)}$ is equal to the minimum length between F_x and F_y, which is given as

$$d_{\min}^{(n)} = \sqrt{\left(d_1^{(n)} \right)^2 + \left(d_2^{(n)} \right)^2}. \tag{4.14}$$

Finally, the estimation of $d^{(n)}$ is given as

$$d^{(n)} = (d_{\max}^{(n)} + d_{\min}^{(n)})/2. \tag{4.15}$$

The above estimation of diameter $d^{(n)}$ is valid for both convex and concave surfaces, since for any positive or negative curvature of the surface, the exact diameter representing the population distribution must lie within the range of $d_{\min}^{(n)}$ and $d_{\max}^{(n)}$. The same computation procedure of diameter $d^{(n)}$ can also be extended to any multidimensionl objective space (Tan et al. 1999b). To achieve a uniformly distributed population along the tradeoff surface, the sharing distance $\sigma_{\text{share}}^{(n)}$ could be computed as half of the distance between neighboring individuals in the $(m-1)$-dimension hypervolume $V_{\text{pop}}^{(n)}$ covered by the population of size N at generation n,

$$N \times \frac{\pi^{(m-1)/2}}{\left(\frac{m-1}{2} \right)!} \times \left(\sigma_{\text{share}}^{(n)} \right)^{m-1} \approx V_{\text{pop}}^{(n)}. \tag{4.16}$$

Substituting (4.9) into (4.16) gives the sharing distance $\sigma_{\text{share}}^{(n)}$ at generation n in term of the diameter $d^{(n)}$ and the population size N as given by

$$\sigma_{\text{share}}^{(n)} = N^{1/(1-m)} \times \frac{d^{(n)}}{2}. \tag{4.17}$$

Clearly, (4.17) provides a simple computation of σ_{share} that is capable of distributing the population evenly along the Pareto front, without the need for any prior knowledge of the usually unknown fitness landscape. Moreover, adopting the computation of sharing distance that is dynamically based upon the population distribution at each generation is also more appropriate and effective than the method of offline estimation with preassumed tradeoff surface as employed in many existing sharing methods, since the tradeoff surface may be changed any time along the evolution whenever the goal setting is altered.

4.3.2 MOEA Program Flowchart

The overall program flowchart of a multiobjective evolutionary algorithm (MOEA) is illustrated in Fig. 4.5. At the beginning of the evolution, a population of candidate solutions is initialized and evaluated according to a vector of objective functions. Based upon the user-defined specifications, such as goals, constraints, priorities, and logical operations, the evaluated individuals are ranked according to the goal-sequence domination scheme (described in Section 4.2.2) in order to evolve the search toward the global tradeoff surface. The resulted rank values are then further refined by the dynamic sharing scheme (described in Section 4.3.1) in order to distribute the nondominated individuals uniformly along the discovered Pareto optimal front. If the stopping criterion is not met, the individuals will undergo a series of genetic operations, which are detailed within the "genetic operations" in Fig. 4.6. Here, simple genetic operations consisting of tournament selection, simple crossover with mating restriction that selects individuals within the sharing distance for mating (Fonseca and Fleming 1995b; 1998a) as well as simple mutation are performed to reproduce offspring for the next generation.

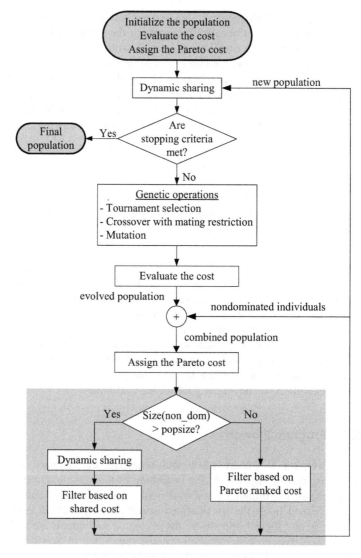

Fig. 4.5. Program architecture of the MOEA.

Genetic Operations for MOEA:

Let $pop^{(n)}$ = population in current generation n.

Step 1. Perform tournament selection to select individuals from $pop^{(n)}$ based on their shared fitness obtained from dynamic sharing scheme. The selected population is called $selpop^{(n)}$.

Step 2. Perform simple crossover and mating restriction for $selpop^{(n)}$. The resulted population is called $crosspop^{(n)}$.

Step 3. Perform simple mutation for $crosspop^{(n)}$. The resulted population is called $evolpop^{(n)}$.

Fig. 4.6. Detailed procedure within the box of "genetic operations" in Fig. 4.5.

After the genetic operations, the newly evolved population is evaluated and combined with the nondominated individuals preserved from the previous generation. The combined population is then subjected to the domination comparison scheme and pruned to the desired population size according to the switching preserved strategy (SPS) (Tan et al. 1999b). This maintains a set of stable and well-distributed nondominated individuals along the Pareto optimal front. In SPS, if the number of nondominated individuals in the combined population is less than or equal to the desired population size, extra individuals are removed according to their rank values in order to promote stability in the evolutionary search toward the final tradeoffs. Otherwise, the nondominated individuals with high niched count value will be discarded in order to distribute the individuals uniformly along the discovered Pareto optimal front. After the process, the remaining individuals are allowed to survive in the next generation and this evolutionary cycle is repeated until the stopping criterion is met.

4.3.3 Convergence Trace for MO Optimization

Convergence trace is an important dynamic behavior that provides useful information of performance observation as well as the stopping criteria for an optimization. For evolutionary single-objective optimization, the convergence behavior is often represented by the performance index versus the number of iterations or generations. Obviously, this representation is not appropriate for MO optimization that has more than one objective to be optimized at all time (Coello Coello 1998). Unlike conventional passive approach of terminating the evolution after a fixed number of generations or manually halting the evolution by means of empirical observation, Van Veldhuizen and Lamont (1998a) propose a relative progress (RP) convergence for MO optimization based on the concept of progress measure (Bäck 1996), which is defined as

$$RP = \ln \sqrt{\frac{G_1}{G_T}}, \tag{4.18}$$

where G_1 is the general distance from the population to the actual tradeoffs at generation 1, and G_T denotes the general distance at generation T. Although this measure quantifies the relative convergence improvement in the evolution, computation of the general distance G at each generation requires a priori knowledge of the actual global Pareto front, which is often unknown in practical optimization problems.

Tan et al. (1999b) present a convergence assessment for MO optimization via the concept of population domination and progress ratio. In the sense of progress toward the tradeoff surface formed by the current nondominated individuals, the progress ratio at any particular generation is defined as the domination of one population to another. Generally, the progress ratio $Pr^{(n)}$ at generation n is defined as the ratio of the number of nondominated individuals at generation n (nondom_indiv$^{(n)}$) dominating the nondominated individuals at generation $(n - 1)$ (nondom_indiv$^{(n-1)}$) over the total number of nondominated individuals at generation n (nondom_indiv$^{(n)}$),

$$Pr^{(n)} = \frac{\text{the number of nondom\_indiv}^{(n)} \; dominating \; \text{nondom\_indiv}^{(n-1)}}{\text{the number of nondom\_indiv}^{(n)}}. \qquad (4.19)$$

In order to reduce jumpy effect due to possible irregular progress ratio at each generation, the $pr^{(n)}$ at generation n can be stabilized by taking the mean of pr values over the last l generations as defined by $pr^{(n)} = \sum_{i=n+1-l}^{n} pr^{(i)} / l$. For a normal convergence, the progress ratio should start from a value close to 1 indicating a high possibility for further improvement of the evolution at the initial stage. As the generation proceeds, the pr is expected to be decreased asymptotically toward a small value approaching zero, showing that the population may be near enough to the final tradeoff surface and there is less possibility to produce any new nondominated individuals dominating the current nondominated individuals. Intuitively, the evolution is said to be nearly converged at generation n if $pr^{(n)} \approx 0$. Therefore, the pr provides information of the relative progress of the population evolves in the direction that is normal to the Pareto front formed by the current nondominated individuals at each generation and can be used as a measure of stopping criterion for MO optimization.

4.4 Simulation Studies

This section illustrates how each of the features, including goal-sequence domination scheme, hard/soft goal and priority specifications, logical operations among multiple goals, and dynamic sharing, enhances the performance of MOEA in MO optimization. Fonseca and Fleming's two-objective minimization problem (Fonseca and Fleming 1993) that allows easy visual observation of the optimization performance is applied here. Besides its nonconvex Pareto optimal front, this test function has a large and nonlinear tradeoff curve that should challenge the MOEA's ability in finding and maintaining the entire front uniformly. The two objective functions, f_1 and f_2, to be minimized are given in Eq. (1.4). The tradeoff line is shown in Fig. 1.1. There are eight parameters $(x_1,\ldots, x_8)$ to be optimized so that f_1 and f_2 are minimal. The parameters are decimally coded in the interval $[-2, 2]$ and concatenated to form the chromosomes. The simulations are run for 70 generations with a population size of 100. Standard mutation with a probability of 0.01 and standard two-point crossover with a probability of 0.7 are used.

To study the merit of the dynamic sharing scheme in MOEA, four different types of simulations have been performed. The first type is without fitness sharing. The second and third employ fixed sharing distances of 0.01 and 0.1, respectively. The fourth uses the dynamic sharing scheme that does not require any predefined sharing distance setting. Figure 4.7 illustrates the respective population distribution in the objective domain at the end of the evolution. It can be observed that all of the four simulations are able to discover the final tradeoff curve, but with some performance differences in terms of the closeness and uniformity of the population distribution along the tradeoff curve.

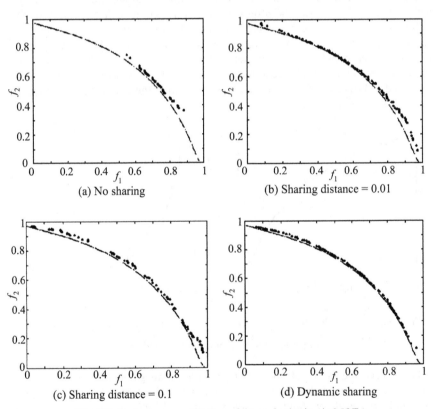

Fig. 4.7. Performance validation of dynamic sharing in MOEA.

For the MOEA without fitness sharing as shown in Fig. 4.7a, the population tends to converge to an arbitrary part of the tradeoff curve. This agrees with the findings of Fonseca and Fleming (1993). For the MOEA with fitness sharing (Goldberg and Richardson 1987), as shown in Figs. 4.7b and 4.7c, the population can be distributed along the tradeoff curve rather well, although the sharing distance of 0.01 provides a more uniform distribution than that of 0.1. This indicates that although fitness sharing contributes to population diversity and distribution along the tradeoff curve, the sharing distance has to be chosen carefully in order to ensure the uniformity of the population distribution. This often involves tedious trial-and-error procedures in order to "guess" an appropriate sharing distance, since it is problem-dependent and based upon the size of the discovered tradeoffs as well as the number of nondominated individuals. These difficulties can be solved with the dynamic sharing scheme, which has the ability to automatically adapt the sharing distance along the evolution without the need of any predefined parameter, as shown in Fig. 4.7d.

Figure 4.8 shows the simulation results of MOEA without goal and priority settings. All individuals in the final population are nondominated, as indicated by the solid dots. These individuals are distributed uniformly along the entire tradeoff surface. Figure 4.8b shows the progress ratio evaluated at each generation of the evolution. As can be seen, the progress ratio is relatively high at the initial stage of the evolution and is decreased asymptotically toward zero as the evolution proceeds or as the population gets closer to the tradeoff surface. The convergence curve saturates at around the generation of 70, which is consistent with Fig. 4.8a, where individuals have been evenly distributed along the Pareto optimal front at about the same generation.

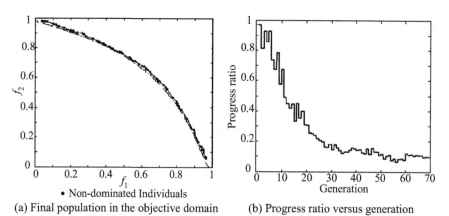

(a) Final population in the objective domain   (b) Progress ratio versus generation

Fig. 4.8. MOEA minimization with SPS.

To observe the effect of switching preserved strategy in MOEA, the above simulation was repeated with different scenarios and settings. Figure 4.9 shows the simulation results without the implementation of SPS, in which the evolution faces difficulty converging to the tradeoff curve. As shown in Fig. 4.9a, the final population is crowded and the nondominated individuals are distributed with some distance away from the tradeoff curve. Compared with Fig. 4.8b, the progress ratio without SPS as shown in Fig. 4.9b converges much slower toward the zero. Simulation results for the MOEA with SPS and filtering solely based upon individuals' rank values are shown in Fig. 4.10. As can be seen, the final population has now managed to converge to the Pareto-optimal front with a low progress ratio at the end of the evolution. However, the nondominated individuals are not evenly distributed and the diversity of the population is poor: They only concentrate on a portion of the entire tradeoff curve (cf. Figs. 4.7d, 4.10a).

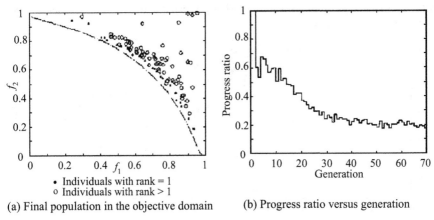

(a) Final population in the objective domain   (b) Progress ratio versus generation

Fig. 4.9. MOEA minimization without SPS.

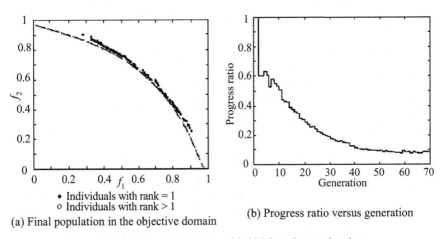

(a) Final population in the objective domain   (b) Progress ratio versus generation

Fig. 4.10. MOEA minimization with SPS based on rank values.

The goal-sequence domination scheme was also validated for problems with different goal settings, including a feasible goal setting of (0.75, 0.75), a feasible but extreme goal setting of (0.98, 0.2), and an infeasible goal setting of (0.7, 0.4) as shown in Figs. 4.11, 4.12, and 4.13, respectively. In the figures, diamonds represent goals, small circles represent the dominated individuals, and solid dots represent nondominated individuals. As desired, the population is seen to concentrate on the preferred region of the tradeoff curve at the end of the evolution, regardless of the unattainable or extreme goal settings. Figures 4.11a and 4.12a illustrate the population distribution at the initial stage of the evolution (generation = 5), where the populations are well guided along the evolution toward the respective goal settings. As shown in Figs. 4.11b, 4.12b, and 4.13, the MOEA is capable of uniformly distributing the nondominated individuals along any tradeoff surface resulting from different goal settings, with the help of the dynamic sharing scheme that automatically computes a suitable sharing distance for optimal population distribution at each generation.

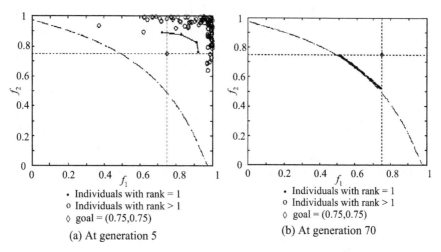

(a) At generation 5

(b) At generation 70

Fig. 4.11. MOEA minimization with a feasible goal setting.

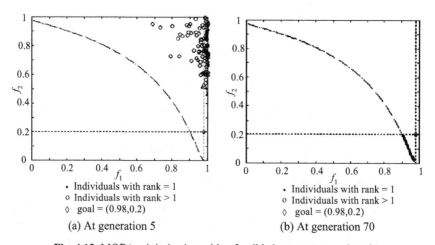

(a) At generation 5

(b) At generation 70

Fig. 4.12. MOEA minimization with a feasible but extreme goal setting.

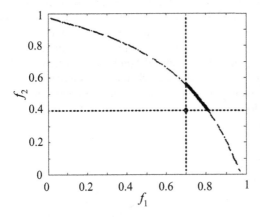

Fig. 4.13. MOEA minimization with an infeasible goal setting.

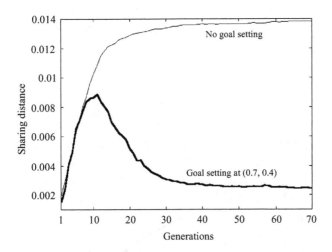

Fig. 4.14. Trace of the dynamic sharing distance along the evolution.

Figure 4.14 shows the trace of sharing distance during the evolution. The thin and thick lines represent the average sharing distances without any goal setting (see Fig. 4.8a for the corresponding Pareto front) and with the goal setting of (0.7, 0.4) (see Fig. 4.13 for the corresponding Pareto front), respectively. Generally, MO optimization without a goal setting has an initially small size of discovered Pareto front, which subsequently grows along with the evolution to approach and cover the entire tradeoff region at the end of evolution. This behavior is explained in Fig. 4.14, where the sharing distance increases asymptotically along the evolution until a steady value of 0.0138 is reached. It should be noted that this value is close to the fixed sharing distance of 0.01 in Fig. 4.7b, which was carefully chosen after trial-and-error procedures. For the case of MOEA with a goal setting of (0.7,

0.4), the sharing distance increases initially and subsequently decreases to 0.0025 along the evolution, which is lower than the value of 0.0138 (without goal setting). The reason is that the concentrated tradeoff region within the goal setting is smaller than the entire tradeoff region (without goal setting) and hence results in a smaller distance for uniform sharing of nondominated individuals. These experiments show that the dynamic sharing scheme can automatically adapt the sharing distance to arrive at an appropriate value for uniform population distribution along the discovered tradeoff regions with different sizes, without the need for any a priori parameter setting.

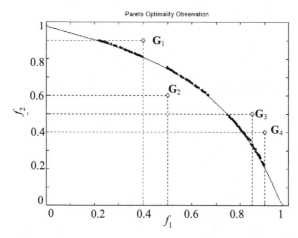

Fig. 4.15. MOEA minimization for $(G_1 \cup G_2 \cup G_3 \cup G_4$

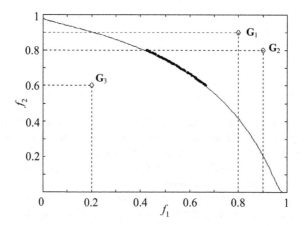

Fig. 4.16. MOEA minimization for $(G_1 \cap G_2 \cap G_3)$.

Figures 4.15 and 4.16 show the MO optimization results that include multiple goal settings specified by logical "OR" ($\cup$) and "AND" ($\cap$) connectives, respectively. For the "OR" operation as shown in Fig. 4.15, the population is automatically distributed and equally spread over the different concentrated tradeoff regions to satisfy the goal settings separately, regardless of the overlapping or feasibility of the goals. With dynamic sharing scheme, the subpopulation size for each goal is in general based upon the relative size of the concentrated tradeoff surface of that goal, and thus individuals are capable of equally distributing themselves along the different concentrated tradeoff regions. For the "AND" operation as illustrated in Fig. 4.16, the whole population evolves toward minimizing all the goals G_1, G_2, and G_3 simultaneously. As a result, the individuals are equally distributed over the common concentrated tradeoff region formed by the three goals, as desired.

Figures 4.17 and 4.18 show the MOEA simulation results for the case of an infeasible goal setting with soft and hard priorities, respectively. In the figures, diamonds represent goals, small circles represent nondominated individuals, and solid dots represent dominated individuals. For the soft priority setting in Fig. 4.17, goals are treated as first priority followed by minimizing f_1 as second priority, i.e., $P_g = [1, 1]$ and $P_f = [2, 0]$. As can be seen, it provides a distributive optimization approach for all goals by pushing the population toward the objective component of f_1 that has a higher priority than f_2, after taking the goal vector into consideration (cf. Figs. 4.3a and 4.17b). In contrast, Fig. 4.18 shows the minimization results with hard priority setting where the priority of f_1 is higher than that of f_2, i.e., $P_g = [1, 2]$ and $P_f = [0, 0]$. Unlike the soft priority optimization in Fig. 4.17, hard priority minimizes the objective of f_1 until the relevant goal component of $g_1 = 0.5$ is satisfied before attaining the objective component of f_2 with the second goal component of $g_2 = 0.5$ as shown in Fig. 4.18 (cf. Figs. 4.3b and 4.18b). As can be seen, objective values with hard priority settings are better with higher priority but are worse with lower priority, as compared to the solutions obtained in soft priority optimization (cf. Figs. 4.17b and 4.18b).

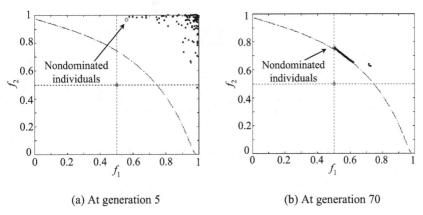

(a) At generation 5   (b) At generation 70

Fig. 4.17. MO minimization with infeasible goal setting: f_1 has soft priority higher than f_2.

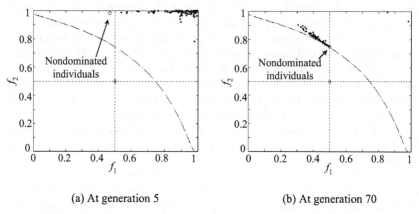

(a) At generation 5   (b) At generation 70

Fig. 4.18. MO minimization with infeasible goal setting: f_1 has hard priority higher than f_2.

Figure 4.19 shows the MOEA minimization result with f_1 being a hard constraint. The population continuously evolves toward minimizing f_2 only after the hard constraint of f_1 has been satisfied. In general, objective components with hard constraints may be assigned as hard priorities in order to meet the hard constraints before minimizing any other objective components.

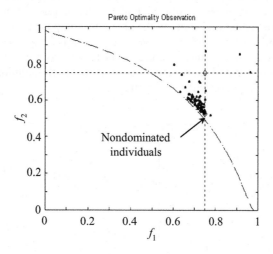

Fig. 4.19. MOEA minimization with hard constraint on f_1.

4.5 Conclusions

This chapter has studied a multiobjective evolutionary algorithm with a goal-sequence domination scheme to allow advanced specifications such as hard/soft priorities and constraints to be incorporated for better decision support in MO optimization. In addition, a dynamic fitness sharing scheme that is simple in computation and adaptively based upon the online population distribution at each generation has been presented. Such a dynamic sharing approach avoids the need for a priori parameter settings or user knowledge of the usually unknown tradeoff surface often required in existing methods. A switching preserved strategy that ensures the stability and diversity of MOEA optimization has also been presented. Besides, a convergence representation by means of population domination at each generation to provide useful information of MO optimization performance and stopping criteria has been presented. The effectiveness of the various features in MOEA has been demonstrated by showing that each of the features contains its specific merits and usage that benefit the performance of MOEA.

5
Dynamic Population Size and Local Exploration for MOEAs

5.1 Introduction

As stated in Chapter 1, evolutionary algorithms have been recognized to be well suited for MO optimization because they can evolve a set of nondominated individuals distributed along the Pareto front. These methods, however, need to "guess" for an optimal constant population size in order to discover the usually sophisticated tradeoff surface. It is known that evolutionary algorithms may suffer from premature convergence if the population size is too small. If the population is too large, however, undesired computational resources may be incurred and the waiting time for a fitness improvement may be too long in practice. Therefore, the selection of an appropriate population size in evolutionary optimization is important and could greatly affect the effectiveness and efficiency of the optimization performance (Schaffer 1985; Alander 1992). In the case of single-objective optimization, various methods for determining an optimal population size from different perspectives have been proposed. Grefenstette (1986) applies a meta-genetic algorithm to control the population size of another genetic algorithm. Smith (1993) and Arabas et al. (1994) propose the approach of determining the population size adaptively according to the "age" of a chromosome. Zhuang et al. (1996) propose an adaptive population size by adapting it to the degree of improvement achieved at each generation.

This chapter presents an incrementing multiobjective evolutionary algorithm (IMOEA) with dynamic population size. Instead of having a constant population to explore the solution space, IMOEA adaptively computes an appropriate population size according to the online evolved tradeoffs and its desired population distribution density. In this way, evolution could begin with a small population size initially as preferable, which is then increased or decreased adaptively based upon the discovered Pareto front at each generation. This approach reduces the computational effort due to unnecessary extra individuals and avoids premature convergence or incomplete tradeoffs resulting from an insufficient number of individuals. The IMOEA incorporates a fuzzy boundary local perturbation technique with a dynamic number of local perturbations per parent. This encourages and reproduces the "incrementing" individuals for better MO optimization, whereas any "extra" individuals will be filtered through the method of switching preserve strategy as discussed in Chapter 4. While maintaining the capability for global search, the scheme enhances the local exploration and fine-tuning of the evolution at each generation so as to fill up any discovered gaps or discontinuities among the nondominated individuals on the tradeoff surface. Details of the IMOEA with fuzzy boundary local perturbation and other features are described in Section 5.2. Qualitative illustrations of the various features in IMOEA are presented in Section 5.3. Conclusions are drawn in Section 5.4.

5.2 Incrementing Multiobjective Evolutionary Algorithm

In general, evolutionary techniques for MO optimization face the common difficulty in determining an optimal population size in order to efficiently explore the solution space as well as to distribute a sufficient number of nondominated individuals on the tradeoff surface. In single-objective evolutionary optimization, the population size is often "guessed" according to the size of the search space in the parameter domain. This is, however, not applicable to MO optimization where the global optimum is not a single solution but is often a set of Pareto optimal points covering the entire tradeoff surface in the objective domain. Moreover, as the exact tradeoffs for MO optimization are often unknown a priori, it is difficult to estimate an optimal number of individuals necessary for effective exploration of the solution space as well as good representation of the tradeoff surface. The issue of dynamic population size in MO optimization remains an interesting problem for researchers in the field of evolutionary computation. Extending from the MOEA studied in Chapter 4, an incrementing multiobjective evolutionary algorithm is presented here to address the problem by adaptively computing an appropriate population size at each generation. The population size in IMOEA is thus dynamic and is increased or decreased based upon the online discovered Pareto front and the desired population distribution density on the tradeoff surface.

5.2.1 Dynamic Population Size

Instead of "guessing" for an optimal population size in evolutionary MO optimization, an adaptation mechanism is employed in IMOEA (Khor et al. 2000; Tan et al. 2001c, 2001d) such that the population size is evolved based upon the online evolved tradeoffs and the required population distribution density defined by the user according to his or her preference on how closely the nondominated individuals should be distributed away from each other on the Pareto front. Consider an m-dimensional objective space, the desired population size, $dps^{(n)}$, with the desired population size per unit volume, ppv, and the approximated tradeoff hyperarea of $A_{to}^{(n)}$ (Tan et al., 1999b) discovered by the population at generation n can be defined as

$$lowbps \leq dps^{(n)} = ppv \times V_{pop}^{(n)} \leq upbps , \qquad (5.1)$$

where $lowbps$ and $upbps$ are the lower and upper bound for the desired population size $dps^{(n)}$, respectively, which can be treated as hard bounds that are defined optionally by the user. For example, the setting of $upbps$ is based largely upon affordable simulation time, as a large value of $upbps$ allows a large population size and subsequently requires a large computational effort. On the other hand, evolution is unable to maintain genetic diversity with too small a setting of $lowbps$. Within the limit of $lowbps$ and $upbps$, the population size will be increased or decreased dynamically according to the discovered tradeoff area of $A_{to}^{(n)}$. If the settings of $lowbps$ and $upbps$ are left undefined, the population size will be freely dynamic adapted by IMOEA according to the discovered area $A_{to}^{(n)}$ of nondominated individuals at generation n. Note that since ppv is defined as a finite positive integer and $A_{to}^{(n)}$ is always bounded by the objective space, the largest size of $dps^{(n)}$ is, thus, always bounded even without the inclusion of $upbps$ in (5.1) (although the value could be large for problems with a large tradeoffs). The definition of population per unit volume, ppv, is to set the desired number of nondominated individuals to be distributed in every unit size of the discovered tradeoff region. The larger the value of ppv, the more the nondominated individuals are desired to be scattered inside every unit size of discovered tradeoff region and, hence, the shorter the distance among each nondominated individual in the objective domain, and vice versa.

As mentioned in Section 4.3.1, the Pareto front for an m-objective optimization problem is in the form of an (m - 1)-dimension hypersurface, which can be approximated as,

$$V_{pop}^{(n)} \approx \frac{\pi^{(m-1)/2}}{\left(\frac{m-1}{2}\right)!} \times \left(\frac{d^{(n)}}{2}\right)^{m-1} , \qquad (5.2)$$

where $d^{(n)}$ is the diameter of the hypersphere at generation n. Clearly, (5.1) and (5.2) provide a simple estimation of the desired population size at each generation according to the online discovered tradeoffs and the desired population density ppv.

5.2.2 Fuzzy Boundary Local Perturbation

This section presents a fuzzy boundary local perturbation (FBLP) scheme (Khor et al. 2000; Tan et al. 2001c, 2001d) that perturbs the set of nondominated individuals to produce the necessary "incrementing" individuals for the desired population size in IMOEA as given by (5.1) and (5.2). In brief, the FBLP is implemented for the following objectives:

1. Produce additional "good" individuals to fill up the gaps or discontinuities among existing nondominated individuals for better representation of the Pareto front;

2. Perform interactive fine learning to overcome weakness of local exploration in an evolutionary algorithm (Dengiz et al. 1997; Liong et al. 1998) and to achieve better convergence for evolutionary MO optimization;
3. Provide the possibility of perturbation beyond the neighborhood to avoid premature convergence or local saturation.

Concerning the first objective, Liong et al. (1998) propose a method that utilizes the limited number of final Pareto optimal solutions found by an evolutionary optimization to train a neural network with the aim of generating more optimal points. The method has several drawbacks, although it has been shown to mimic the evolutionary generated optimal points well in certain cases. Since the neural network learns from examples, network training that relies on the limited number of points on Pareto front found by the evolutionary optimization may be insufficient and result in overfitting. Although this problem can be overcome by including inferior points in the learning, the trained neural network in this case is less likely to mimic the Pareto front since learning has been influenced by other inferior points. Besides, the function between candidate parameters and objective values may be discontinuous due to the usually involved hard constraints among the MO, thus adding to the learning difficulties of the network. Concerning the design complexity, this approach requires a two-stage learning process as well as to "guess" for an appropriate network structure and initial weights that often lead to heavy commitments in the algorithm.

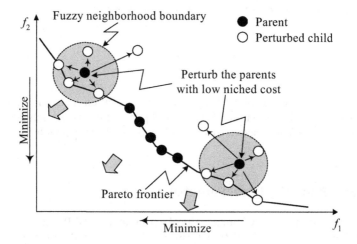

Fig. 5.1. FBLP for nondominated parents with low niched cost (apart from other parents).

As shown in Fig. 5.1, a simple and effective way to achieve the above three objectives is to generate more Pareto optimum points within the evolution itself without going through the two-stage neural network learning process. These additional Pareto points can be obtained via the method of fuzzy boundary local perturbation at each generation. Note that only parent individuals that are being selected for reproduction from the tournament selection will be perturbed with the FBLP and the selection criterion for the tournament is based solely on the individuals' niched cost in the objective domain instead of the cost of objective functions in order to encourage uniform distribution. Therefore, parents with low niched cost (located apart from other parents) will be given higher probability to be perturbed as compared to those with a high niched cost (located close to other parents).

As shown in Fig. 5.2, the neighborhood boundary for the parents to be perturbed is fuzzy in such a way that the probability of perturbation is higher within the neighborhood region than outside the neighborhood. Without loss of generality, consider a decimal coding scheme with only one parameter being coded in an n-digit chromosome $X = \{x_i: i = 1, 2,..., n\}$, where i is the coding index such that $i = 1$ represents the most significant index and $i = n$ is the least significant index of the chromosome. A probability set $P = \{p_i: i = 1, 2,..., n\}$ that indicates the perturbation probability for each element of the chromosome X, with a value of "1" represents "always perturb," a value of "0" implies "never perturb," and their intermediate values can be defined and represented by the following sigmoid function (Cox 1994):

$$p_i = \begin{cases} b\left[2\left(\dfrac{i-1}{n-1}\right)^2 + a\right] & 1 \le i \le \beta, \\ b\left[1 - 2\left(\dfrac{i-n}{n-1}\right)^2 + a\right] & \beta < i \le n, \end{cases} \qquad \forall i = 1, 2,..., n; \; n > 1. \qquad (5.3)$$

As given in (5.3), the probability value of p_i has a lower bound of "ab" and an upper bound of $(ab + b)$. For simplicity, the coefficients "a" and "b" are chosen in the range of $0 \le b \le 0.7$ and $0 \le ab \le 0.02$, which are set according to the desired perturbation probability for the upper and the lower bounds. The value of β is defined based on the desired boundary of the digit x_β in the parameter space, which can be selected as $\lceil n/2 \rceil$ as adopted in this chapter.

In Fig. 5.2, the more significant a digit in the parameter X, the lower its perturbation probability in FBLP. This increases the possibility for the generated offspring to lie within their parents' neighborhood rather than outside the neighborhood. Note that FBLP differs in two aspects as compared to other local search methods in single-objective evolutionary optimization (Dengiz et al. 1997; Hagiwara 1993). The first is that, unlike simple mutation, the perturbation probabilities in FBLP vary according to the significance of the genes in a chromosome for ease of implementation. In addition, there is no hard boundary of the neighborhood size in the perturbation, which gives a nonzero chance to produce offspring that are far away from their parents in order to maintain diversity. The second is that FBLP produces a number of offspring from each selected parent without immediate cost evaluation as to determine the acceptance or rejection for each of the perturbed individual, which can be regarded as an extension of mutation with at least one (instead of one) locally perturbed offspring per parent.

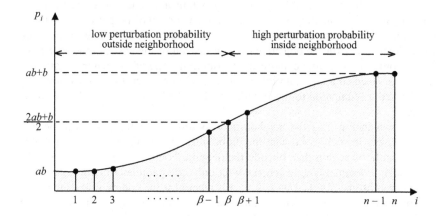

Fig. 5.2. The perturbation probability for a one-parameter chromosome in FBLP.

Although a large number of perturbations per individual in FBLP often provide a fast convergence and broad local explorations at each generation, additional computational effort is necessary in order to carry out these perturbations. To address the issue, the number of perturbations in FBLP is made dynamic and adaptive to the online optimization conditions based upon the function of progress ratio as described in Chapter 4. There are two advantages in applying the progress ratio to determine the number of offspring per parent in FBLP. First, the number of perturbations per individual in FBLP can be self-adjusted based on the feedback of the resulting progress ratio to regulate the improvement rate of the evolution. Intuitively, it is appropriate to set a low number of offspring per parent with less computational effort if the progress ratio is already above a satisfactory level indicating a high improvement rate. If the progress ratio lies below the satisfactory level, however, the number of perturbations per individual may be increased so as to reproduce more "fitter" individuals for better improvement rate. Second, local fine-tuning at the initial stage of the evolution is often not as essential as compared to the final stage, since the problem of chromosome stagnation often occurs toward the final stage of the evolution (Hagiwara 1993). It is, thus, desirable to limit the number of local perturbations at the initial stage and widen the search gradually as the evolution approaches the final tradeoffs, i.e., the number of perturbations should follow the inverse trend of the progress ratio along the evolution.

Concerning these reasons, the number of perturbations per individual in FBLP is set inversely to the progress ratio of the evolution as illustrated in Fig. 5.3. For simplicity, the number of perturbations per individual np is defined according to the function of progress ratio pr as formulated by Eq. (5.4).

According to (5.4), np has an inverse relationship with pr and is bounded by upper bound ($ubnp$) and lower bound ($lbnp$). The coefficient α denotes the boundary between satisfactory and unsatisfactory level of pr, which could be set as 0.5 for simplicity. $ubnp$ and $lbnp$ could be determined based upon the maximum affordable perturbation effort for each individual and the minimum number of perturbations needed for neighborhood exploration, respectively. For simplicity, they could be set as (5.5).

$$
np(pr) = \begin{cases} (ubnp - lbnp)\left[1 - 2\left(\dfrac{pr}{n}\right)^2 + \dfrac{lbnp}{ubnp - lbnp}\right] & 0 \le pr \le \alpha, \\[3mm] (ubnp - lbnp)\left[2\left(\dfrac{pr - n}{n}\right)^2 + \dfrac{lbnp}{ubnp - lbnp}\right] & \alpha < pr \le 1. \end{cases} \tag{5.4}
$$

$$
1 \le lbnp < ubnp \le 5. \tag{5.5}
$$

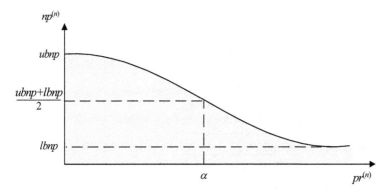

Fig. 5.3. Number of perturbations per individual $np^{(n)}$ versus progress ratio $pr^{(n)}$.

5.2.3 Program Flowchart of IMOEA

The overall program flowchart of IMOEA (Khor et al. 2000; Tan et al. 2001c, 2001d) is shown in Fig. 5.4. The dynamic sharing method for niched cost estimation is applied here to provide a simple computation of σ_{share} at each generation, which is capable of distributing the population uniformly along the Pareto front without a priori knowledge in setting the σ_{share}. The detailed procedures within the box of genetic operations for IMOEA in the program flow are shown in Fig. 5.5. The number of individuals selected for reproduction in the tournament selection is dynamic so that the desired number of offspring could be generated. Since the desired population size for next generation is $dps^{(n+1)}$, and FBLP generates a perturbed individual size of $np^{(n)}$ per each individual in the current generation, the total number of tournament selected individuals $nsi^{(n)}$ is also dynamic at each generation as given by

$$nsi^{(n)} = \begin{cases} \left\lceil \dfrac{dps^{(n+1)}}{np^{(n)}} \right\rceil & \text{for } np^{(n)} > 0, \\[2ex] dps^{(n+1)} & \text{for } np^{(n)} = 0. \end{cases} \tag{5.6}$$

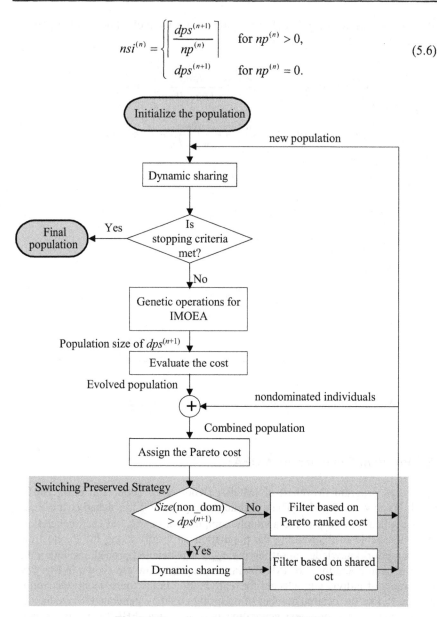

Fig. 5.4. Overall program flowchart of IMOEA.

Instead of simple mutation, fuzzy boundary local perturbation is performed in IMOEA with dynamic number of local perturbations per each parent to encourage or reproduce the "incrementing" individuals needed for a better tradeoff representation. While maintaining the global search capability, the scheme enhances the local exploration and fine-tuning of the evolution at each generation so as to fill up any discovered gaps or discontinuities among the nondominated individuals that are located far away from each other on the tradeoff surface. As shown in Fig. 5.4, the evolved population with the desired population size of $dps^{(n+1)}$ will be combined with the reserved nondominated individuals at generation n to form a combined population that has a size greater than or equal to $dps^{(n+1)}$. Individuals in the combined population are then selected by means of switching preserved strategy (discussed in Chapter 4) for the next generation such that a stable and well-distributed Pareto front could be maintained at each generation.

Genetic Operations for IMOEA:

Let $dps^{(n)}$ = the size of population at current generation n
 $pop^{(n)}$ = population at current generation n.
Step 1. From current $pop^{(n)}$, the desired population size in next generation is computed according to the adaptation mechanism in (5.1):
$$dps^{(n+1)} = ppv \times V_{pop}{}^{(n)}.$$
Step 2. Compute progress ratio $pr^{(n)}$ at current generation and then compute the number of perturbation per parent $np^{(n)}$ from (5.4).
Step 3. Perform tournament selection to select $nsi^{(n)}$ number of individuals from $pop^{(n)}$ based on their niched cost obtained from dynamic sharing scheme. The selected population is called $selpop^{(n)}$.
Step 4. Perform simple crossover with crossover probability $p_c = 0.7$ and mating restriction for $selpop^{(n)}$ using the dynamic sharing distance in step 3. The resulted population is called $crosspop^{(n)}$.
Step 5. Perform FBLP with $np^{(n)}$ number of perturbations for each individual in $crosspop^{(n)}$ via the probability set p as shown in Fig. 5.2. The resulted population is called $evolpop^{(n)}$.

Fig. 5.5. Detailed procedures within the box of "genetic operations for IMOEA" in Fig. 5.4.

5.3 Simulation Studies

In this section, various features of IMOEA are examined qualitatively and different cases are used to represent different combinations of settings in IMOEA. The MO problem used in this study is Fonseca and Fleming's two-objective minimization problem as described in Chapter 1. Table 5.1 summarizes seven different cases under study, with certain properties enabled/disabled to evaluate the performance of respective features. In the table, ppv denotes the population distribution density, SPS is the switching preserved strategy, while l is the number of generations before generation n on which the average value of $pr^{(n)}$ at generation n is computed.

Simulation in case 1 (IMOEA with fixed population size and without FBLP) has a population size of 10, while others applied the dynamic population size with an initial population size of 10 in each case and a predefined population per unit volume, ppv, of 100 for Cases 3 and 4, while 200 for Cases 2 and 5–7. FBLP is included in all cases, except Cases 1 and 4, with similar settings of $ubnp$, $lbnp$, b, ab, and β to Section 5.2.2. The number of generations l used in averaging the pr are set as one in Case 5 and set as three for all other cases except Case 1. Simulation in Case 6 is performed without SPS, while Case 7 has a goal setting of $(f_1, f_2) =$ (0.9, 0.5) to be attained in the optimization. For consistency, the evolutions are run until generation 70 is achieved for all cases. The absolute CPU time taken for each simulation is also recorded to show the computational effort needed in each case. Note that performances for each case are compared qualitatively here by direct observation on the population distribution in the objective domain and, hence, only simulation results of one run in each case are shown in this section to avoid heavy display of almost identical graphs. All simulations considered are implemented with the same coding scheme where each parameter is represented by a three-digit decimal and concatenated to form the chromosomes. Standard two-point crossover with a probability of 0.7 and standard mutation with a probability of 0.01 are used. All sharing is performed in the phenotype space and no sharing distance is required to be predefined since the dynamic sharing scheme (discussed in Chapter 4) is implemented in all cases.

Table 5.1. Comparison Results of IMOEA with Different Settings

| Case | Settings | | | | | | | Results | |
	Popsize	Initial popsize	ppv	FBLP	SPS	l	Goal setting	Final popsize	Simulation time (sec)
1	Fixed	10	—	No	Yes	—	No	10	34
2	Dynamic	10	200	Yes	Yes	3	No	302	6.4×10^3
3	Dynamic	10	100	Yes	Yes	3	No	146	5.3×10^3
4	Dynamic	10	100	No	Yes	—	No	162	5.5×10^3
5	Dynamic	10	200	Yes	Yes	1	No	304	6.6×10^3
6	Dynamic	10	200	Yes	No	3	No	192	5.8×10^3
7	Dynamic	10	200	Yes	Yes	3	Yes	70	2.6×10^3

Progress ratio for the simulation in Case 1 is shown in Fig. 5.6a, indicating that the population has a nearly zero value of pr with almost no further improvements toward the end of the evolution at generation 70. All the individuals are nondominated as represented by the solid circle in Fig. 5.6b. However, Case 1 fails to discover the tradeoffs neither in normal nor tangent directions to the Pareto front since insufficient number of individuals is adopted in this case. Therefore, a larger size of population is needed in order to explore the solution space more thoroughly. In practice, a suitable population size is not easy to be predefined accurately if the fitness landscape and the size of the true Pareto front are not known beforehand.

As mentioned, the suitable population size was found to be larger than 10 after observing an insufficient population size in Case 1, i.e., it requires a trial-and-error process or a priori knowledge in setting an optimal population size for MO optimization. This problem can be overcome by adapting a dynamic population size for online adaptation as in IMOEA, which estimates an appropriate and bounded population size at each generation to discover the entire tradeoffs based on the desired population distribution density. The IMOEA is applied in Case 2 with a small initial population size of 10, similar to the initial population size in Case 1, and a predefined *ppv* of 200 that is determined based on the user-desired distribution density of Pareto front. As shown in Fig. 5.7a, the population size of Case 2 starts with a small initial population size of 10 and increases or decreases adaptively based on the online growing Pareto front. In the final generation, the population size of IMOEA maintains at 302 when the entire tradeoffs have been discovered. Therefore, the population size of IMOEA is adapted online based upon the discovered size of Pareto front and leads gradually to the optimal population size to meet the desired distribution density of Pareto front. Figure 5.7b presents the final population, which is distributed uniformly along the entire tradeoff curve although it initially has an insufficient population size of 10 as shown in Case 1.

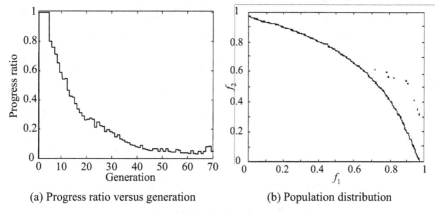

(a) Progress ratio versus generation   (b) Population distribution

Fig. 5.6. Simulation results of Case 1.

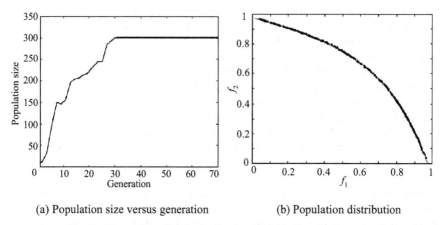

(a) Population size versus generation   (b) Population distribution

Fig. 5.7. Population distribution in the objective domain for Case 2.

Case 3 illustrates performances of the IMOEA with a smaller setting of population size per unit volume by reducing the value of *ppv* from 200 in Case 2 to 100. Figures 5.8(a) and (b) show the trace of population size at each generation and the population distribution at the end of the evolution in Case 3, respectively. It can be seen from the results in Table 5.1 that the final population in this case is 146, which is smaller than the final population size in Case 2 (302) since a smaller value of desired *ppv* (100) than that of Case 2 (200) is set in this case. This shows that IMOEA is capable of adaptively determining the required population size to reach the desired population distribution density along the Pareto front in MO optimization space, as desired.

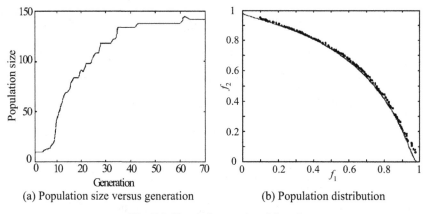

(a) Population size versus generation   (b) Population distribution

Fig. 5.8. Simulation results of Case 3.

The simulation performed in Case 4 is to examine the effect of incorporating FBLP in IMOEA. In this case, all the parameter settings are similar to Case 3 except that FBLP is not implemented. Figures 5.9(a) and (b) show the corresponding trace of population size at each generation and the population distribution at the end of the evolution, respectively. As listed in Table 5.1, the final population size is 162, which is about the same as that in Case 3. However, the final Pareto front found in Case 4 is more discontinuous than that in Case 3 [cf. Figs. 5.9(b) and 5.8(b)]. Therefore, it is obvious that without the incorporation of local exploration with FBLP, the gaps or discontinuities among the nondominated individuals are more difficult to be filled up so as to achieve a better representation of the Pareto front. Besides, as can be seen in Fig. 5.9(b), the nondominated individuals are also quite hard to evolve forward when they are close to the actual Pareto front if no FBLP is embedded.

The relationship between progress ratio and the number of perturbations per parent in FBLP can be observed in Figs. 5.10 and 5.11. In general, the progress ratio is high at the initial stage and results in a small number of perturbed individuals per parent. As evolution proceeds, the value of progress ratio drops asymptotically and provides a larger number of perturbations according to (5.4) in order to broaden local exploration and to recover any gaps or discontinuities among the evolved Pareto front. These two figures also unveil that the progress ratio and the number of perturbed individuals for Case 5, where l is one, are more hilly and fluctuating than that of Case 2 where l is three, since a smaller number of l is set in Case 5.

To show the effectiveness of SPS in IMOEA, simulation in Case 2 is repeated in Case 6 without incorporating the SPS. As shown in Fig. 5.12(b), the algorithm in Case 6 faces difficulties in distributing all individuals uniformly and fails in converging to the final tradeoffs at the end of the evolution. Moreover, the evolved population in Case 6 only manages to cover certain portion of the trade-offs with a slow convergence of progress ratio as shown in Fig. 5.12(a). This illustrates the effectiveness of SPS in promoting rapid convergence toward the final tradeoffs as well as preserving consistency and diversity of the population along the Pareto front.

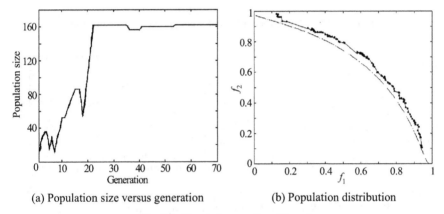

(a) Population size versus generation   (b) Population distribution

Fig. 5.9. Simulation results of Case 4.

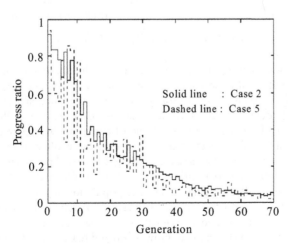

Fig. 5.10. Progress ratio versus generation.

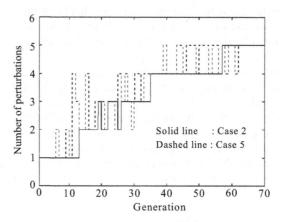

Fig. 5.11. Number of perturbed individuals per parent versus generation.

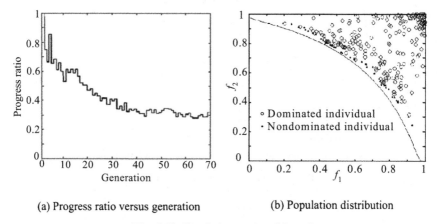

(a) Progress ratio versus generation   (b) Population distribution

Fig. 5.12. Simulation results of Case 6.

In Case 7, a goal setting of $(f_1, f_2) = (0.9, 0.5)$ is incorporated. Figure 5.13(b) shows the distribution of nondominated individuals at 4 different stages along the evolution. As can be seen in Fig. 5.13(a) and (b), the population size starts to grow from an initial population size of 10 and reaches 70 at the end of the evolution based on the limited size of the focused tradeoff curve and the desired population distribution density in the objective domain. Along the evolution, the population size of IMOEA varies and increases according to the online discovered Pareto front before satisfying the goal setting (Stages 1 to 3). When at least one individual satisfies the goal after 20 generations, the population size drops to the lower bound immediately due to the sudden decrease of Pareto front covered by the small amount of nondominated individuals inside the goal region. As evolution proceeds, the population size starts to grow again and reaches 70 at Stage 4, after a substantial number of individuals have evolved into the goal compound to cover the final focused tradeoffs. This shows that the IMOEA is capable of evolving an appropriate population size starting from a small initial population with less computational overhead to effectively represent the entire final tradeoffs with or without any goal setting. Note that the final population size of 70 in IMOEA also indicates the existence of tradeoffs in this problem; otherwise, there should only be a single optimal solution and the desired population size should be reduced to *lowbps* due to the zero tradeoffs in the objective domain.

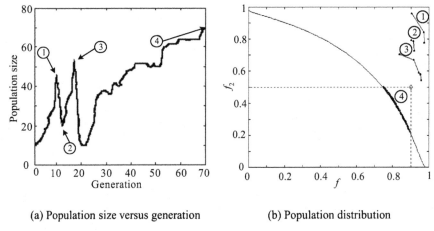

(a) Population size versus generation   (b) Population distribution

Fig. 5.13. Simulation results of Case 7.

5.4 Conclusions

An incrementing multiobjective evolutionary algorithm that has a dynamic population size based on the online discovered Pareto front and its desired population distribution density has been presented in this chapter. The algorithm implemented the concept of Pareto optimal domination with adaptive niche induction technique to evolve a set of nondominated individuals uniformly distributing on the tradeoff surface. The method of fuzzy boundary local perturbation with dynamic local fine-tuning has been incorporated to achieve broader neighborhood explorations as well as to eliminate any gaps or discontinuities along the Pareto front for better convergence and tradeoffs representations. Numerous simulations with different algorithm settings have been carried out to examine the effects of including the various features in IMOEA, such as the adaptive mechanism of dynamic population size, FBLP, SPS, etc. It has been shown that each of these features has its own specific usage, which produces overall optimized solutions in terms of Pareto domination and population diversity as well as the uniform distribution of the nondominated solutions when combined together as applied in IMOEA.

5.3 Conclusions

6

A Distributed Cooperative Coevolutionary Multiobjective Algorithm

6.1 Introduction

Although many successful MOEAs have been proposed over the years (Knowles and Corne 2000a; Corne et al. 2000; Deb et al. 2002a; Zitzler et al. 2001; Tan et al. 2001c), the computational cost involved in terms of time and hardware for evolving a complete set of tradeoff solutions in MO optimization often become insurmountable as the size or complexity of the problem to be solved increases. Meanwhile, studies have shown that coevolutionary mechanisms can increase the efficiency of the optimization process significantly (Potter and De Jong 1994, 2000; Moriarty 1997; Liu et al. 2001). Therefore, one promising approach to overcome the limitation of MOEAs is to incorporate the mechanism of coevolution by decomposing a complex MO optimization problem into smaller problems via a number of subpopulations co-evolving for the set of Pareto optimal solutions in a cooperative way.

Neef et al. (1999) introduced the concept of coevolutionary sharing and niching into multiobjective genetic algorithms by adapting the niche radius through competitive coevolution. Parmee and Watson (1999) used multiple populations where each population optimizes one objective that is related to the problem. The individual fitness of each population is then adjusted by comparing the variable values of identified solutions related to a single-objective with the solutions of other populations. Lohn et al. (2002) embodied the model of competitive coevolution in MO optimization, which contains population of candidate solutions and target population with the target objective vectors. Keerativuttiumrong et al. (2002) extended the approach of cooperative coevolutionary genetic algorithm (Potter and De Jong 1994, 2000) for MO optimization by evolving each species with MOGA (Fonseca and Fleming 1993) in a rather elementary way.

This chapter presents a cooperative coevolutionary algorithm (CCEA) to evolve multiple solutions in the form of cooperative subpopulations for MO optimization. Incorporated with various features like archiving, dynamic sharing, and extending operator, the CCEA is capable of maintaining search diversity in the evolution and distributing the solutions uniformly along the Pareto front. Exploiting the inherent parallelism of cooperative coevolution, the CCEA is further formulated into a computing structure suitable for concurrent processing that allows intercommunications of subpopulations residing in multiple computers over the Internet.

The remainder of this chapter is organized as follows: Section 6.2 describes the principle of CCEA for MO optimization. The implementation of software infrastructure necessary to support a distributed CCEA using the resource of networked computers is presented in Section 6.3. Section 6.4 examines the different features of CCEA and provides a comprehensive comparison of CCEA with other MOEAs. The performance improvement of the distributed CCEA running on multiple networked computers is also studied in Section 6.4. Conclusions are drawn in Section 6.5.

6.2 A Cooperative Coevolutionary Algorithm

6.2.1 Coevolution Mechanism

Recent advances in evolutionary computation show that the introduction of ecological models and coevolutionary architectures are effective ways to broaden the use of traditional evolutionary algorithms (Rosin and Belew 1997; Potter and De Jong 2000). Coevolution can be classified into competitive coevolution and cooperative coevolution. While competitive coevolution tries to make individuals more competitive through evolution, the cooperative coevolution aims to find individuals from which better systems can be constructed. Many studies (Angeline and Pollack 1993; Rosin and Belew 1997) show that competitive coevolution leads to an "arms race," where two populations reciprocally drive one another to increase levels of performance and complexity. The model of competitive coevolution is often compared to predator–prey or host–parasite interactions, where preys (or hosts) implement the potential solutions to the optimization problem, while the predators (or parasites) implement individual "fitness cases." In a competitive coevolutionary algorithm, the fitness of an individual is based on direct competition with individuals of other species that evolve separately in their own populations, e.g., increased fitness for one of the species implies a diminution in the fitness for the other species. Such an evolutionary pressure tends to produce new strategies in the populations involved in order to maintain their chances of survival.

The basic approach of cooperative coevolution is "divide-and-conquer" (Potter and De Jong 2000), which divides a large system into many modules and evolves the modules separately. These modules are then combined again to form the whole system. The cooperative coevolutionary algorithms involve a number of independently evolving species that together form a complex structure for solving difficult problems. The fitness of an individual depends on its ability to collaborate with individuals from other species. In this way, the evolutionary pressure stemming from difficulty of the problem favors the development of cooperative strategies and individuals. Potter and De Jong (1994) present a cooperative coevolutionary genetic algorithm with improved performance on many benchmark functions. The approach was also successfully applied to the applications of string matching and neural network designs (Potter and De Jong 2000). Moriarty (1997) applied a cooperative coevolutionary approach to evolve neural networks, where each individual in one species corresponds to a single hidden neuron of a neural network as well as its connections with input and output layers. This population co-evolves alongside with a second population that encodes sets of hidden neurons in its individuals (i.e., individuals from the first population) to form a neural network. Liu et al. (2001) used cooperative coevolution to speed up the convergence of a fast evolutionary programming for solving large-scale problems with dimensions ranging from 100 to 1000.

6.2.2 Adaptation of Cooperative Coevolution for MO Optimization

6.2.2.1 Cooperation and Rank Assignment

Given a single-objective optimization problem with n parameters, each parameter can be assigned a subpopulation, and these n subpopulations can co-evolve individuals contained in each of them (Potter and De Jong 1994, 2000; Liu et al. 2001). CCEA extends the idea of assigning one subpopulation to each parameter to evolve multiple nondominated individuals along the Pareto front for MO optimization. Figure 6.1 depicts the principle of cooperation and rank assignment in CCEA, where individuals in a subpopulation i is cooperated with representatives from other subpopulations to form the complete candidate solutions.

As shown in the figure, each subpopulation optimizes only one parameter in the evolution. The best r individuals in a subpopulation are defined as the representative set of that subpopulation. To evaluate an individual in a subpopulation, a representative is selected randomly from the representative set of every other subpopulation, and these representatives are combined with the individual under evaluation to form a complete candidate solution. Then this candidate solution is mapped onto an objective vector by the objective functions, which is used to evaluate how well the selected individual cooperates with other subpopulations for producing good solutions. The Pareto ranking scheme by Fonseca and Fleming (1995b) can be applied here to give each individual a scalar rank value, where the rank of an individual partially reflects the distance between the objective vector of that individual and the current approximated Pareto front. The set of Pareto optimal solutions in CCEA is obtained by incorporating an archive to store the nondominated individuals discovered along the evolution. The archive works as an elitism mechanism that ensures a good convergence in CCEA. Besides, it also serves as a comparison set for rank assignment of individuals from the subpopulations.

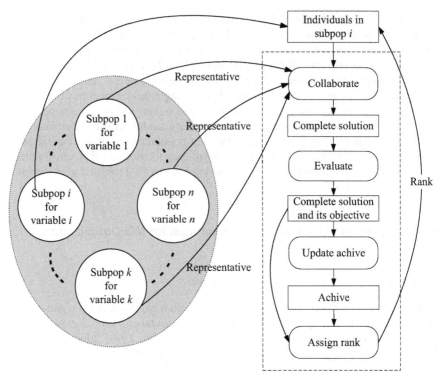

Fig. 6.1. Cooperation and rank assignment in CCEA.

6.2.2.2 Archive Updating

The size of archive, *archive_size*, can be adjusted according to the desired number of individuals to be distributed on the tradeoffs in the objective domain. As illustrated in Fig. 6.2, the archive will be updated once a complete candidate solution is formed. If the candidate solution is not dominated by any members in the archive, it will be added to the archive, and any archive members dominated by this solution will be discarded from the archive. When the maximum archive size is reached, a truncation method based on niche count (*nc*) is used to eliminate the most crowded archive members in order to maintain diversity of individuals in the archive. To distribute the nondominated individuals equally along the Pareto front, the dynamic sharing scheme by Tan et al. (2003b) is incorporated in CCEA. Note that a partial order is used in CCEA to compare the strengths of individuals, i.e., for any two individuals i and j, $i \geq_n j$ if $\mathrm{rank}(i) < \mathrm{rank}(j)$ or $\{\mathrm{rank}(i) == \mathrm{rank}(j)$ and $nc(i) < nc(j)\}$.

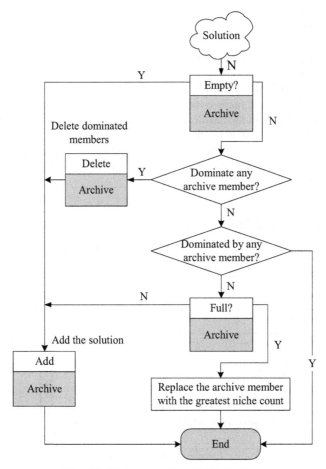

Fig. 6.2. The process of archive updating.

6.2.3 Extending Operator

An extending operator is used in CCEA to improve the smoothness and spread of nondominated individuals in covering the entire Pareto front uniformly. Ordinarily, the less populated regions are the gaps or boundaries in the archive. The extending operator is thus designed to guide the evolutionary search to concentrate on these underrepresented regions. At the initial stage of evolution, the CCEA focuses on finding the nondominated individuals to fill up the archive and to achieve a good preliminary approximation to the Pareto front. When the archive size is full, the archive member that resides in the least populated region based upon the niche count is discovered, which is subsequently cloned and added to the evolving subpopulations in order to explore the underrepresented regions thoroughly. Detailed description of the extending operator is given as follows:

The Extending Operator for CCEA:
Let c be the number of clones.
Step 1.   If the archive is not full, exit.
Step 2.   Calculate the niche count of each member in the archive and find the member with the smallest niche count, e.g., the member that resides in the least populated region.
Step 3.   Clone c copies of this archive member to the subpopulations, where each part of this member is cloned into its corresponding subpopulation.

6.2.4 Flowchart of CCEA

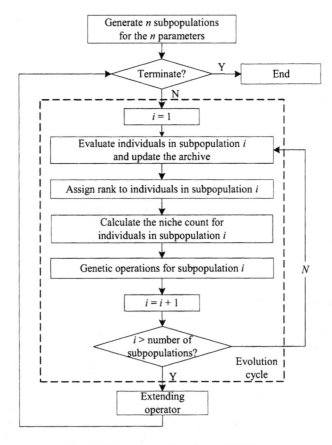

Fig. 6.3. The program flowchart of CCEA.

As depicted in the program flowchart of CCEA in Fig. 6.3, n subpopulations are randomly initialized for an n-parameter problem, each of which optimizes only one parameter. In the evolution cycle, the n subpopulations are evolved in a sequential way. The genetic operations in CCEA consist of tournament selection, uniform crossover, and bit-flip mutation. Once an evolution cycle is completed, the extending operator finds the archive member residing in the least populated region, which is subsequently cloned and added to the evolving subpopulations in order to explore the underrepresented regions thoroughly and to distribute the nondominated individuals uniformly along the Pareto front.

6.3 A Distributed Cooperative Coevolutionary Algorithm

6.3.1 Distributed Evolutionary Computing

It is known that the computational cost for an evolutionary optimization in terms of time and hardware increases as the size and complexity of the problem increase. One approach to overcome such a limitation is to exploit the inherent parallel nature of EA by formulating the problem into a distributed computing structure suitable for parallel processing, i.e., to divide a task into subtasks and to solve the subtasks simultaneously using multiple processors. This divide-and-conquer approach has been applied in different ways, and many parallel EA implementations have been reported in literature (Cantú-Paz 1998; Goldberg 1989b; Rivera 2001).

As categorized by Rivera (2001), there are four possible strategies to parallelize EAs, i.e., global parallelization, fine-grained parallelization, coarse-grained parallelization, and hybrid parallelization. In global parallelization, only the fitness evaluations of individuals are parallelized by assigning a fraction of the population to each processor. The genetic operators are often performed in the same manner as traditional EAs since these operators are not as time-consuming as the fitness evaluation. This strategy preserves the behavior of traditional EA and is particularly effective for problems with complicated fitness evaluations. The fine-grained parallelization is often implemented on massively parallel machines, which assigns one individual to each processor and the interactions between individuals are restricted into some neighborhoods. In coarse-grained parallelization, the entire population is partitioned into subpopulations. This strategy is often complex since it consists of multiple subpopulations and different subpopulations may exchange individuals occasionally (migration). In hybrid parallelization, several parallelization approaches are combined. The complexity of these hybrid-parallel EAs depends on the level of hybridization.

6.3.2 A Distributed CCEA (DCCEA)

The availability of powerful networked computers presents a wealth of computing resources to solve problems with large computational effort. As the communication amount in coarse-grained parallelization is small as compared to other parallelization strategies, it is a suitable computing model for distributed networks with limited communication speeds. This parallelization approach is considered here, where large problems are decomposed into smaller subtasks that are mapped into the computers available in a distributed system.

To design the CCEA suitable for distributed computing, several issues are considered, such as variant communication overhead, different computation speeds, and network restrictions. A prototype model of DCCEA with six subpopulations over three peer computers is illustrated in Fig. 6.4. As shown in the figure, each parameter is assigned a subpopulation, and these subpopulations are further partitioned into groups depending on the number of available peers. Without loss of generality, the six subpopulations are divided into three groups, each of which is assigned to a peer computer. Note that each peer contains its own archive and representatives, which evolves its subpopulations sequentially in an approach similar to CCEA.

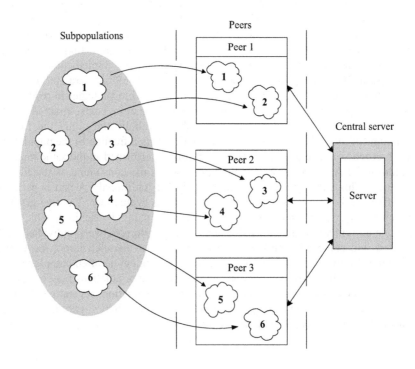

Fig. 6.4. The model of DCCEA.

Inside a peer, the complete candidate solutions generated through the collaboration consistently update the archive in the peer. The subpopulations in the peer then update their corresponding peer representatives once in every cycle. The cooperation among peers is indirectly achieved through the exchange of archive and representatives between the peers and a central server. In DCCEA, the communication time among peers is a conspicuous part of the whole execution time. To reduce the communication overhead, the exchange of archive and representatives between a peer and the central server only occurs every several generations as determined by exchange interval. Since the peers are often not identical, the cooperation among peers will become ineffective if there is a big difference for the evolution progress among the peers, e.g., the poor cooperation among peers may deteriorate the performance of DCCEA. To make the peers cooperate well in the evolution, the peers are synchronized every several generations as determined by synchronization interval. Note that the exchange and synchronization intervals in DCCEA can be fixed or computed adaptively along the evolution.

6.3.3 Implementation of DCCEA

The DCCEA has been designed and embedded in a distributed computing framework named Paladin-DEC (Tan et al. 2002b, 2003a) that was built upon the foundation of Java technology offered by Sun Microsystems and was equipped with application programming interfaces (APIs) and technologies from J2EE. The J2EE is a component-based technology provided by Sun for the design, development, assembly, and deployment of enterprise applications. The unique advantage of Java programming language, such as platform independence and reusability, makes the approach attractive.

As shown in Fig. 6.5, the Paladin-DEC software consists of two main blocks, i.e., the servant block and workshop block that are connected by remote method invocation over the Internet inter-ORB protocol (RMI-IIOP). The servant functions as an information center and backup station through which peers can check their identifications or restore their working status. The workshop is a place where peers (free or occupied) work together in groups, e.g., the working peers are grouped together to perform a specified task, while the free ones wait for new jobs to be assigned. The servant contains three different servers, i.e., logon server, dispatcher server, and database server. The logon server assigns identification to any registered peers. It also removes the information and identification of a peer when it is logged off as well as synchronizes the peer's information to the dispatcher server. The dispatcher server is responsible for choosing the tasks to be executed and the group of peers to perform the execution. It also handles the transfer of peers' information to/from the database server. Besides, the dispatcher server also synchronizes the information, updates the peer's list, and informs the database server for any modification. Whenever a task is available, the dispatcher server will transfer the task to a group of selected peers.

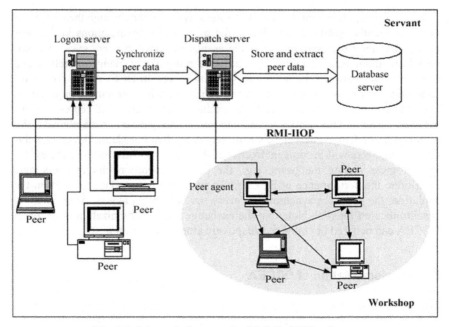

Fig. 6.5. Schematic framework of Paladin-DEC software.

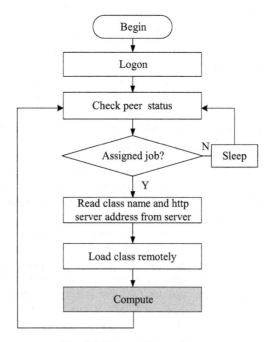

Fig. 6.6. The workflow of a peer.

The working process of a peer begins when it logs on to the server by sending a valid email address to the server. The peer computers are then pooled and wait for the tasks to be assigned by the server. Once a peer detects that a task has been assigned, it will extract relevant information from the server, such as class name and path, as well as the http server address before loading the class remotely from the server. If the class loaded is consistent with the Paladin-DEC system, it will be allowed to initiate the computation procedure. Figure 6.6 depicts the working process of a peer, where the description of the module "Compute" is shown in Fig. 6.7.

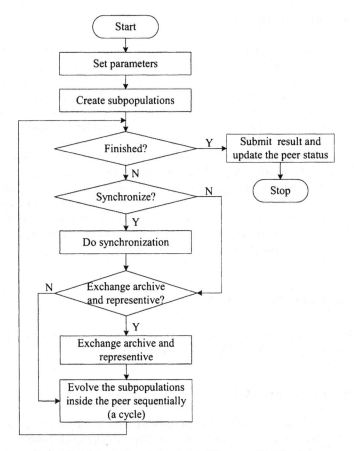

Fig. 6.7. Detailed description of the module "Compute" in Fig. 6.6.

Once a peer starts the computation procedure, it first initializes the parameters, such as generation number, number and size of subpopulations, crossover rate, and mutation rate. The peer then creates the subpopulations assigned to it. When a peer reaches a synchronization point, it suspends its evolution until the server signals that all the peers have reached the synchronization point. At each generation, a peer checks whether it should exchange the archive and representatives between the peer and server. If the conditions of exchange are satisfied, the peer initiates a session in the server and exchanges/updates the archive and representatives between the peer and server. The peer then evolves its subpopulations sequentially for one generation after these procedures. If a peer meets the termination conditions, it will initiate a session to submit the results and restores itself to the ready status. If the user cancels a running job, those peers involved in the job will stop the computation and set themselves to the ready status.

6.3.4 Workload Balancing

As the processing power and specification for various computers in a network may be different, the feature of workload balancing that ensures the peers are processed in a similar pace is important in DCCEA. Besides having a long simulation time, the poor cooperation among computers will also deteriorate the performance of DCCEA if a heavy workload is assigned to the peer that has a relatively low processing power as compared to others. Intuitively, workload balancing for a distributed system could be difficult because the working environment in a network is often complex and uncertain. The DCCEA resorts to a simple workload balancing strategy by assigning workload to peers according to their respective computational capabilities. As stated in Section 6.3.3, when a peer is first launched, it uploads its configuration information to the server, including hardware configuration of the peer such as CPU speed, RAM size, etc. Based on the information, the dispatch server performs a simple task scheduling and assigns different tasks to the respective peers according to their processing powers.

6.4 Simulation Studies

In this section, various simulations are carried out to examine the effect of extending operator in CCEA and the performance of DCCEA.

6.4.1 Performance Metrics

Four different quantitative performance metrics for MO optimization are used here (Van Veldhuizen and Lamont 1999; Deb 2001; Zitzler et al. 2000). The first metric is generational distance (GD), which measures how "far" the solution set is away from the true Pareto front. The second metric is spacing (S), which measures how "equally" members are distributed in the solution set. The third metric is maximum spread (MS), which measures how "well" the true Pareto front is covered by the solution set. The fourth metric is hypervolume ratio(HVR), which calculates the normalized volume (in the objective domain) that is covered by the nondominated solution set (Van Veldhuizen and Lamont 1999). More details of these metrics are given in Section 8.2 of Chapter 8.

6.4.2 MO Test Problems

Nine test problems are used here to evaluate the performance of CCEA, including ZDT1, ZDT2, ZDT3, ZDT4, ZDT6, FON, KUR, TLK, and DTL2. Details of these problems, except DTL2, are given in Section 8.3 of Chapter 8.

The test problem of DTL2 was designed by Deb et al. (2002b) to evaluate the MOEAs' ability for solving problems with a large number of objectives, which is given as

$$Minimize(f_1, f_2, \ldots, f_M)$$

$$\begin{cases} f_1(x) = (1 + g(x_M))\cos(x_1\pi/2)\cdots\cos(x_{M-1}\pi/2) \\ f_2(x) = (1 + g(x_M))\cos(x_1\pi/2)\cdots\sin(x_{M-1}\pi/2) \\ \vdots \\ f_M(x) = (1 + g(x_M))\sin(x_1\pi/2) \\ g(x_M) = \sum_{x_i \in x_M}(x_i - 0.5)^2 \end{cases} \qquad (6.1)$$

where $M = 5$, $x_M = \{x_M, \ldots, x_{M+9}\}$, $x_i \in [0,1]$, $\forall i = 1, 2, \ldots, M+9$.
All points on the tradeoffs satisfy the equation below:

$$\sum_{i=1}^{M} f_i^2 = 1. \qquad (6.2)$$

6.4.3 Simulation Results of CCEA

This section presents the simulation results of CCEA, which is implemented with a binary coding scheme of 30 bits per decision variable, tournament selection, uniform crossover, and bit-flip mutation. In the simulation, 30 independent runs (with random initial populations) are performed on each of the nine test functions in order to study the statistical performance, such as consistency and robustness of CCEA. The number of function evaluations for each simulation run is fixed and the configuration of CCEA is shown in Table 6.1.

Table 6.1. The Configuration of CCEA (Continued on Next page)

Populations	Subpopulation size is 20; archive size is 100
Chromosome length	30 bits per decision variable
Selection	Binary tournament selection
Crossover method	Uniform crossover
Crossover rate	0.8
Mutation method	Bit-flip mutation
Mutation rate	2/L for ZDT1, ZDT2, ZDT3, ZDT4, ZDT6, TLK, and DTL2, where L is the chromosome length; 1/30 for FON and KUR, where 30 is the bit number per variable

Table 6.1. (Continued) The Configuration of CCEA

Hypergrid size	2^3 per dimension for DTL2; 2^5 per dimension for other problems
Representative number	2 for FON and KUR; 1 for other problems
Number of evaluations	120,000

6.4.3.1 Dynamic Behaviors of CCEA

The dynamic behaviors of CCEA for test problems ZDT4 and ZDT6 are illustrated in Fig. 6.8, which shows the various metric values along the number of function evaluations. The problems of ZDT4 and ZDT6 are usually difficult to be tackled by MOEAs, due to the features of multiple local Pareto fronts in ZDT4 and nonuniform distributions in ZDT6. As shown in the figure of *GD*, the CCEA is capable of escaping from the harmful local optima in the evolution. The results also show that the CCEA performs well in terms of the metrics of *S*, *MS*, and *HVR*.

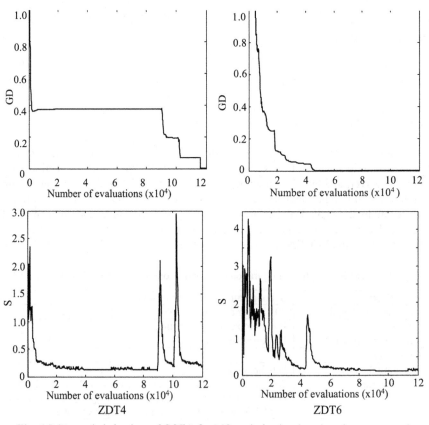

ZDT4   ZDT6

Fig. 6.8. Dynamic behaviors of CCEA for MO optimization (continued on next page).

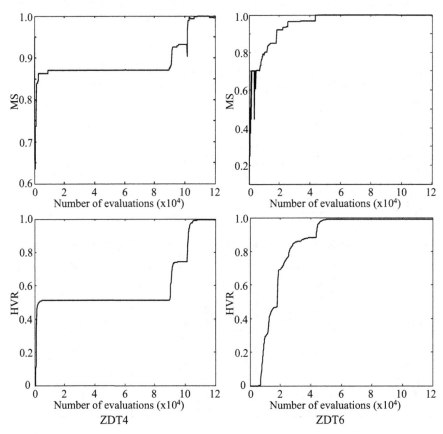

Fig. 6.8. (Continued) Dynamic behaviors of CCEA for MO optimization.

6.4.3.2 Effect of Extending Operator

To study the effect of the extending operator, the simulations of CCEA without extending operator, with extending operator (clone number $c = 1$), and with extending operator ($c = 2$) were run for 30 times with different initial populations, respectively. Tables 6.2, 6.3, and 6.4 list the median values of generational distance, spacing, and maximum spread, respectively. In most cases, the extending operator works well and improves the performance of CCEA. It can be observed that the results of extending operator with $c = 1$ are better than that of $c = 2$. For the test problem of ZDT3 with discontinuous Pareto front, the extending operator is able to reduce the value of spacing significantly. Besides, it also reduces the value of spacing and improves the performance of maximum spread for the problem of FON. Generally, the results for other test problems are rather consistent and illustrate that the extending operator is able to improve the smoothness and maximum spread of nondominated individuals in CCEA.

Table 6.2. Median Generational Distance with and Without Extending Operator

Problem	CCEA without extending operator	CCEA with extending operator ($c = 1$)	CCEA with extending operator ($c = 2$)
ZDT1	1.80E-04	1.32E-04	1.76E-04
ZDT2	2.52E-04	2.15E-04	1.44E-04
ZDT3	7.01E-04	4.05E-04	4.29E-04
ZDT4	1.87E-01	1.85E-01	1.85E-01
ZDT6	5.28E-07	4.92E-07	4.95E-07
FON	2.66E-02	1.47E-02	1.34E-02
KUR	1.37E-02	1.24E-02	1.49E-02
TLK	2.69E-01	2.69E-01	2.68E-01
DTL2	1.15E-03	8.57E-04	1.03E-03

Table 6.3. Median Spacing with and Without Extending Operator

Problem	CCEA without extending operator	CCEA with extending operator ($c = 1$)	CCEA with extending operator ($c = 2$)
ZDT1	0.1299	0.1376	0.1354
ZDT2	0.1312	0.1274	0.1376
ZDT3	0.2469	0.2140	0.2129
ZDT4	0.1267	0.1339	0.1358
ZDT6	0.1373	0.1246	0.1307
FON	0.8289	0.1901	0.1544
KUR	0.6542	0.6589	0.6703
TLK	1.1074	1.1074	1.1125
DTL2	0.1255	0.1214	0.1208

Table 6.4. Median Maximum Spread with and Without Extending Operator

Problem	CCEA without extending operator	CCEA with extending operator ($c = 1$)	CCEA with extending operator ($c = 2$)
ZDT1	0.9931	0.9935	0.9947
ZDT2	0.9989	0.9988	0.9990
ZDT3	0.9973	0.9981	0.9978
ZDT4	0.9358	0.9355	0.9352
ZDT6	0.9992	0.9992	0.9992
FON	0.7202	0.7742	0.8577
KUR	0.9975	0.9981	0.9964
TLK	0.9826	0.9830	0.9830
DTL2	0.9957	0.9971	0.9977

6.4.4 Simulation Results of DCCEA

The test environment of DCCEA consists of 11 PCs connected via a campus local area network. Table 6.5 lists the configuration of these PCs, where the server runs on PIV 1600/512 and the peers are run on other PCs. The test problems of ZDT1, ZDT2, ZDT3, ZDT4, and ZDT6 that have a large number of decision variables are applied here to study the speedup of DCCEA in program execution. The parameters of DCCEA are listed in Table 6.6.

Table 6.5. The Configuration of PCs for the Test Environment of DCCEA

PC	CPU (MHz)/RAM (MB)
1	PIV 1600/512
2	PIII 800/512
3	PIII 800/512
4	PIII 800/256
5	PIII 933/384
6	PIII 933/128
7	PIV 1300/128
8	PIV 1300/128
9	PIII 933/512
10	PIII 933/512
11	PIII 933/256

Table 6.6. The Parameters of DCCEA

Populations	Subpopulation size 20; archive size 100
Chromosome length	30 bits for each decision variable
Selection	Binary tournament selection
Crossover rate	0.8
Crossover method	Uniform crossover
Mutation rate	$2/L$, where L is the chromosome length
Mutation method	Bit-flip mutation
Number of evaluations	120,000
Exchange interval	5 generations
Synchronization interval	10 generations

To minimize the bias in the simulation results, 30 independent runs with randomly generated initial populations were performed. The median run times of the 30 simulation runs for different test problems are listed in Table 6.7 and plotted in Fig. 6.9. It can be observed that the median run times are reduced as the number of peers is increased. In the case of ZDT1, the median run time for 5 peers (each peer with 6 subpopulations) is 109 seconds, which is about one third of the 270 seconds required by 1 peer (each peer with 30 subpopulations). When the number of peers is more than 5, the increased communication cost counteracts the reduction of computation cost as shown in Fig. 6.9, e.g., the saturation for the speedup of DCCEA is achieved for the test problems.

The four median metrics of the 30 simulation runs are plotted in Fig. 6.10. It can be observed that the median metrics for the five test problems have no distinct changes, in spite of some small fluctuations on the curves, as the number of peers is increased. This illustrates that the DCCEA is effective in reducing the simulation run time without sacrificing the performance of CCEA as the number of peers is increased.

Table 6.7. Median Run Times for Different Number of Peers (Unit: Second)

Number of peers	ZDT1	ZDT2	ZDT3	ZDT4	ZDT6
1	270	242	189.5	209	138
2	177.5	142.5	128.5	170	137
3	134	121.5	101	142	124
4	120	109.5	97	139	121
5	109	90	88	134	121
6	96	80	67	123	108
7	94	73	68.5	111	110
8	80	74	65	115	109.5
9	78	72	64	114	109.5
10	78	76	68	115	110.5

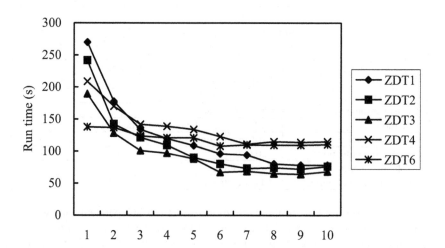

Fig. 6.9. Median run times for different number of peers.

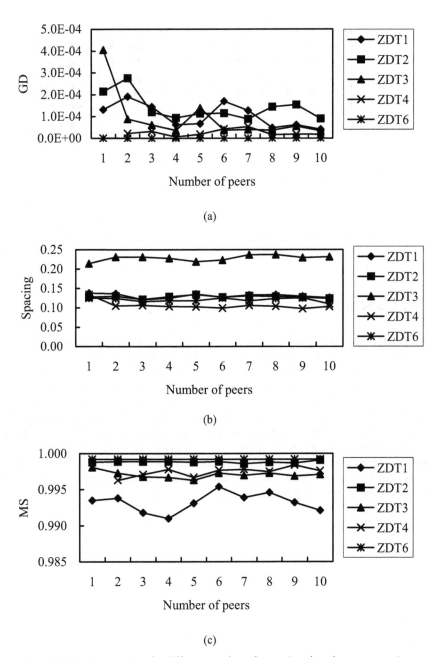

Fig. 6.10. Median metrics for different number of peers (continued on next page).

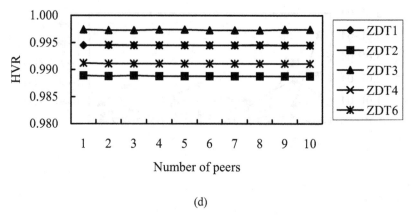

(d)

Fig. 6.10. (Continued) Median metrics for different number of peers.

6.5. Conclusions

This chapter has presented a cooperative coevolutionary algorithm, where a number of subpopulations are co-evolved in a cooperative way for the set of Pareto optimal solutions in MO optimization. Incorporated with various features like archiving, dynamic sharing, and extending operator, the CCEA is capable of maintaining search diversity in the evolution and distributing the solutions uniformly along the Pareto front. Exploiting the inherent parallelism of cooperative coevolution, the CCEA has been formulated into a computing structure suitable for concurrent processing that allows intercommunications of subpopulations residing in multiple computers over the Internet. It has been shown that the DCCEA is able to reduce the simulation runt time without sacrificing the performance of CCEA as the number of peers is increased.

7
Learning the Search Range in Dynamic Environments

7.1 Introduction

Evolutionary algorithms (EAs) are proven optimization and machine learning techniques based on the adaptive mechanism of biological systems (Goldberg 1989a; Holland 1975). Since EAs are operated on coded chromosomes, a predefined search range in the parameter domain is required in a priori to an evolution process. However, the parameter range or the global optimum in a usually multimodal multidimension search space is unknown for many real-world problems. Instead of "guessing" for a specific search range, a passive approach is to start the evolution over a large search space, which is reduced gradually based on human perception of promising subspace by observing scattering of the evolved candidate solutions. Such an approach is, however, tedious and workable if the search space assumed comprising the global optimal solutions.

Yokose et al. (1999) propose the approach of having a large number of bits per chromosome at the initial stage of evolution in order to search for a wider region without aggravating the computational speed. As the evolution proceeds, the search space is decreased gradually according to the value of objective function and the restriction of number of bits. However, the approach is performed according to an analytical model (Yokose et al. 1999) and applicable only to single-objective optimization problems.

This chapter presents an adaptive search space scheme that shrinks or expands the search range adaptively to promote the evolution toward more promising regions, even if these regions are outside the initial predefined search space. Details of the adaptive search space scheme are described in Section 7.2. Section 7.3 examines the effectiveness of the scheme for evolutionary optimization in dynamic environments. Conclusions are drawn in Section 7.4.

7.2 Adaptive Search Space

One of the requirements in evolutionary optimization is that the boundary of all feasible regions in the parameter domain must be predefined a priori to an evolution process (Venkat et al. 1989; Cingoski et al. 1997; Vavak et al. 1997; Yokose et al. 1999; Khor et al. 2001b). To address the issue, this section presents a boundary shrinking and expanding mechanism to explore the search space dynamically for both single-objective and MO problems. The scheme is inspired by the concept of knowledge generation through the investigation in the human brain, in which an inductive–deductive learning process takes places.

According to Box (1998), studies of the human brain over the last few decades confirmed that the brain is divided into two parts constructed to perform jointly the inductive–deductive learning process. For the majority of people the left brain is particularly concerned with deductive, analysis, and rational thinking, while the right brain is more concerned with induction as well as knowledge combination and interpolation in a creative manner. Therefore, the generation of new knowledge through investigation takes place as an iterative inductive–deductive learning process.

It is believed that the above phenomenon has some similar properties to the evolutionary optimization process (Khor et al. 2001b). Analogously, genetic operations such as crossover and mutation can be viewed as the basis of inductive learning in a human brain, where the induction and recombination of knowledge take place. If the candidate solutions are regarded as knowledge stored in a human brain, the evolution toward the global optimum is similar to the route of the investigation process, while the parameter search space in evolutionary optimization can be viewed as the experimental region of interest in human brain. The region of interest may change through the deductive learning process, and the search space in evolutionary optimization can be dynamic and learned in a deductive manner where analysis and reasoning take place.

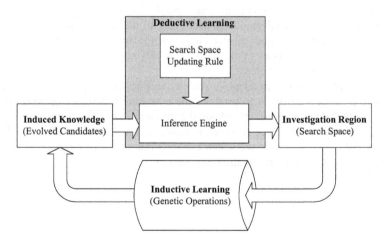

Fig. 7.1. Overall structure of iterative inductive–deductive learning.

Figure 7.1 depicts the general structure of inductive–deductive learning for evolutionary optimization. In each block, the bold text represents the terminology in a human brain learning process, which is analogous to the terminology in an evolutionary optimization process. At each generation, the genetic evolution performs an inductive learning where knowledge in the form of candidate solutions is induced through the genetic operations for previous solutions. Then statistical information is acquired from the distribution of induced candidates and applied to the deductive learning process. In deductive learning, analysis and reasoning are performed based on heuristic rules to determine the next search space of interest in the parameter domain for inductive learning.

Figure 7.2 illustrates the flowchart of updating rule for deductive search space. From the information on current distribution of evolved candidate solutions (given by *maxpar*, *minpar*, and *prange*), the current search space of interest (in terms of *curlowbd* and *curuppbd*) is updated to the new search space of interest (in terms of *newlowbd* and *newuppbd*) based on the updating rule of deductive search space and the parameter *pstep* as depicted in Fig. 7.2. Consider an n-dimensional parameter search space and $\forall \, i = 1, 2,..., n$, the notations applied in the rule can be defined as follows:

i. Search space of interest,
- *curlowbd*(i) = current lower boundary of parameter search space in the ith dimension.
- *curuppbd*(i) = current upper boundary of parameter search space in the ith dimension.
- *newlowbd*(i) = new lower boundary of parameter search space in the ith dimension.
- *newuppbd*(i) = new upper boundary of parameter search space in the ith dimension.

ii. Distribution of candidate solutions,
Let $X_j(i)$ denotes the ith parameter of the jth evolved individual vector in the individual list of N_c candidates (Khor et al. 2001a),
- *maxpar*(i) = max($X_j(i)$, $\forall \, j = 1, 2, ..., N_c$),
- *minpar*(i) = min($X_j(i)$, $\forall \, j = 1, 2, ..., N_c$),
- *prange*(i) = *maxpar*(i) - *minpar*(i).

iii. Parameter for the updating rule,
pstep(i) = additive step size of parameter search space in the ith dimension.

The search space updating rule as depicted in Fig. 7.2 is categorized as deductive since it does not involve any creative induction of knowledge. Instead, the search space is guided through a step-by-step heuristic reasoning approach. Such a dynamic search space mechanism directs the evolution toward finding the optimal solutions even if they are not comprised in the initial search space. Since fitness information of the evolved candidates is not required in the updating rule, the adaptive search space approach can be directly applied to most evolutionary algorithms, for both single-objective and MO optimization problems.

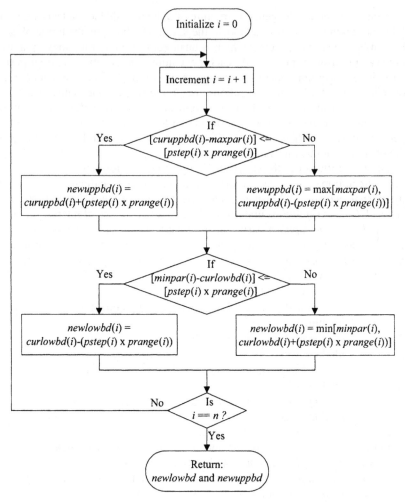

Fig. 7.2. Deductive search space updating rule.

7.3 Simulation Studies

7.3.1 Single-Objective Optimization

To illustrate effectiveness of the dynamic search space scheme, a single-objective maximization problem is considered here. It aims to find a global peak surrounded by many harmful local peaks in a large two-dimensional parameter space. The objective function to be maximized is

$$f(x_1,x_2) = f_1 + f_2 + f_3,$$ (7.1a)

where

$$f_1(x_1,x_2) = 4 \times 10^{-6} x_1^2 \left(8.4 \times 10^{-6} x_1^2 - 5.33 \times 10^{-12} x_1^4\right)$$ (7.1b)
$$+ 10^{-6} x_2^2 \left(4 - 4 \times 10^{-6} x_2^2\right),$$

$$f_2(x_1,x_2) = 5e^{-0.19\sqrt{x_1^2 + x_2^2}},$$ (7.1c)

$$f_3(x_1,x_2) = 0.7\left[-2\sin(0.02x_1)\sin(0.02x_2) - \sin(0.04x_1)\sin(0.04x_2)\right].$$ (7.1d)

The fitness landscape is shown in Fig. 7.3, where the ranges of parameters x_1 and x_2 are [−1000, 500] and [−1000, −500], respectively. Besides a sharp global peak, there are many local peaks scattering over the parameter space. Figure 7.4 depicts the contour plot of the zoomed-in fitness landscape in the parameter domain. As shown by a pair of black arrows, the global peak is located at $x_1 = 0$ and $x_2 = -666.7$, with a fitness value of $f = 6$ at the global peak.

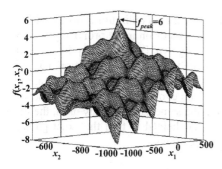
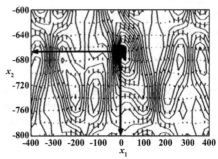

Fig. 7.3. The fitness landscape.

Fig. 7.4. Contour zoomed into the peak location (x_2 versus x_1).

Assume that the exact location of the global optimum is unknown and the search space is confined and chosen such that the global optimum is excluded. Therefore, it is impossible to find the global peak for any optimization if the search range is fixed along the evolution. An exploratory multiobjective evolutionary algorithm (EMOEA) (Khor et al. 2001a) without incorporating any dynamic search space scheme is used in this simulation. It implements a decimal coding scheme (Tan et al. 1999b) with two digits per decision variable, standard two-point crossover with a probability of 0.7, and standard mutation with a probability of 0.01. The size of elite list N_t and individual list N_c (population size) in EMOEA is 1 and 50, respectively. The parameter range of x_1 and x_2 is [−1000, −900] and [−1000, −950], respectively, which are set purposely to exclude the global peak. The simulation was run for 300 generations and the best solution found at the end of the evolution has a fitness value of 3.2591 that is not the global optimum, as expected.

Even if the predefined search space is large enough such that the global optimum is included by "luck," the resolution of the search points may be insufficient to represent the exact global optimum accurately. This can be illustrated by repeating the above simulation with a different fixed search space of $[-1000, 500]$ for x_1 and $[-1000, -500]$ for x_2. At the end of the evolution, the best solution found is 4.9978, which is not the exact global optimum due to the insufficient resolution of genetic representation. Although the resolution can be increased at the expense of a larger chromosome length, it subsequently requires more computational effort in the evolution. An effective approach is thus to adapt the search space dynamically toward more promising regions along the evolution, instead of confining the evolution to a predefined search range. Based on the overall iterative inductive–deductive learning, the search space is then expanded to include other promising regions or shrunk for higher resolution of the solutions. To illustrate the effectiveness of this approach, the simulation of EMOEA with deductive search space updating rule considers the following two cases:

(i) Case 1

In Case 1, an initial search space that includes the global optimum is used to demonstrate the ability of the approach to shrink and focus on more promising search regions. For this purpose, an initial search range of $[-1000, 500]$ for x_1 and $[-1000, -500]$ for x_2 is used: It has been illustrated in previous simulation that the exact global peak is hard to find based on this setting using a fixed search range. Figure 7.5 illustrates the convergence trace of the evolution in Case 1. As shown in the figure, with other parameters remaining the same as previously used, the inclusion of adaptive search space in EMOEA has helped to find the exact global peak with a fitness value of 6 after about 50 generations.

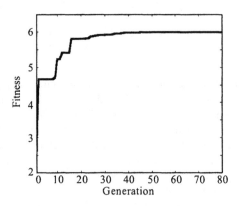

Fig. 7.5. Convergence trace in Case 1.

The trace of search range along the evolution is unveiled for parameter x_1 in Fig. 7.6(a) and parameter x_2 in Fig. 7.6(b). In both figures, the shaded regions represent the trace of the search range, while the bold lines show the trace of the best solution found along the evolution. It can be observed that although the initial search range is large, the iterative inductive–deductive learning has successfully shrunk the search range to improve the resolution in finding the exact global optimum.

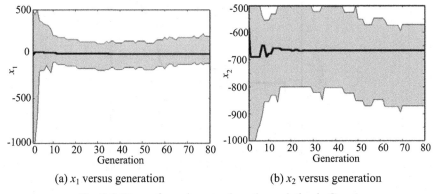

(a) x_1 versus generation   (b) x_2 versus generation

Fig. 7.6. Trace of search range along the evolution in Case 1.

To further compare the adaptive and fixed-space approaches, the search space of the above problem is expanded significantly to the range of $[-10^8, 10^8]$ for both x_1 and x_2. Figure 7.7 shows the mean of the convergence traces over 30 repeated simulations with randomly generated initial populations. In the figure, the negative part of the y-axis denotes the value of $-\log(-f)$, as the range of the negative part of f is extremely large. By applying the dynamic search space, the evolution is able to focus on promising regions adaptively in order to achieve better and more accurate solutions. Besides, it also contributes to a faster convergence in terms of the number of generations [Fig. 7.7(a)] and the CPU time [Fig. 7.7(b)].

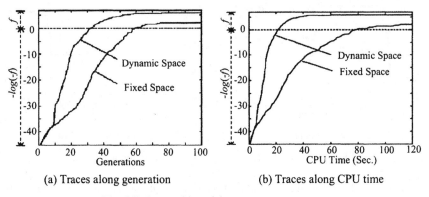

(a) Traces along generation   (b) Traces along CPU time

Fig. 7.7. Comparison of the convergence traces.

(ii) Case 2

In Case 2, the initial search space is defined to exclude the global optimum purposely, which is set as [−1000, −900] for x_1 and [−1000, −950] for x_2. Figure 7.8 shows the convergence trace of the evolution in Case 2. As shown in the figure, the EMOEA with deductive search space updating rule is able to find the exact global peak with a fitness value of 6 after about 280 generations.

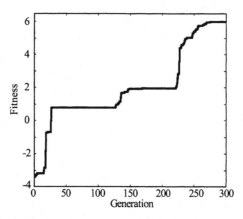

Fig. 7.8. Convergence trace in Case 2.

The trace of search range along the evolution is unveiled for parameter x_1 in Fig. 7.9(a) and for parameter x_2 in Fig. 7.9(b). The figure is plotted in a format similar to that of Fig. 7.6. Although the global optimum is not comprised in the initial search space, the iterative inductive–deductive learning approach makes the search space dynamic to include the global optimum by shrinking or expanding the space of interest adaptively along the evolution.

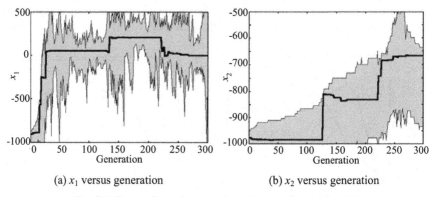

(a) x_1 versus generation   (b) x_2 versus generation

Fig. 7.9. Trace of search space along the evolution in Case 2.

These results show that the iterative inductive–deductive learning plays two major roles, i.e., to shrink the search space dynamically for better resolution of genetic representation in order to facilitate the evolution toward finding more accurate solutions; and to offset the search space dynamically to a new space that contains better solutions by means of shrinking and expanding the current search range in the evolution.

7.3.2 MO Optimization I

The two-objective minimization problem FON as described in Chapter 1 is used for the simulation study here. To illustrate the effect of *pstep* (additive step size of parameter search space) on the performance of adaptive search space, simulations are carried out with different settings of *pstep*. The size of elite list N_t and individuals list N_c is 20 and 100, respectively. The initial search range for the eight parameters is $[-2, -1.5]$, which is defined purposely to exclude the global optimum in the initial search space. Figure 7.10 depicts the overlapping convergence trace of search ranges for all the eight parameters resulting from the different settings of *pstep*. The results show that a higher *pstep* will give a more chaotic convergence trace and a faster response to drive the evolution toward more promising search regions, since it is more sensitive to expand than to shrink the search space as described in Section 7.2.2.

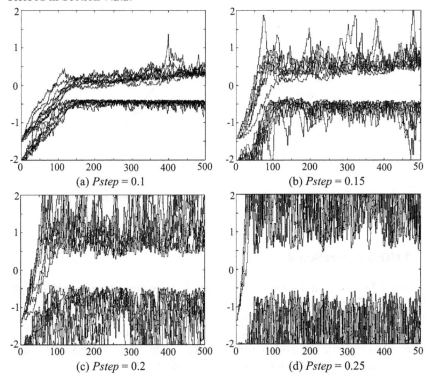

Fig. 7.10. Trace of search range with different settings of *Pstep* (continued on next page).

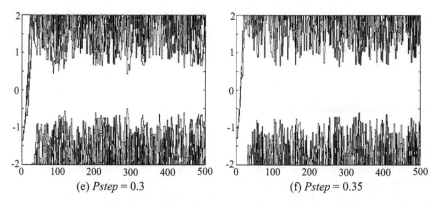

(e) *Pstep* = 0.3   (f) *Pstep* = 0.35

Fig. 7.10. (Continued) Trace of search range with different settings of *Pstep*.

Figure 7.11 illustrates the distribution of nondominated individuals at the end of the evolution for the case of *pstep* = 0.2. It can be observed that all the nondominated individuals are distributed uniformly along the tradeoff curve, although the global optimum is not comprised in the initial search space.

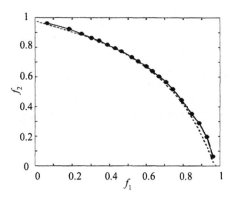

Fig. 7.11. Distribution of nondominated individuals along the tradeoff curve.

7.3.3 MO Optimization II

As stated by Merz and Freisleben (1998), it is important to consider high-dimensional fitness landscape for performance evaluation of evolutionary algorithms. By extending the single-objective minimization problem proposed by Schaffer et al. (1989) to two-dimension search space, the test problem of (7.2) is presented to evaluate the evolutionary optimization in a high-dimensional search space with plenty of local optima as formulated below:

$$f_1 = x_1, \tag{7.2a}$$

$$f_2 = \frac{1}{x_1}\left\{1+\left(\sum_{i=2}^{11}x_i^2\right)^{0.25}\left[\sin^2\left(50\left(\sum_{i=2}^{11}x_i^2\right)^{0.1}\right)+1.0\right]\right\}. \tag{7.2b}$$

The problem involves an 11-dimensional search space with a search range of [0.1, 1] for x_1 and [−100, 100] for $x_i \; \forall \; i = 2, 3, ..., 11$. The value of N_c, N_t, and *pstep* is set as 30, 10, and 2, respectively, while other parameters in the simulation remain the same as previously used. Figure 7.12 shows the trace of adaptive search space for parameter 1 in part (a) and parameters 2 to 11 overlapping each other in part (b). The shaded region represents the range of the respective dimension confined by the dynamic search boundary. It can be seen that the search space is expanded adaptively in the dimension of parameter 1 in order to distribute the nondominated individuals along the Pareto front, while the search space is shrunk asymptotically in the dimension of x_2-x_{11} in order to achieve better accuracy of the solutions, as desired.

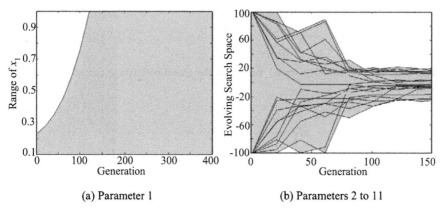

(a) Parameter 1   (b) Parameters 2 to 11

Fig. 7.12. Trace of adaptive search space with an initial search range of [0.1. 0.23] for x_1 and [−100, 100] for x_2 to x_{11}.

The above simulation was repeated for an initial search range of [−100, −70] for parameters x_2 to x_{11}, which was chosen purposely to exclude the global optimum. Figure 7.13 illustrates the trace of adaptive search space for the parameters of x_2 to x_{11}, where each rectangle represents the graph of parameter value versus generation number. The scale of each rectangle is [−100, 100] for the y-axis and [0, 5000] for the x-axis. The shaded regions represent the bounded search space of interest in the respective dimension of the parameter along the evolution. The simulation results show that the search range of parameters x_2 to x_{11} is refined gradually and moved toward the region of the global optimum that is located at zero for x_2 to x_{11}, although there exist many local optima in the parameter domain. Figure 7.14 illustrates the distribution of nondominated individuals at the end of the evolution. Similar to the results obtained in Fig. 7.11, the nondominated individuals are distributed closely along the tradeoff curve, although the global optimum is not comprised in the initial search space.

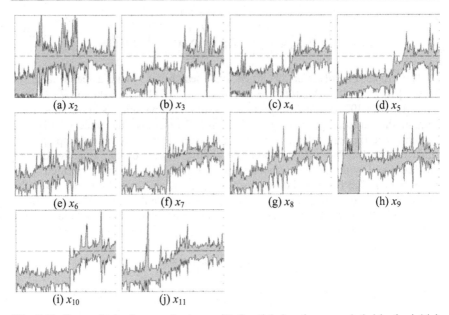

Fig. 7.13. Trace of adaptive search space with the global optimum excluded in the initial search space.

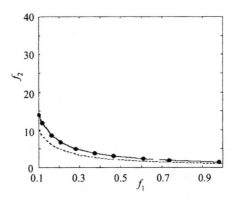

Fig. 7.14. Distribution of nondominated individuals along the tradeoff curve.

7.4 Conclusions

This chapter has presented a dynamic search space scheme with iterative inductive–deductive learning for evolutionary optimization in dynamic environments. By shrinking or expanding the search space adaptively, it promotes the evolution toward more promising search regions, even if these regions are outside the initial predefined search space. If the global optimum is comprised in the initial search space, the approach is able to shrink the search space dynamically for better resolution of genetic representation in order to facilitate the evolution toward finding more accurate solutions. It has been shown that the dynamic search space approach can handle different fitness landscapes and distribute nondominated individuals uniformly along the tradeoff curve for MO optimization, even if there are many local optima in the high-dimensional search space or the global optimum is not comprised in the initial predefined search space.

8
Performance Assessment and Comparison of MOEAs

8.1 Introduction

Since Schaffer's pioneering work, evolutionary techniques for MO optimization have been gaining significant attention, and various MOEAs with different features and characteristics have been proposed. It is thus interesting to study the capabilities of these algorithms and to identify the strength and weakness of each approach (Zitzler et al. 2000; Deb et al. 2002a; Tan 2002a). As pointed out by Zitzler et al. (2000), such a comparative study will bring to light the advantages and shortfalls of existing MOEAs. In this chapter, the performances of 10 MOEAs are studied and compared based upon 10 test problems with different types of optimization difficulties. The performance metrics concerning different aspects in MO optimization are formulated in Section 8.2. Section 8.3 describes the MO test problems with different optimization difficulties and challenges. Section 8.4 discusses the performances of MOEAs both statistically and qualitatively. Conclusions are drawn in Section 8.5.

8.2 MO Performance Metrics

A number of quantitative performance metrics for MO optimization have been proposed by Deb (1999b), Shaw et al. (1999), Van Veldhuizen and Lamont (1998b, 1999), Zitzler and Thiele (1999), and so on. As stated by Shaw et al. (1999), these quantitative metrics mainly examine the MO optimization performance in two aspects, i.e., the spread across the Pareto optimal front and the ability to attain the global tradeoffs. In this section, five different quantitative performance metrics for MO optimization are presented as follows (Van Veldhuizen 1999; Deb 2001; Zitzler et al. 2000; Tan et al. 2002a):

Generational Distance (GD)

The metric of generational distance represents how "far" the known Pareto front (PF_{known}) is away from the true Pareto front (PF_{true}), which is defined as

$$GD = (\frac{1}{n}\sum_{i=1}^{n} d_i^2)^{1/2} , \tag{8.1}$$

where n is the number of members in PF_{known}, d_i is the Euclidean distance (in the objective domain) between the member i in PF_{known} and its nearest member in PF_{true}.

Spacing (S)

The metric of spacing measures how "evenly" members in PF_{known} are distributed. It is defined as

$$S = [\frac{1}{n}\sum_{i=1}^{n}(d_i' - \overline{d}')^2]^{1/2} / \overline{d}', \text{ where } \overline{d}' = \frac{1}{n}\sum_{i=1}^{n} d_i' , \tag{8.2}$$

where n is the number of members in PF_{known}, d_i' is the Euclidean distance (in the objective domain) between the member i in PF_{known} and its nearest member in PF_{known}.

Maximum Spread (MS)

The metric of maximum spread measures how "well" the PF_{true} is covered by the PF_{known} through hyperboxes formed by the extreme function values observed in the PF_{true} and PF_{known} (Zitzler et al. 2000). In order to normalize the metric, it is modified as

$$MS = \sqrt{\frac{1}{M}\sum_{m=1}^{M}[\frac{\min(f_m^{max}, F_m^{max}) - \max(f_m^{min}, F_m^{min})}{F_m^{max} - F_m^{min}}]^2} , \tag{8.3}$$

where M is the number of objectives; f_m^{max} and f_m^{min} are the maximum and minimum of the mth objective in PF_{known}, respectively; F_m^{max} and F_m^{min} are the maximum and minimum of the mth objective in PF_{true}, respectively.

Hypervolume (HV) and Hypervolume Ratio (HVR)

The metric of hypervolume calculates the "volume" in the objective domain covered by the set of nondominated individuals for an MO minimization problem (Van Veldhuizen and Lamont 1999; Zitzler and Thiele 1999; Deb 2001). It is defined as

$$HV = \text{volume}(\bigcup_{i=1}^{n} v_i) . \tag{8.4}$$

For each member i in the nondominated solution set, a hypercube v_i is constructed with a reference point W and the member i as the diagonal corners of the hypercube. The reference point is found by constructing a vector of the worst objective function values. In geometry, the volume of an object is the amount of space occupied by the object. Then HV is the amount of space occupied by the union of hypercubes constructed by the nondominated solutions and the reference point.

To reduce the bias and to normalize the metric, Van Veldhuizen and Lamont (1999) define the metric of hypervolume ratio as a ratio of the hypervolume of PF_{known} and the hypervolume of PF_{true}, which is given as

$$HVR = HV(PF_{known})/HV(PF_{true}).$$ (8.5)

Average Best Performance (*ABP*)

The metric of average best performance measures the ability of tracking the optimal region in a changing environment for time-dependent objective functions. It is defined as the average of the best solutions found at each generation,

$$ABP(T) = \frac{1}{T}\sum_{t=1}^{T} g*(t),$$ (8.6)

where $g*(t)$ is the performance of the best individual given at generation t (Branke 1999), and T is the number of generations.

8.3 MO Test Problems

According to Branke (1999), test problems should be simple, easy to describe, easy to analyze, and tunable in their parameters. On one hand, they should be complex enough to allow conjectures to the real world; on the other hand, they should be simple enough to allow gaining new insights into the optimization algorithm. Concerning the formation of test problems, Deb (1999b) points out a few features that could pose difficulties for MOEAs in maintaining population diversity and converging to the final tradeoffs. These features include multimodality, deception, isolated optima, and collateral noise.

This section describes the set of test problems used for performance assessment of MOEAs. The features of these problems are summarized in Table 8.1, and the corresponding Pareto fronts in the objective domain are shown in Fig. 8.1. Widely adopted in the literature, these test problems were designed with different MO optimization difficulties and challenges (Knowles and Corne 2000a; Corne et al. 2000; Deb et al. 2002a; Tan et al. 2002a; Zitzler et al. 2000, 2001).

Table 8.1. Features of the Test Problems

	Test Problem	Features
1	ZDT1	Pareto front is convex.
2	ZDT2	Pareto front is nonconvex.
3	ZDT3	Pareto front consists of several noncontiguous convex parts.
4	ZDT4	Pareto front is highly multimodal, where there are 21^9 local Pareto fronts.
5	ZDT6	The Pareto optimal solutions are nonuniformly distributed for the global Pareto front. The density of the solutions is low near the Pareto front and high away from the front.
6	FON	Pareto front is nonconvex.
7	KUR	Pareto front consists of several noncontiguous parts.
8	POL	Pareto front and Pareto optimal solutions consist of several noncontiguous parts.
9	TLK	Noisy landscape.
10	TLK2	Nonstationary environment.

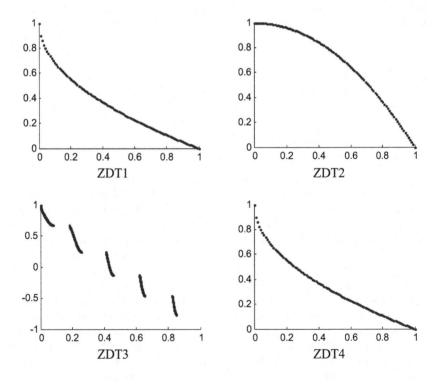

Fig. 8.1. The optimal Pareto fronts of the test problems (continued on next page).

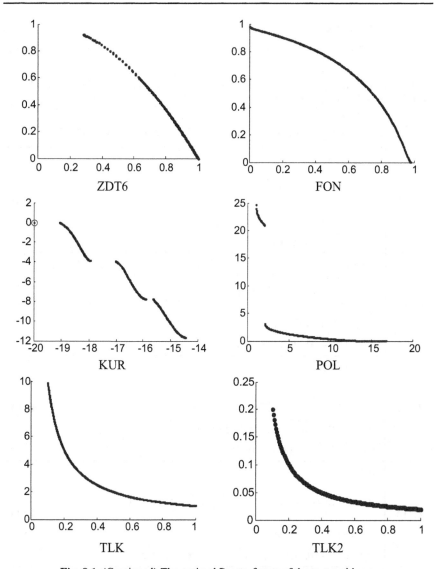

Fig. 8.1. (Continued) The optimal Pareto fronts of the test problems.

8.3.1 Test Problems of ZDT1, ZDT2, ZDT3, ZDT4, and ZDT6

These test problems were designed by Zitzler et al. (2000), where each of the problems is structured in a similar manner and consists of three functions (Deb 1999a):

$$\text{Minimize } T(x) = (f_1(x_1), f_2(x))$$
$$\text{subject to } f_2(x) = g(x_2,\ldots,x_m)h(f_1(x_1), g(x_2,\ldots,x_m)) \tag{8.7}$$
$$\text{where } x = (x_1,\ldots,x_m).$$

The definitions of f_1, g, h in ZDT1, ZDT2, ZDT3, ZDT4, and ZDT6 are listed in Table 8.2.

Table 8.2. Definitions of f_1, g, h in ZDT1, ZDT2, ZDT3, ZDT4, and ZDT6

ZDT1	$f_1(x_1) = x_1$ $g(x_2,\ldots,x_m) = 1 + 9 \cdot \sum_{i=2}^{m} x_i /(m-1)$ $h(f_1,g) = 1 - \sqrt{f_1/g}$ where $m = 30$, and $x_i \in [0,1]$.	(8.8)
ZDT2	$f_1(x_1) = x_1$ $g(x_2,\ldots,x_m) = 1 + 9 \cdot \sum_{i=2}^{m} x_i /(m-1)$ $h(f_1,g) = 1 - (f_1/g)^2$ where $m = 30$, and $x_i \in [0,1]$.	(8.9)
ZDT3	$f_1(x_1) = x_1$ $g(x_2,\ldots,x_m) = 1 + 9 \cdot \sum_{i=2}^{m} x_i /(m-1)$ $h(f_1,g) = 1 - \sqrt{f_1/g} - (f_1/g)\sin(10\pi f_1)$ where $m = 30$, and $x_i \in [0,1]$.	(8.10)
ZDT4	$f_1(x_1) = x_1$ $g(x_2,\ldots,x_m) = 1 + 10(m-1) + \sum_{i=2}^{m} (x_i^2 - 10\cos(4\pi x_i))$ $h(f_1,g) = 1 - \sqrt{f_1/g}$ where $m = 10$, $x_1 \in [0,1]$, and $x_2,\ldots,x_m \in [-5,5]$.	(8.11)
ZDT6	$f_1(x_1) = 1 - \exp(-4x_1)\sin^6(6\pi x_1)$ $g(x_2,\ldots,x_m) = 1 + 9 \cdot [(\sum_{i=2}^{m} x_i)/(m-1)]^{0.25}$ $h(f_1,g) = 1 - (f_1/g)^2$ where $m = 10$, and $x_i \in [0,1]$.	(8.12)

8.3.2 Test Problems of FON, KUR, and POL

A brief description for the test problems of FON, KUR, and POL is given as follows:

i. FON
The FON is a two-objective minimization test problem that has been widely used in the literature (Fonseca and Fleming 1995b; Tan et al. 1999b, 2002a; Van Veldhuizen and Lamont 1999). Besides having a nonconvex Pareto front, this problem has a large and nonlinear tradeoff curve that is suitable for challenging an algorithm's ability to find and maintain the entire Pareto front uniformly. The problem contains eight parameters, $x_1,\ldots,x_8$, as described in Chapter 1. Due to the symmetry and tradeoff of the two objectives, the Pareto optimal solutions for this problem are points given by (Fonseca 1995b)

$$x_1 = x_2 = \cdots = x_8, \quad \frac{-1}{\sqrt{8}} \le x_1 \le \frac{1}{\sqrt{8}}. \tag{8.13}$$

ii. KUR
The KUR is a difficult two-objective optimization problem proposed by Kursawe (1990). As illustrated in Fig. 8.1, the Pareto front consists of three distinct and disconnected regions. The parameter values that correspond to the disconnected Pareto fronts are also disconnected in the parameter domain.

iii. POL
The POL is a two-parameter and two-objective test problem proposed by Poloni et al. (2000). It has a discontinuous Pareto front for which a large portion, i.e. the lower region, is constituted by the boundary solutions in the search space.

Table 8.3. Definitions of f_1 and f_2 in FON, KUR, and POL (Continued on Next Page)

	Minimize(f_1, f_2)	
FON	$\begin{cases} f_1(x_1,\ldots,x_8) = 1-\exp[-\sum_{i=1}^{8}(x_i - 1/\sqrt{8})^2] \\ f_2(x_1,\ldots,x_8) = 1-\exp[-\sum_{i=1}^{8}(x_i + 1/\sqrt{8})^2] \end{cases}$ where $-2 \le x_i < 2, \forall i = 1,2,\ldots,8.$	(8.14)
KUR	Minimize(f_1, f_2) $\begin{cases} f_1(x) = \sum_{i=1}^{2}[-10\exp(-0.2\sqrt{x_i^2 + x_{i+1}^2})] \\ f_2(x) = \sum_{i=1}^{3}[|x_i|^{0.8} + 5\sin(x_i^3)] \end{cases}$ where $-5 \le x_i < 5, \forall i = 1,2,3.$	(8.15)

Table 8.3. (Continued) Definitions of f_1 and f_2 in FON, KUR, and POL

	Minimize(f_1, f_2)
POL	$$\begin{cases} f_1(x) = 1 + (A_1 - B_1)^2 + (A_2 - B_2)^2 \\ f_2(x) = (x_1 + 3)^2 + (x_2 + 1)^2 \\ A_1 = 0.5\sin 1 - 2\cos 1 + \sin 2 - 1.5\cos 2 \\ A_2 = 1.5\sin 1 - \cos 1 + 2\sin 2 - 0.5\cos 2 \\ B_1 = 0.5\sin x_1 - 2\cos x_1 + \sin x_2 - 1.5\cos x_2 \\ B_2 = 1.5\sin x_1 - \cos x_1 + 2\sin x_2 - 0.5\cos x_2 \end{cases}$$ (8.16) where $-\pi \le x_i \le \pi, \forall i = 1, 2.$

8.3.3 Test Problem of TLK

This problem evaluates the robustness of evolutionary algorithms in a noisy environment in the sense that disappearance of individuals from the population has little influence on the overall evolution results (Collard and Escazut 1995). A noisy two-objective optimization problem with three variables is given as (Tan et al. 2002a)

Minimize(f_1, f_2)

$$f_1 = x_1,$$

$$f_2 = \frac{1}{x_1}\left\{1 + \left(x_2'^2 + x_3'^2\right)^{0.25}\left[\sin^2\left(50\left(x_2'^2 + x_3'^2\right)^{0.1}\right) + 1.0\right]\right\}.$$

(8.17)

Instead of "real" parameters, the optimization is performed based on the "corrupted" parameters with additive noise elements

$$x_i' = x_i + N(\sigma, \mu),$$

(8.18)

where $0.1 \le x_1 \le 1$, $-100 \le x_i \le 100 \ \forall i = 2, 3$, and $N(\sigma, \mu)$ is a white noise. The distribution density of the noise is "normal" as given by

$$P(x \mid N(\sigma, \mu)) = \frac{1}{\sqrt{2\pi\sigma^2}}\exp\left(-\frac{(x - \mu)^2}{2\sigma^2}\right),$$

(8.19)

where μ and σ^2 are the mean and variance of the probability density distribution, respectively. Here, μ and σ are given as 0 and 0.1, respectively. Note that the difficulty of the problem is increased with different patterns of well depths and heights of the barrier between the wells as formulated in (8.17) (Schaffer et al. 1989). The 2-dimension cross section of $f_2(x)\cdot x_1$ through the origin is shown in Fig. 8.2. It can be observed that there exist a lot of local optima around the global optimum. The Pareto front is shown by the curve in Fig. 8.3, where the shaded area represents the unfeasible search region in the objective domain.

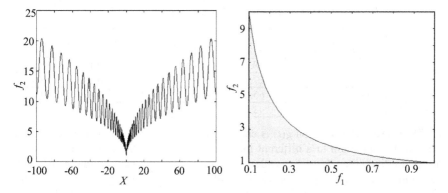

Fig. 8.2. Central cross section of $f_{4,2}$.

Fig. 8.3. Pareto front in the objective domain.

8.3.4 Test Problem of TLK2

The TLK2 is extended from the test problem of nonstationary environment proposed by Branke (1999), which provides an artificial multidimension landscape consisting of several peaks, where the height, width, and position of each peak are varied as the environment changes. The problem of TLK2 is given as

$$f_1 = x_1,$$ (8.20a)

$$f_2 = \frac{1}{x_1 \cdot g(t)},$$ (8.20b)

$$g(t) = \max_{i=1...5} \left[\frac{H_i(t)}{1 + W_i(t)\sum_{j=1}^{5}\left(x_{j+1} - X_{ij}(t)\right)^2} \right],$$ (8.20c)

where $0.1 \le x_1 \le 1$, $0 \le x_i \le 100$ $\forall i = 2,...,6$, and X_i is the coordinate of peak i.

The coordinates, height H and width W, of each peak are initialized according to Table 8.4. At every Δe generation, the height and width of each peak are changed by adding a random Gaussian variable. The location of each peak is moved by a vector v of fixed length s in a random direction, i.e., the parameter s controls the severity of change and the parameter Δe determines the frequency of change. Here, the two parameters are set as $s = 1$ and $\Delta e = 50$. A change in the peak can be described as

$$\sigma \in N(0,1),$$ (8.21a)

$$H_i(t) = H_i(t-1) + 7 \cdot \sigma,$$ (8.21b)

$$W_i(t) = W_i(t-1) + 0.01 \cdot \sigma,$$ (8.21c)

$$X_i(t) = X_i(t-1) + v.$$ (8.21d)

Table 8.4. Initial Parameters of the Peaks

	X_{i1}	X_{i2}	X_{i3}	X_{i4}	X_{i5}	W_i	H_i
Peak 1	8.0	64.0	67.0	55.0	4.0	0.1	50.0
Peak 2	50.0	13.0	78.0	15.0	7.0	0.1	50.0
Peak 3	9.0	19.0	27.0	67.0	24.0	0.1	50.0
Peak 4	68.0	87.0	65.0	19.0	43.0	0.1	50.0
Peak 5	78.0	32.0	43.0	54.0	65.0	0.1	50.0

The multimodal function $g(t)$ is changed with the time t, which may result in a shift of the optimum to a different location. In this case, the evolutionary search needs to "jump" or "cross" a valley in order to find the new optimum. At each generation, the highest peak is scaled to 50 in order to maintain the global Pareto front in the objective domain. The rest of the peaks are multiplied by the same scale as the highest peak. Note that all the individuals are reevaluated at every generation in order to detect if there are any changes in the fitness landscape.

8.4 Simulation Studies

This section presents the simulation results of MOEAs, including their ability to discover and distribute nondominated solutions uniformly along the entire Pareto front; to escape from harmful local optima; and to minimize the effect of noise induced from the environment. The 10 MOEAs included in the simulation are VEGA (Schaffer 1985), HLGA (Hajela and Lin 1992), MOGA (Fonseca and Fleming 1993), NPGA (Horn and Nafpliotis 1993), CCEA (presented in Chapter 6), PAES (Knowles and Corne 1999, 2000a), PESA (Corne et al. 2000), NSGAII (Deb et al. 2002a), SPEA2 (Zitzler et al. 2001), and IMOEA (Tan et al. 2001c). All the algorithms are implemented with the same binary coding scheme of 30 bits per decision variable, tournament selection, uniform crossover, and bit-flip mutation. To study the statistical performance like consistency and robustness of the algorithms, 30 simulation runs with randomly generated initial populations are performed for each algorithm and each test function presented in the previous section. The configuration of these algorithms is listed in Table 8.5.

Figures 8.4 to 8.7 summarize the simulation results for each test problem with respect to the performance metrics of generational distance (GD), spacing (S), maximum spread (MS), and hypervolume ratio (HVR). The distribution of the results from the 30 independent runs is represented in the box plots format (Chambers et al. 1983), which is applied to visualize the distribution of a sample set. In the box plot, a thick horizontal line within the box encodes the median while the upper and lower ends of the box are the upper and lower quartiles. Dashed appendages illustrate the spread and shape of distribution, and dots represent the outside values.

Table 8.5. The Configuration of MOEAs

Population size	1 in PAES; initial population size 20, maximum population size 100 in IMOEA; subpopulation size 20 in CCEA; 100 in other MOEAs
Archive (or secondary population) size	100
Chromosome length	30 bits for each decision variable
Selection	Binary tournament selection
Crossover rate	0.8
Crossover method	Uniform crossover
Mutation rate	$2/L$ for ZDT1, ZDT2, ZDT3, ZDT4, ZDT6, and TLK2, where L is the chromosome length; 1/30 for FON, KUR, POL, and TLK, where 30 is the bit number of one variable
Mutation method	Bit-flip mutation
Hypergrid size	32 per dimension
Niche radius	0.01 in the normalized objective domain
Number of evaluations	120,000

With respect to the metric of *GD*, HLGA is particularly weak in approaching the true tradeoff curve for almost all the test problems. It can be observed that the performances of nonelitist algorithms, such as VEGA, MOGA, and NPGA, fall behind those of the elitist algorithms. For the problem of TLK, it can be seen that VEGA, HLGA, MOGA, and NPGA are affected severely by the noise. The results also show that PESA gives good performance for most problems, while CCEA, IMOEA, NSGAII, and SPEA2 are generally competitive in terms of *GD*.

Concerning the metric of *S*, it can be seen that CCEA and IMOEA give the smallest values of *S* for almost all the test problems, showing their ability to distribute nondominated individuals uniformly along the Pareto front. Besides, NSGAII and SPEA2 also give excellent performance in terms of the population distribution. The results also show that the performance of PAES (nonpopulation-based approach) is less competitive for most test problems, while PESA performs fairly for problems such as FON, KUR, POL, and ZDT6.

Concerning the metric of *MS*, it is observed that NSGAII and SPEA2 give the best performance in terms of variance and consistency. The performance of CCEA is shown to be significantly superior to others for the problem of ZDT4, due to its capability of dealing with multimodality in a problem. The results also show that IMOEA and PESA perform rather well for many test problems, while HLGA is among the worst performers in terms of *MS*. From the moderate performance of PAES, it is believed that the incorporation of elitism alone is insufficient for preserving population diversity without a population of solutions.

Taking into account the convergence and diversity, *HVR* provides a qualitative measure for the general quality of the solutions. It can be observed that the performance of CCEA is outstanding for the problem of ZDT4, while IMOEA produces excellent results except for the problems of ZDT4 and TLK. The results also show that NSGAII and SPEA2 are competitive for all the test problems, which are consistent with their previously good performances based on other measures.

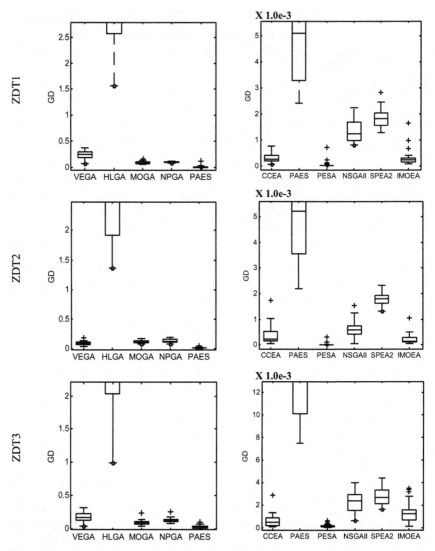

Fig. 8.4. Box plots for the metric of generational distance (*GD*) of the solution sets (continued on next page).

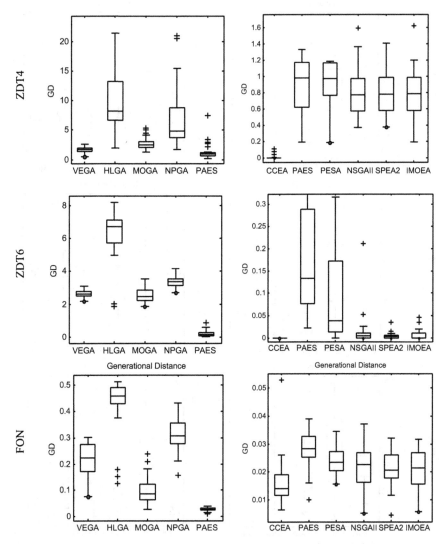

Fig. 8.4. Box plots for the metric of generational distance (*GD*) of the solution sets (continued on next page).

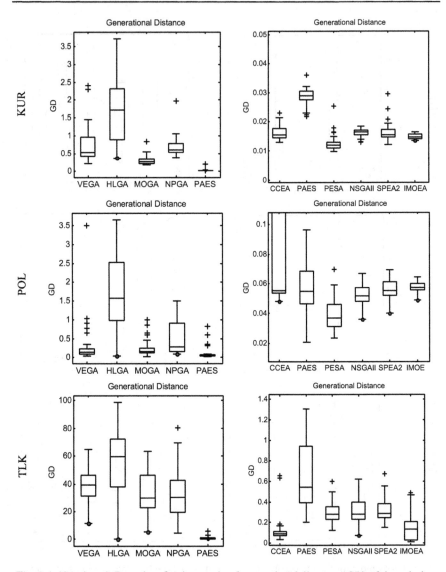

Fig. 8.4. (Continued) Box plots for the metric of generational distance (*GD*) of the solution sets.

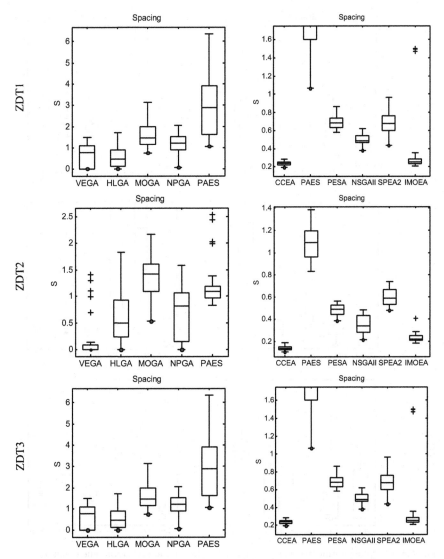

Fig. 8.5. Box plots for the metric of spacing (S) of the solution sets (continued on next page).

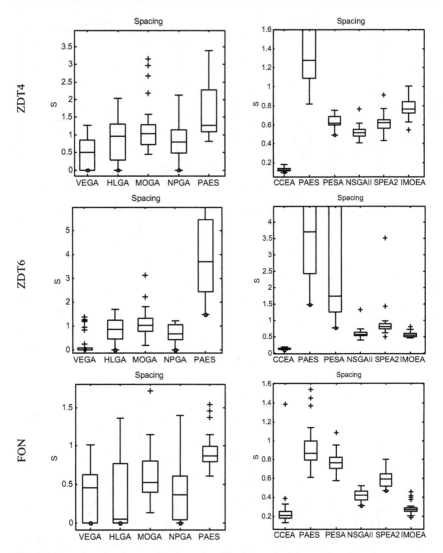

Fig. 8.5. Box plots for the metric of spacing (S) of the solution sets (continued on next page).

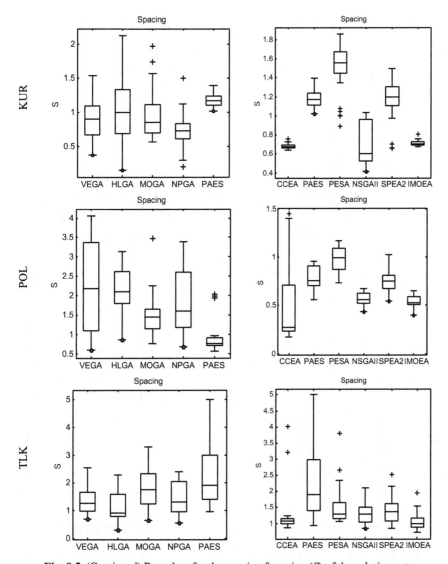

Fig. 8.5. (Continued) Box plots for the metric of spacing (S) of the solution sets.

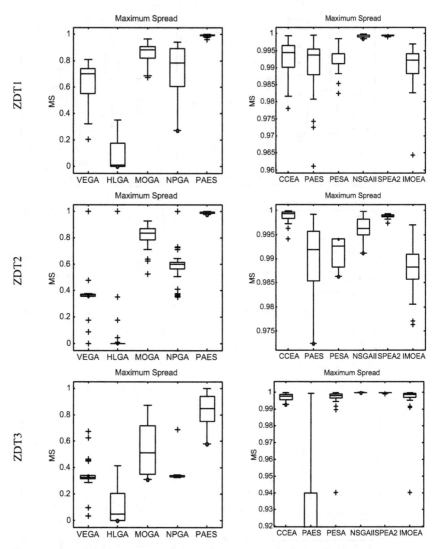

Fig. 8.6. Box plots for the metric of maximum spread (*MS*) of the solution sets (continued on next page).

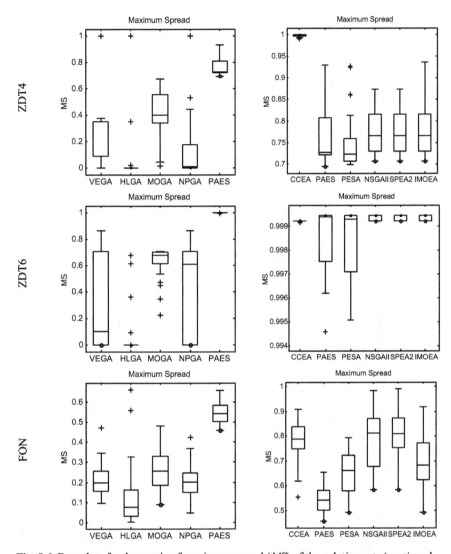

Fig. 8.6. Box plots for the metric of maximum spread (*MS*) of the solution sets (continued on next page).

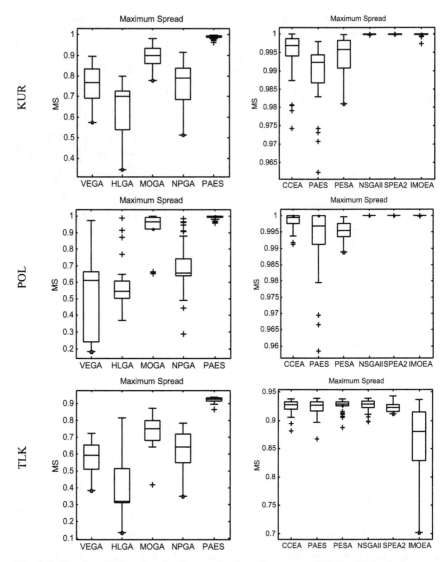

Fig. 8.6. (Continued) Box plots for the metric of maximum spread (*MS*) of the solution sets.

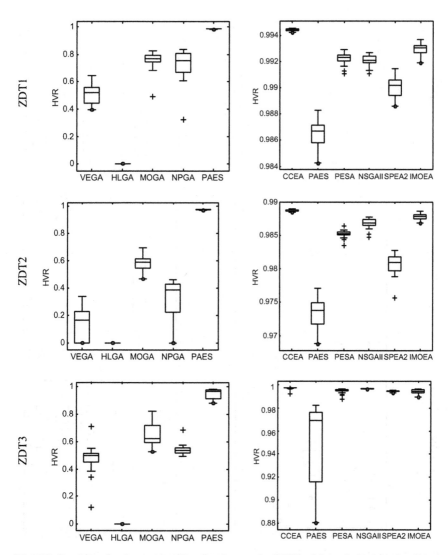

Fig. 8.7. Box plots for the metric of hypervolume ratio (*HVR*) of the solution sets (continued on next page).

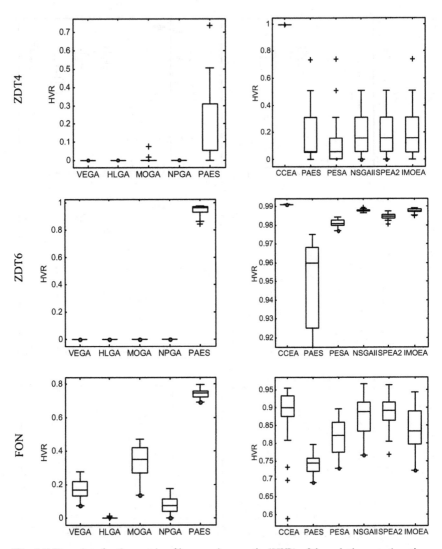

Fig. 8.7. Box plots for the metric of hypervolume ratio (*HVR*) of the solution sets (continued on next page).

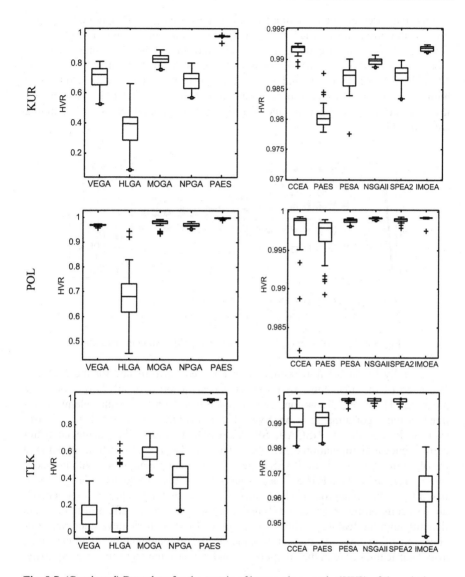

Fig. 8.7. (Continued) Box plots for the metric of hypervolume ratio (*HVR*) of the solution sets.

Figure 8.8 depicts the trace of average best performance (*ABP*) along the evolution for the problem of TLK2, where a nonstationary fitness environment is considered. Although the trends of *ABP* for all algorithms tend to become smoother along the evolution, it can be seen that the performances of PAES, PESA, NSGAII, SPEA2, IMOEA, and CCEA are superior to others, with a relatively high value of *ABP*. It can also be observed that the *ABP* of HLGA is relatively low, indicating its poor performance for tracking the optimal region in a changing environment.

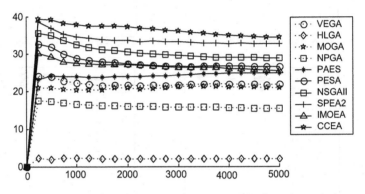

Fig. 8.8. Trace of average best performance (*ABP*) along the evolution.

Generally the simulation results show a mixed performance for the MOEAs, i.e., none of the algorithms performed the best in terms of all the performance measures. However, discussions can be made based on the feature elements applied in the algorithms. It is observed that algorithms incorporated with elitism such as PAES, PESA, NSGAII, SPEA2, IMOEA, and CCEA, achieved better convergence and population distribution along the discovered Pareto front. Among the algorithms with elitism, PAES appears to be a simple approach with competitive performance. But PAES is less superior possibly due to its nonpopulation-based local search approach. The results also show that algorithms without elitism are less competitive in terms of *GD* and more sensitive to the effect of noise. Note that although the feature of elitism is useful for MOEAs to achieve good performance and robustness in noisy environments, the implementation of elitism may also significantly burden the computation and increase the algorithmic complexity.

8.5 Conclusions

This chapter has given a preliminary study on the performance of MOEAs based upon a number of performance metrics, such as generational distance, spacing, maximum spread, hypervolume ratio, and average best performance. Ten MO test problems with different optimization difficulties and challenges have been used in the study, including nonconvex Pareto front, high-dimension search space, multiple local optima, discontinuous Pareto front, deception with harmful local optima, noisy landscape, and nonstationary environments. The simulation results show a mixed performance for the MOEAs, i.e., none of the algorithms performed the best in terms of all the performance measures. In general, the feature of elitism (as implemented in PAES, PESA, NSGAII, SPEA2, IMOEA, and CCEA) is useful for MOEAs to achieve better convergence and population distribution along the Pareto front. However, the implementation of elitism can also significantly burden the computation and increase the algorithmic complexity for MOEAs.

9
A Multiobjective Evolutionary Algorithm Toolbox

9.1 Introduction

Although MOEAs have been recognized to be effective tools for solving optimization problems, the users often require certain programming expertise with considerable time and effort in order to write a computer program for implementing the often sophisticated algorithm according to their need. This work could be tedious and needs to be done before users can start their design task for which they should really be engaged in. A simple solution is to get a ready-to-use evolutionary optimization toolbox, which is often developed for general purposes but has the potential to be applied to any specific application. Generally there are two types of MOEA toolboxes that are available in the market: (1) The key functions of the evolutionary algorithm are coded separately in the toolbox where the users can build their own programs by calling the relevant functions; (2) a ready-to-use toolbox where the user merely writes a "model" file that specifies the objective function corresponding to his or her particular optimization problem, and plugs the file into the toolbox for immediate solutions.

Existing evolutionary algorithm toolboxes include the genetic and evolutionary algorithm toolbox (GEATbx) for use with Matlab (The Mathworks 1998), which is developed by Pohlheim (1998) and is commercially available. The toolbox is modular and contains some evolutionary functions that could be used for users' own programs. The interface with GEATbx can be performed via either command-line interpretation or simple GUIs. The genetic algorithms for optimization toolbox (GAOT) developed by Houck et al. (1995) at North Carolina State University requires the simulation settings to be specified in different variables, and the user is required to input a long string of variables before each simulation. Similar to GEATbx, the GAOT requires users to be familiar with Matlab and evolutionary computing in order to understand the various functions as well as to specify the decision variables in relevant m-files, since these toolboxes are mainly the text-based-driven with limited GUI supports. The FlexToolGA developed from the Flexible Intelligence Group (1999) is a ready-to-use toolbox that is also implemented in Matlab and is commercially available. This toolbox is mainly designed for single-objective problems and does not provide full support for identifying the entire tradeoffs in MO optimization.

This chapter presents an optimization toolbox that is built upon the MOEA algorithm (Tan et al. 1999b) as described in Chapter 4. The MOEA toolbox is ready for immediate use with minimal knowledge needed in Matlab or evolutionary computing. It is fully equipped with interactive GUIs and powerful graphical displays for ease-of-use and efficient visualization of different simulation results. Besides the ability of evolving a family of nondominated solutions along the Pareto front, each of the objective components can have different goal settings or preferences to guide the optimization for individual specification rather than pre-weighting the MO function manually. The toolbox also contains various analysis tools for users to compare, examine, or analyze the results at anytime during the simulation. This chapter is organized as follows: Section 9.2 presents the design and various features of MOEA toolbox. Conclusions are drawn in Section 9.3.

9.2 Roles and Features of MOEA Toolbox

The interactive GUI-based MOEA toolbox (Tan et al. 2001e) was developed under the Matlab programming environment. Matlab is a popular, high-performance programming language used for technical computing. It integrates computation, visualization, and programming in an easy-to-use environment, where problems and solutions can be expressed in familiar mathematical notation. It is chosen as the software environment for the MOEA toolbox implementation due to the following reasons (Houck et al. 1995): (1) It provides many built-in auxiliary functions useful for function optimization in engineering and nonengineering applications; (2) it is portable and is efficient for numerical computations; (3) it provides powerful and easy-to-use graphic utilities; (4) it provides the application program interface (API) to interact with data and programs that are external to the Matlab environment; (5) it is capable of generating optimized code for embedded systems, rapid prototyping, and hardware-in-the-loop design. Although execution speed in Matlab may be slow as compared to other low-level programming languages like C/C++, function files in Matlab that require extensive computational effort can be compiled into "mex" files using software like Matcom (The Mathworks 1999) for faster program execution, if so desired.

9.2.1 GUIs of MOEA Toolbox

The MOEA toolbox is designed based upon the technique of evolutionary computing and the concept of Pareto's optimality for effective MO optimization. Interfacing with the toolbox is through powerful GUI windows. Most simulation settings can be done by manipulating labeled graphical controls that have tool tips attached for easy function identification. The toolbox also provides many help documentations in HTML (HyperText Markup Language) format and some simple *m*-file templates to assist users in writing "model" files. Besides, it is capable of representing simulation results in various formats, such as text files or graphical displays for the purpose of results viewing and analysis. The file-handling capability of the toolbox also allows users to store or retrieve simulation data. The main features of the toolbox are summarized below:

- Support both single-objective and multiobjective optimization;
- The ability to focus on finding Pareto optimal solutions with powerful graphical displays;
- Fixed and dynamic population size for optimal representation of Pareto front;
- Handle both hard and soft constraints;
- Goal and priority information for better support of decision making in MO optimization;
- Powerful GUIs and easy linking to other program workbench;
- Step-by-step guidance to interface with "model" files;
- Comprehensive HTML help files and tutorials.

The main toolbox GUI window can be called from the Matlab workspace by the command "begin". This GUI can be minimized into a smaller window so that it occupies less space on the screen for easy access. Many other toolbox GUI windows, including the help files or simulation setup files, can be easily accessed through the buttons on this GUI. There are two types of setup available in the toolbox, i.e., the "Quick" setup and the "Guided" setup. The GUI of "Quick" setup is shown in Fig. 9.1, which provides all simulation settings, such as the number of objectives and decision variables, generation and population size, selection strategy, and so forth to be easily accessible within one GUI window. The options of fixed and dynamic niching schemes (Goldberg and Richardson 1987; Tan et al. 1999b) are also included in this GUI. These schemes determine whether sharing distance is fixed or adaptively estimated based upon the online population distribution at each generation. The "Quick" setup also includes features to incorporate random strings or reuse strings from the last evolution if necessary. Besides, the "model" file or Simulink (The Mathworks 1999) can be loaded directly through this GUI to achieve easy linking between MOEA toolbox and application setups.

For new users who have minor or no experience in setting up the parameters for simulation, an alternative "Guided" setup GUI window as shown in Fig. 9.2 is available to assist them by going through the whole setup process step by step with guidance information provided. The sparse multipage arrangement in "Guided" setup also allows more information to be incorporated into the GUI window. Note that all parameter settings of "Quick" and "Guided" setups are interlinked, i.e., users may switch between these two GUI windows anytime as they wish, where all current settings in one setup window are automatically transferred to another. All settings in these two setups can also be saved into a file for reloading purposes. From the "Quick" setup or "Strings" setting in "Guided" setup as shown in Fig. 9.3(a), the "Model Parameter Options" GUI window as shown in Fig. 9.3(b) can be opened to set up all decision variables involved in the optimization. Note that the toolbox does not have a limit to the number of decision variables that it can handle, although such a limit may be imposed by the limited system resources. As shown in Fig. 9.3(b), settings over every 10 decision variables can be easily accessed through the navigational controls in the toolbox.

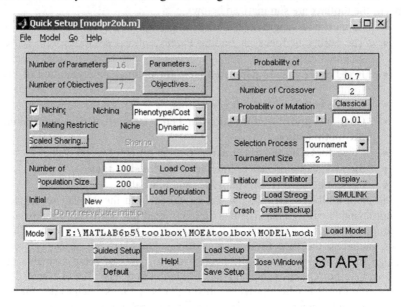

Fig. 9.1. GUI window for quick setting of simulation parameters.

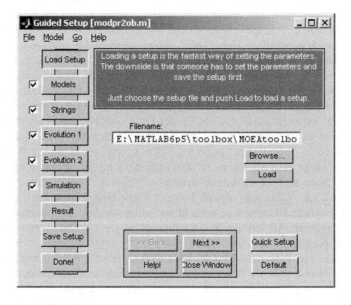

Fig. 9.2. The "Guided" setup with loading setup details.

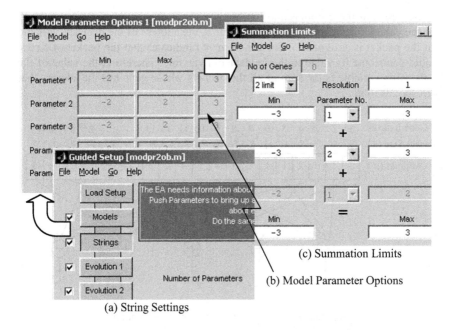

(a) String Settings

(b) Model Parameter Options

(c) Summation Limits

Fig. 9.3. Decision variable settings and linear constraint handling.

Figure 9.3(c) shows the "Summation Limits" GUI window, which is a primitive version of packet distribution method (Tan et al. 2001e) for handling simple constraints with linear decision variables. This GUI window allows linear constraint specifications of the following format:

$$T_L \le T = \sum_{i=1}^{n} p_i \le T_H, \tag{9.1}$$

$$p_{1L} \le p_1 \le p_{1H},$$
$$p_{2L} \le p_2 \le p_{2H},$$
$$\vdots$$
$$p_{nL} \le p_n \le p_{nH},$$

where T = summation of all decision variables; T_L = lower summation limit; T_H = upper summation limit; p_i = decision variable i; p_{iL} = lower limit for decision variable i; p_{iH} = upper limit for decision variable i; n = number of decision variables. These constraints are automatically coded into the genetic structure of strings in the simulation, i.e., all strings in the population reproduced after the crossover and mutation operations remain as feasible strings, which avoids the need of repairing or rejecting any infeasible strings through specialized genetic operators. Figure 9.4 shows the genetic structure as given by

$$P_i = P_{iL} + \sum_{j=1}^{g} \left(\begin{cases} s_j & \text{if } a_j = i, \\ 0 & \text{else.} \end{cases} \right) \tag{9.2}$$

The genes in the chromosome represent packets of prespecified sizes, $s_1...s_g$, and the value of each gene, $a_1...a_g$, determines the address of the decision variable that the packet is assigned to. For gene j, $a_j = i$ indicates that the packet of size s_j should contribute its value to the ith decision variable. Therefore, the value of the ith decision variable is the sum of all the packets whose gene has the address that corresponds to it.

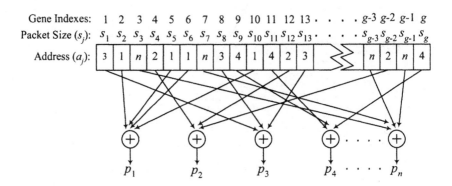

Fig. 9.4. General structure of packet representation.

As shown in Fig. 9.5, the "Objective" setup window that specifies the setting of objective functions for the optimization problem can be called from either the "Quick" or "Guided" setup. Similar to the setting of decision variables, there is no limit on the number of objectives although the limited system resources may impose such a limit. This GUI window is built to provide an easy and complete setup for each objective component involved in the optimization, which includes the support for setting of goal, priority, and hard/soft constraints (Tan et al. 1999b). Note that the setting of a single specification (consists of a set of objective components with goal, priority, and constraint) can also be extended to multiple specifications with logical "AND"/"OR" operations to accommodate more complex decision making in the toolbox as shown in Fig. 9.5.

Figure 9.6 shows the "Population Handling" GUI window of the MOEA toolbox. This GUI window allows strings or decision variables to be manually edited, removed, or replaced by random ones as necessary. Any string in the population can be selected with its decision variables being displayed on the left side of the window. At each generation, the fitness as well as the decision variables of the selected string are available for viewing or editing on the right half of the window. This GUI window is useful for providing online or offline results analysis via strings editing, where users can have better interaction and understanding of the changing environment in the simulation. Note that strings for the entire population can also be created via the "Population Handling" GUI, which could then be saved and reloaded as an initial population for other setups.

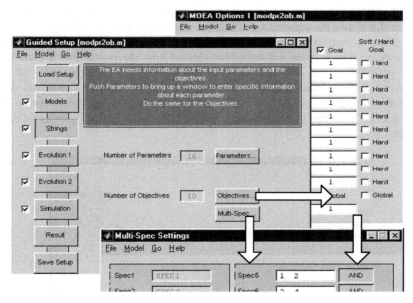

Fig. 9.5. "Objective" setup window with settings of goal, priority, and logical "AND"/"OR" operations.

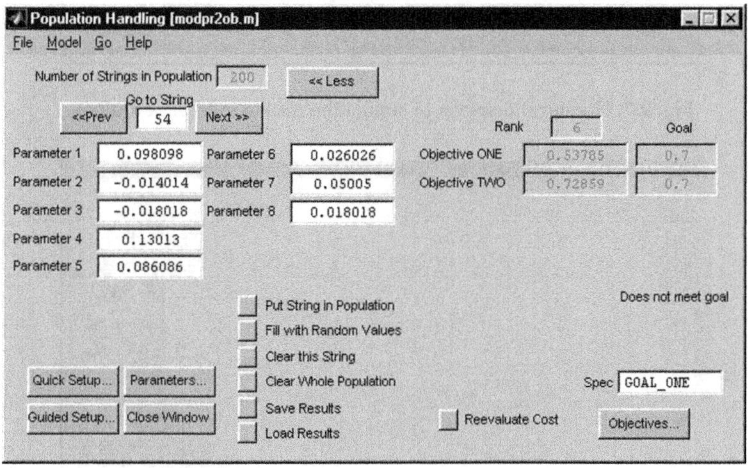

Fig. 9.6. GUI window for strings manipulation.

Using the MOEA toolbox, simulation results can be represented in various plotting for graphical analysis or visualization. These plots can be updated at each generation for which users can interactively manipulate controls to adjust the displays. One of the graphical display windows is shown in Fig. 9.7, where strings can be arranged in an ascending order based on any selected optimization criteria. Figure 9.8 shows the convergence trace for single-objective or multiobjective optimization as well as the number of strings meeting the goal setting over some generations, which gives a quantitative idea of how the population is evolving over generations. For MO optimization, the convergence trace is measured by means of progress ratio (Tan et al. 1999b). The GUI also allows simulation data such as strings in a population, fitness of strings as well as progress ratio to be saved as a "mat" file in Matlab or as a "text" file to be loaded by external programs.

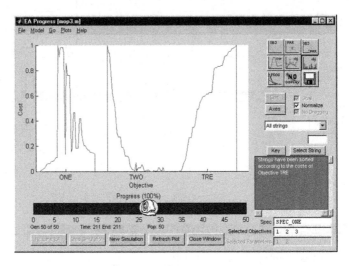

Fig. 9.7. Graphical displays of simulation results in MOEA toolbox.

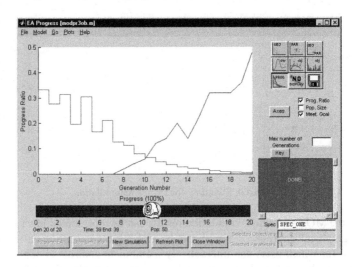

Fig. 9.8. Convergence trace for the evolution progress.

The MOEA toolbox also comes with comprehensive online help files in HTML format, which can be easily accessed via button/link in each GUI window or the menu bar as shown in Fig. 9.9. Whenever the Help command is called, the relevant help document will be opened via the default Web browser in the system. The information contained in the help files include

- General information on evolutionary algorithms and MO optimization;
- Step-by-step demonstration of the toolbox;
- Guides to GUIs of the toolbox and writing of Matlab and Simulink "model" files;
- List of possible error messages and ways of handling them.

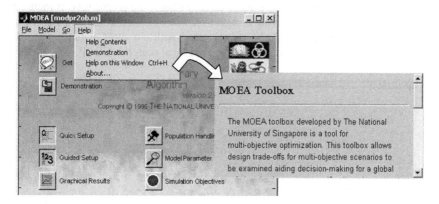

Fig. 9.9. Toolbox link from the main window to the help file contents.

9.2.2 Advanced Settings

Figure 9.10(a) shows the GUI window for evolutionary parameter settings, where crossover and mutation rates can be set graphically. There are two types of selection methods available in the toolbox, i.e., the roulette wheel and tournament selection schemes. Three types of mutation operator are provided in "Mutation Settings" GUI window as shown in Fig. 9.10(b). The first type is the classical mutation operator, where a gene is randomly mutated if a random generated number is smaller than the probability of mutation. The second type is approximate-number mutation, where a number of randomly selected genes, equal to the rounded product of the total number of genes and the probability of mutation, are mutated randomly.

The third mutation method is called fuzzy boundary local perturbation (FBLP) (Tan et al. 2001c), which can be used for producing strings to fill up discontinuities among nondominated strings along the Pareto front. Each string in FBLP is perturbed in such a way that the resultant string from the perturbation is likely to be situated within a short distance from the original one. The number of perturbations for each string is related to the status of progress ratio (Tan et al. 2001c), which is generally large for a small progress ratio and vice versa. A high progress ratio means that the performance of evolution is improving a lot and is likely to be far away from the tradeoff. A local search at this stage is less meaningful since the evolution is less likely to reproduce strings on or near to the tradeoff region. In contrast, the progress ratio is generally low when the evolution is approaching the tradeoff, and thus it is more meaningful to increase the number of perturbations at this stage in order to obtain more neighboring strings for better tradeoff representation. This relation is adjustable in the toolbox as shown in Fig. 9.10(b). When FBLP is performed on a string, mutation probability for each gene depends on its position in the respective decision variable. For each decision variable, the closer the gene to the LSG (least significant gene), the higher the probability of mutation is assigned to this gene. By giving a higher chance of mutation for less significant genes, perturbed strings are likely to be located within a short distance from the original string, thereby fulfilling the purpose of local search in FBLP.

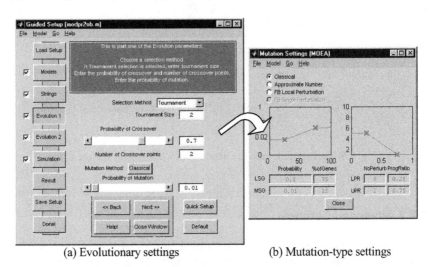

(a) Evolutionary settings   (b) Mutation-type settings

Fig. 9.10. Settings of evolutionary operators and mutation types.

At the stage of "Evolution 2" in "Guided" setup as shown in Fig. 9.11(a), several advanced evolutionary settings are available. The "niche induction" technique by means of a sharing function (Deb and Goldberg 1989) is used to evolve an equally distributed population along the Pareto front or multiple optima for evolutionary optimization. To avoid the need of a priori knowledge for predefining a sharing distance, the toolbox includes the dynamic sharing scheme (Tan et al. 1999b) which can adaptively compute for a suitable sharing distance at each generation. Since each decision variable or objective may have different desired scaling value, the toolbox provides a "Niching Distance Scaling" GUI window where the scale of each decision variable or objective can be easily specified as shown in Fig. 9.11(b). Mating restriction (Fonseca and Fleming 1995b) is included in the toolbox to restrict mating of strings in order to prevent reproduction of highly un-fit strings as well as to maintain the population diversity. If the mating restriction is enabled, two strings will be selected for mating if they are located within a certain distance, e.g., the sharing distance; otherwise a random string is selected for mating if no such strings are found.

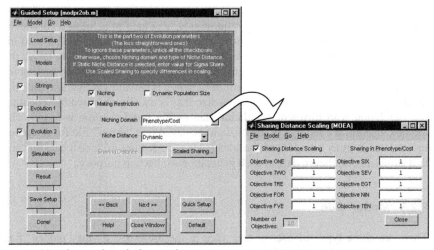

(a) Advanced evolution settings   (b) Sharing distance scaling

Fig. 9.11. Settings of evolutionary operators and sharing distance scaling.

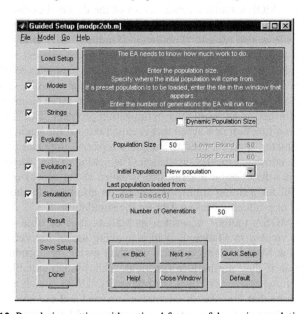

Fig. 9.12. Population setting with optional feature of dynamic population size.

The MOEA toolbox also allows users to load an initial population, generate a new population of random strings, or use a combination of both before any simulations. The initial population can be loaded from a file generated from last simulation session or entered via the "Population Handling" GUI. As shown in Fig. 9.12, the feature of dynamic population size (Tan et al. 2001c) is included in the toolbox, which is particularly useful for automatically estimating an optimal population size at each generation to sufficiently explore the search space as well as to represent the Pareto front effectively. Intuitively, it is hard to achieve a good evolution if the population size is too small with loosely distributed strings due to insufficient exchange of genetic information. If the population size is too large, the evolution may take extra computational effort with greater demands on system resources and simulation time. The merit of dynamic population is that it avoids the need of presetting a constant population size that is usually obtained by repeating the simulation with different population size until a good solution is found. The toolbox also allows settings in the GUIs to be saved in a "setup" file for reference or use later in other simulations, besides having the feature of "crash backup" file that stores all simulation data at each generation for backup purpose.

9.2.3 "Model" File

There are three types of user-written files in the toolbox, i.e., the "model" file, "initiator" file, and "streog" file. According to the users' optimization problem on hand, the "model" file that specifies the objective function must be written in order to determine the fitness function of each string in the population before any simulation. The MOEA toolbox sends values of the decoded decision variables to this "model" file and expects a cost vector to be returned for each of the strings. The "model" file is also used in "Population Handling" GUI to allow any manual examination, modification, or re-evaluation of strings of interest in a population. Besides providing help files in HTML format, several templates for the writing of "model" files are included in the toolbox. There are also notes, guides, and reminders in the form of comments in each template to assist users in writing the "model" file for his or her particular optimization problem. The "initiator" file is optional and is a function or a script that is called once at the beginning of simulation. This "initiator" may be used to initiate a separate graphical display window or to initialize constants for the simulation. The setting of the "streog" file is also optional and is a function or a script that is called at the end of each generation, which is useful for plotting simulation results on graphical display generated by the "initiator" or producing backup data for the simulation.

Since the MOEA toolbox is written in Matlab, it is capable of running any "model" files created in Matlab as well as making use of the versatile functions and resources in Matlab. Users can also call their own C or Fortran "model" files from Matlab as if they are built-in functions. This Matlab callable C or Fortran program is defined as a "mex" file (The Mathworks 1998), which is a dynamically linked subroutine that the Matlab interpreter can load and execute. Details of creating and executing a "mex" file are available in the Matlab application program interface guide (The Mathworks 1998). The merit of a "mex" file is that it executes faster than its *m*-file equivalent, and hence reduces the overall simulation time. Alternatively, a "model" file can also be written as an *m*-file and easily be compiled into a "mex" file with the help of Matcom (The Mathworks 1999) for similar purposes.

The MOEA toolbox can run a model built with Simulink, which is a GUI-based software in Matlab for modeling, simulation, and analysis of dynamic systems. The toolbox provides a special template containing comments and sample codes that assist users in creating "model" files for running Simulink models. There are also various functions that allow *m*-files to modify the parameters of Simulink functions or to run the simulation in Simulink. The Simulink model can be loaded by typing its model name at the Matlab command window before running the simulation. An "initiator" file can also be used to load a Simulink model in a new window if none already exists. For example, consider a Simulink model with step response simulation of a first-order system as shown in Fig. 9.13. The model is saved as a file named "Fstorder.mdl", and the "initiator" file that opens this model consists of a command line "Fstorder".

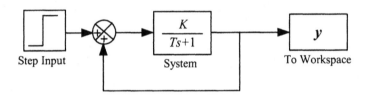

Fig. 9.13. Simulink model of a first-order system (filename: Fstorder).

In the model file, the following lines can be written to describe the system:

```
% A sample model file
    Time = 1 : 0.1 : 1000;
    num = [K];
    den = [T 1];
    set_param("Fstorder/Syst", ...
        "Numerator", ['['num2str(num)']'], ...
        "Denominator", ['['num2str(den)']'])
sim("Fstorder", t, [], []);
```

where "Fstorder" is the name of Simulink "model" file, "Syst" is the name of blocks that represent the system, "Time" is the simulation time index, "*K*" and "*T*" are the parameters of "num" and "den" that define the first-order system, respectively. Note that after each "model" evaluation in Simulink, the step response data of the first-order system will be returned to the main function in Matlab, as desired.

9.3 Conclusions

This chapter has presented a GUI-based MOEA toolbox, which is equipped with many useful features for advanced supports in MO optimization. The toolbox is ready for immediate use with minimal knowledge needed in evolutionary computing. It can represent simulation results in various formats, such as text files or interactive graphical displays for results viewing and analysis. To use the toolbox, the user merely needs to provide a simple "model" file that specifies the objective functions corresponding to his or her particular optimization problem. Other aspects like decision variable settings, optimization process monitoring, or graphical results analysis can be performed easily through the embedded GUIs in the toolbox. To achieve a faster program execution, conversion of the toolbox into standalone executable software is important. For this, a link to Matlab can be provided in the toolbox so that the user is able to access the built-in auxiliary functions in Matlab if necessary.

10
Evolutionary Computer-Aided Control System Design

10.1 Introduction

With the rapid development of control theories and algorithms in the past few decades, many control schemes ranging from the most straightforward proportional plus integral plus derivative (PID), phase lead/lag, and pole-placement schemes to more sophisticated optimal, adaptive, and robust control algorithms have been available to control engineers. Each of these control schemes, however, employs a different control characteristic or design technique that is often restricted to one particular problem or addresses only a subset of performance issues. To design an optimal controller using these methods, the control engineer often needs to select an appropriate control law that best suits the application on hand, and to determine a set of optimal controller parameters for the specified control structure based on the control law chosen (Li et al. 1995).

A practical approach is to design a controller by meeting the multiple performance requirements and constraints simultaneously, instead of satisfying a specific control scheme or in a particular domain (Nye and Tits 1986; Ng 1989; Li et al. 1995; Li et al. 1996; Tan and Li 1997). As pointed out by Limebeer (1991), there are several considerations for evaluating the merits of control system design methodologies:

- Are unavoidable design tradeoffs made clear, and how easily can the designer explicitly make these tradeoffs?
- Are the types of specifications that arise naturally from the physical problem easily incorporated into the design procedure?
- How well does the controller meet the design specifications; does the controller exhibit any characteristic that is not directly arrived at using other design methodologies?

Since the work of Fonseca and Fleming (1994), various evolutionary control system design methodologies have been proposed (Chipperfield and Fleming 1995, 1996; Schroder et al. 1997; Tan and Li 1997; Fonseca and Fleming 1998b; Fleming and Chipperfield 1998a, 1998b; Liu and Mills 1998; Silva and Fleming 1998; Thompson and Fleming 1999). Using such an evolutionary design approach, control engineers can address practical performance requirements such as rise time and overshoots in the time domain, and formulate the robustness specifications such as disturbance rejection and plant uncertainty in the frequency domain (Chiang and Safonov 1992; Doyle et al. 1992; Stoorvogel 1992).

This chapter studies the application of the MOEA toolbox presented in Chapter 9 for computer-aided control system design (CACSD) of linear time-invariant (LTI) systems by unifying various LTI approaches to satisfy performance requirements in both the time and frequency domains. Besides the flexibility of specifying a low-order control structure that simplifies the design and implementation tasks, such a design approach allows the control engineer to interplay and examine different tradeoffs among the multiple design specifications. A general evolutionary CACSD architecture is presented in Section 10.2, which includes the problem formulation of control system as well as the formation of practical design specifications. The evolutionary design of a practical multi-input–multi-output (MIMO) ill-conditioned distillation control system is illustrated in Section 10.3. Conclusions are drawn in Section 10.4.

10.2. Performance-based Design Unification and Automation

10.2.1 Design Architecture

A general evolutionary CACSD paradigm for a unified LTI control (ULTIC) system is illustrated in Fig. 10.1. The design cycle accommodates three different modules: the interactive human decision-making module (control engineer), the optimization module (MOEA toolbox), and the control module (system and specifications). According to the performance requirements and any a priori knowledge on the problem on hand, the control engineer may specify or select the desired specifications from a template (Tan et al. 2001e) to form a multicost function in the control module, which need not be convex or confined to a particular control scheme. These ULTIC design specifications may also incorporate different performance requirements in the time and frequency domain or other system characteristics such as poles and zeros, as desired. Subsequently, response of the control system is simulated based on the plant model and candidate controller H recommended from the optimization module in order to determine the different cost values for each design specification in the multicost function.

According to the evaluation results of cost functions in the control module and the design guidance such as goal and priority information from the decision-making module, the optimization module (MOEA toolbox) automates the ULTIC design process and intelligently searches for the "optimal" controller parameters that best satisfy the set of performance specifications. The online optimization progress and simulation results, such as design tradeoffs and convergence, are displayed graphically and feedback to the decision-making module. In this way, the overall ULTIC design environment is supervised and monitored closely, allowing the control engineer to make appropriate actions, such as examining the competing design tradeoffs, altering the design specifications, adjusting priority and/or goal settings that are too stringent or generous, or modifying the control structure if necessary. This man–machine interactive design and optimization process may continue until the control engineer is satisfied with the required performance. The merit of this approach is that the design problem and interaction with the optimization process are closely linked to the application environment. The control engineer, for most of the part, is not required to deal with any details that are related to the optimization algorithm.

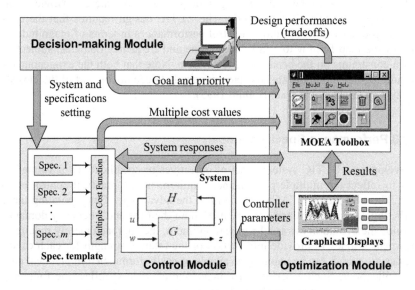

Fig. 10.1. A general evolutionary CACSD architecture.

10.2.2 Control System Formulation

A general configuration for posing control system performance specifications is shown in the control module in Fig. 10.1. The operator G is a 2×2 block matrix mapping the inputs w and u to the outputs z and y (Dahleh and Diaz-Bobillo 1995):

$$\begin{bmatrix} z \\ y \end{bmatrix} = \begin{bmatrix} G_{11} & G_{12} \\ G_{21} & G_{22} \end{bmatrix} \begin{bmatrix} w \\ u \end{bmatrix}. \tag{10.1}$$

The actual process or plant is represented by the submatrix G_{22} (e.g., the nominal model G_0), which is linear time-invariant and may be unspecified except for the constraint that it lies within a given set Π ("uncertainty modeling"). H is the

ULTIC controller to be designed in order to satisfy all specifications and constraints in the system, which is given as

$$H_{i,j}(s) = \frac{p_{i,j,n}s^{n-m-1} + \cdots + p_{i,j,m+2}s + p_{i,j,m+1}}{p_{i,j,m}s^{m} + \cdots + p_{i,j,2}s + p_{i,j,0}}, \tag{10.2}$$

where i, j denotes the respective elements in the transfer matrix and $p_{i,j,k} \in \Re^{+} \ \forall \ k \in \{0, 1, ..., n\}$ are the coefficients to be determined in the design; y is the signal accessible by the controller; and u is the output of the controller, which often has a hard constraint saturation range, such as limited drive voltage or current. The mapping from the exogenous inputs w (e.g., disturbances, noise, reference commands, etc.) to the regulated outputs z (e.g., tracking errors, control outputs, measured outputs, etc.) contains all the input–output maps of interest (Doyle et al. 1992; Dahleh and Diaz-Bobillo 1995). The ULTIC design requires that the controller H provides some optimized control performances in terms of magnitude or norm of the map from w to z in both the time and frequency domains, subject to certain constraints on the behavior of the system. Note that both the exogenous inputs and regulated outputs are auxiliary signals that need not be part of the closed-loop system (Dahleh and Diaz-Bobillo 1995).

10.2.3 Performance Specifications

In developing a ULTIC system, a set of objectives or specifications is formed in order to reflect the multiple performance requirements by practical control engineers. The evolutionary CACSD design has the advantage of incorporating these conflicting specifications and constraints in both the time and frequency domains. To guide the evolution toward the global optimum, the approach merely requires a performance index to provide information of the relative strength for each candidate design, which can be naturally available or easily formulated in practical control applications. Such a performance index should at least reflect the following qualitative requirements (Tan and Li 1997):

i. Stability

Stability is often the first concern in any control system design, which can be determined by solving the roots of the characteristic polynomials. The cost of stability can then be defined as the total number of unstable closed-loop poles or the positive poles on the right-hand side of the s-plane as given by $Nr\{\text{Re}(eig) > 0\}$, i.e., no right-hand poles on the s-plane indicates that the system is stable and vice versa. Alternatively, it may be formulated by maximizing the relative stability of eigenvalues as denoted by $q_{relative} = \min_{i}\left[\text{Re}(eig_i)/|eig_i|\right]$, or by minimizing the absolute stability of eigenvalues given as $q_{absolute} = \min_{i}\left[\text{Re}(eig_i)\right]$ (Joos and Finsterwalder 1999).

ii. Step Response Specifications

Practical control engineers often address system transient and steady-state performances in terms of time domain specifications, since it is straightforward to visualize these performances by means of a constrained graphical step response as shown in Fig. 10.2. For a single-input–single-output (SISO) system, the performance requirement of steady-state accuracy can be defined as $e_{ss} = 1 - y(t)_{t\to\infty}$, where y is the output of the system and e_{ss} is the steady-state error. Similarly, other time domain transient specifications such as overshoot, rise time, and settling time for a step response can be defined as $M_p = \sup_{t\geq 0} y(t) - 1$, $t_r = \{\min(t): y(t) > y_r, y_r$ is a threshold$\}$ and $t_s = \{\min(t): |y(t) - 1| < 0.05$ for $t \geq T$, T is the time constant$\}$, respectively, where t denotes the time index.

For MIMO systems, the diagonal entries in the closed-loop transfer matrix are the transfer functions from the command inputs to their associated variables, which may be required to meet the various specifications such as limits on overshoot and rise time. The off-diagonal entries of the closed-loop transfer matrix are the transfer functions from the commands to other variables. It is generally desirable that the magnitude of these transfer functions is small so that each command input does not impose excessive influence over other variables. This constraint on command interaction can be addressed by ensuring there is no steady-state interaction for constant commands via the specification of $e_{ss\_dcpl}(i) = \sup_{j=1..m, j\neq i} |y_{dcpl}(\infty)_{i,j}|$, where m is the number of the interconnected channels and $y_{dcpl}(i, j)$ is the measure output i due to the coupling effect from input j in the system. Besides, other specifications like $amp_{dcpl}(i) = \sup_{j=1..m, j\neq i} |y_{dcpl}(t)_{i,j}|$, for all $t \geq 0$, can also be incorporated to limit the command interaction in a coupled closed-loop system.

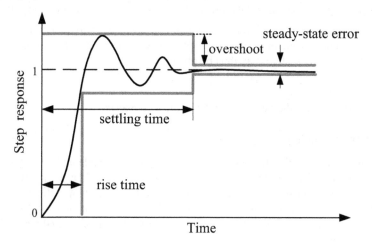

Fig. 10.2. General envelope specification on a step response.

iii. Disturbance Rejection

The disturbance rejection problem is defined as follows: Find a feedback controller that minimizes the maximum amplitude (e.g., H_∞ norm) of the regulated output over all possible disturbances of bounded magnitude (Dahleh and Diaz-Bobillo 1995). A general structure that represents the disturbance rejection for a broad class of control problems is given in Fig. 10.3, which depicts the case where the disturbance d enters the system at the plant output. The mathematical representation is given as

$$y = z = G_0 u + W_1 d, \tag{10.3}$$

$$\frac{y}{d} = W_1 \left(I + G_0 H \right)^{-1} = W_1 S.$$

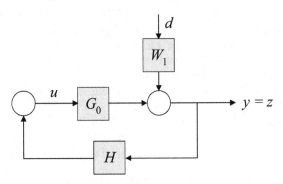

Fig. 10.3. A disturbance rejection problem.

The matrix S is known as the *sensitivity function* and the maximum singular values of S determines the disturbance attenuation, since S is in fact the closed-loop transfer function from disturbance d to the measured output y. W_1 is the desired disturbance attenuation factor, which is a function of frequency to give a different attenuation factor at each frequency. The disturbance attenuation specification for a ULTIC system may thus be given as

$$\bar{\sigma}(S) < \left\| W_1^{-1} \right\|_\infty \Rightarrow \left\| W_1 S \right\|_\infty < 1, \tag{10.4}$$

where $\bar{\sigma}$ defines the largest singular value of a matrix.

iv. Robust Stability

It is important that the designed closed-loop system is stable and provides guaranteed bounds on performance deterioration in the face of "large" plant variations that may occur in practical applications. A robust stability specification requires that some design specifications must hold, even if the plant G_0 is replaced by any G_{pert} from the specified set Π of possible perturbed plants (Dahleh and Diaz-Bobillo 1995).

Small Gain Theorem: Suppose the nominal plant G_0 in Fig. 10.4 is stable with the multiplicative uncertainty Δ being zero. Then the size of the smallest stable Δ for which the system becomes unstable is (Zames 1966)

$$\bar{\sigma}(\Delta) = \frac{1}{\bar{\sigma}(T)} = \left\| \frac{I + G_0 H}{G_0 H} \right\|_\infty . \tag{10.5}$$

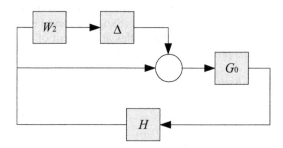

Fig. 10.4. Stability robustness problem with multiplicative perturbation.

The singular value Bode plot of the *complementary sensitivity function T* can be used to measure the stability margin of a feedback system in the face of multiplicative plant uncertainties. The multiplicative stability margin is, by definition, the "size" of the smallest stable Δ that destabilizes the system as shown in Fig. 10.4. According to the small gain theorem, the smaller $\bar{\sigma}(T)$ is, the greater the size of the smallest destabilizing multiplicative perturbation will be and, hence, the larger the stability margin of the system. The stability margin of a closed-loop system can thus be specified via the singular value inequalities such as (Dahleh and Diaz-Bobillo 1995)

$$\bar{\sigma}(T) < \| W_2^{-1} \|_\infty \Rightarrow \| W_2 T \|_\infty < 1, \tag{10.6}$$

where $\| W_2^{-1} \|_\infty$ is the respective size of the largest anticipated multiplicative plant uncertainties.

Note that the approach of treating mixed sensitivity specifications for disturbance rejection (S) and robust stability (T) separately is less conservative than the method of combining them via a "stacking procedure" (Skogestad and Postlethwaite 1996), which is usually used in classical loop-shaping design techniques resulting in the following overall specifications:

$$\| N \|_\infty = \max [\bar{\sigma}(N)] < 1; \quad N = \begin{bmatrix} W_1 S \\ W_2 T \end{bmatrix}, \tag{10.7a}$$

$$\text{where} \quad \bar{\sigma}(N) = \sqrt{|W_1 S|^2 + |W_2 T|^2} . \tag{10.7b}$$

It has been shown by Skogestad and Postlethwaite (1996) that the stacking procedure does not allow the performance bound to be specified on individual transfer functions, and one way to address this conservativeness is to treat the individual transfer functions separately via an MO design optimization approach.

v. Actuator Saturation

In a practical control system, the size of actuator signals should be limited since a large actuator signal may be associated with excessive power consumption or resource usage, apart from its drawback as a disturbance to other parts of the systems if not subject to hardware limitation (Skogestad and Postlethwaite 1996). A general structure for saturation nonlinearities at the input of the plant is shown in Fig. 10.5. To pose this problem, a saturation function is defined as

$$\text{Sat}(u) = \begin{cases} u & |u| \leq U_{max}, \\ U_{max}\,\text{sgn}(u) & |u| \geq U_{max}. \end{cases} \tag{10.8}$$

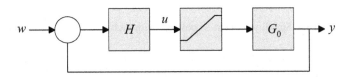

Fig. 10.5. Saturation nonlinearities at the plant input.

Let the plant be $G_0u = G_0 \cdot \text{Sat}(u)$; the objective is to design a ULTIC controller H that satisfies all the design specifications with an allowable control effort of $\max(u) \leq U_{max}$, so as to stay in the linear region of the operation. Note that performances of the closed-loop system, such as tracking accuracy and disturbance attenuation, are bounded by the actuator saturation specification, i.e., a smaller control effort often results in a poorer performance of tracking and disturbance rejection due to the limited control gain operating in a linear region.

vi. Minimal Controller Order

It is desirable that a ULTIC controller is designed as simple as possible, since a simple controller often requires less computation or implementation effort than a higher-order controller (Schroder et al. 1997). Hence, the order of the ULTIC controller can be included as one of the design specifications in order to find the smallest-order controller that satisfies the performance requirements for the closed-loop system.

The performance and robustness specifications that are formulated above cover the usual design requirements in practical control applications. Note that other design specifications such as phase/gain margin, time delay, noise rejection, and so on, can also be added in a similar way, if desired. The simultaneous optimization of multiple ULTIC design parameters to satisfy the conflicting design specifications often leads to a multidimension and multimode design space characterized by the MO performance indices. These as well as other practical constraints make it difficult to use conventional analytical or numerical optimization techniques in existing CACSD packages. The MOEA toolbox presented in Chapter 9 is thus applied to automate the CACSD design by unifying various LTI approaches under performance satisfactions in both the time and frequency domains.

10.3 Evolutionary ULTIC Design Application

In this section, an MIMO ill-conditioned distillation system is used to illustrate the evolutionary CACSD methodology using an MOEA toolbox. The problem was originated from Zames (1966) and studied later in (Skogestad et al. 1989; Postlethwaite et al. 1991; Zhou and Kimura 1991; Diggelen and Glover 1992; Limebeer et al. 1993). The distillation column has 5 inputs (flows: reflux L, boilup V, distillate D, bottom flow B, and overhead vapor V_T) and 5 outputs (compositions and inventories: top composition y_D, bottom composition x_B, condenser holdup M_D, reboiler holdup M_B, pressure p). This control problem usually has no inherent control limitation caused by RHP-zeros, but the plant has poles in or close to the origin that need to be stabilized. Moreover, the 5×5 RGA matrix may have some large elements for high-purity separations (Zames 1966), and the composition measurements are often expensive and unreliable (Skogestad et al. 1989). Hence in most cases, the distillation column is first stabilized by closing three decentralized SISO loops for level and pressure,

$$y_{\text{closed}} = [M_D \quad M_B \quad p]^{\text{T}}, \tag{10.9}$$

and the remaining outputs are

$$y_{\text{opened}} = [y_D \quad x_B]^{\text{T}}. \tag{10.10}$$

Consider a distillation process in "LV" configuration with two inputs (reflux L and boilup V), two outputs (product compositions y_D and x_B), and two disturbances (feed flow-rate x_B and feed composition z_F). The five-state model of "LV" configuration consists of a state-space realization as given by

$$G_0(s) = \begin{bmatrix} A & B \\ C & D \end{bmatrix}, \quad G_0^d(s) = \begin{bmatrix} A & B_d \\ C & D \end{bmatrix}, \tag{10.11}$$

where $G_0(s)$ and $G_0^d(s)$ denotes the transfer matrix from the inputs (L and V) and the disturbances (x_B and z_F), respectively, to the outputs (y_D and x_B). This five-state model was obtained via a model reduction of the original model with 82 states (Skogestad et al. 1989). The process to be controlled is the distillation column with reflux flow and boils up as manipulated inputs and product compositions as outputs.

The set of performance requirements for this distillation control system is listed in Table 10.1 (Skogestad et al. 1989; Postlethwaite et al. 1991; Zhou and Kimura 1991; Diggelen and Glover 1992; Limebeer et al. 1993). These design specifications, treated as the design objectives in MO optimization, can be easily set via the "Objective Setup" GUI in the toolbox. Although determination of the priority settings in Table 10.1 may be a subjective matter and depends on the performance requirements, ranking the priorities is only optional and can be ignored for a "minimum-commitment" design (Guan and MacCallum 1996). If, however, an engineer commits to prioritizing the objectives, it is a much easier task than pre-weighting the different design specifications as required by conventional function aggregation approaches.

Table 10.1. Design Specifications for the MIMO Ill-Conditioned Distillation System

	Design specification			Goal	Priority
Frequency	1. Stability (closed-loop poles)		$Nr[\text{Re}(eig)] > 0\}$	0	1
	2. Plant uncertainty		$\bar{\sigma}\,(W_2T)$	1	2
	3. Closed-loop sensitivity		$\bar{\sigma}\,(W_1S)$	1	2
	4. Actuator saturation		$\bar{\sigma}\,[W_3HS]$	1	2
	5. Disturbance rejection for G_0^d		$\bar{\sigma}\,(S\,G_0^d)$	1	2
	6. $\bar{\sigma}\,(G_0H)$ for $\omega \geq 150$			1	2
	7. $\bar{\sigma}\,(HS)$ for $\omega \geq 150$			1	2
Time	**Tracking performance**	8. Undershoot	$1-\min(y_{11}, y_{22})$ for $t>30$ mins	0.1	3
		9. Overshoot	$\max(y_{11}, y_{22})$ for all t	1.1	3
		10. SS error (e_{ss})	$\max(|y_{11}(\infty)-1|, |y_{22}(\infty)-1|)$	0.01	3
	Interaction and coupling effect	11. amp_{dcpl}	$\max(y_{12}, y_{21})$ for all t	0.5	3
		12. $e_{ss\ dcpl}$	$\max(|y_{12}(\infty)-1|, |y_{21}(\infty)-1|)$	0.01	3

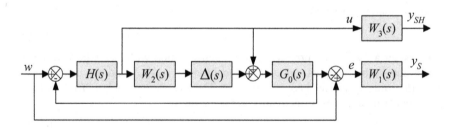

Fig. 10.6. ULTIC design block diagrams of the ill-conditioned distillation system.

Note that all the specifications in Table 10.1 can be tackled in both the time and frequency domains directly using the evolutionary CACSD approach, without the need of domain transformation or worrying about any ill-conditioning problem (Skogestad et al. 1989). Although the actuator saturation requirement (the fourth specification in Table 10.1) can be specified in the time domain, it is here formulated in the frequency domain for consistency with other approaches (Skogestad et al. 1989). The overall ULTIC design block diagrams of the distillation control system are shown in Fig. 10.6. Without loss of generality, the following full-matrix control structure with a simple first-order transfer function is sufficient and adopted (Dahleh and Diaz-Bobillo 1995):

$$H(s) = \begin{bmatrix} H_{11}(s) & H_{12}(s) \\ H_{21}(s) & H_{22}(s) \end{bmatrix}, \tag{10.12}$$

where $H_{i,j}(s) = \dfrac{p_{3,i,j}s + p_{2,i,j}}{p_{1,i,j}s + p_{0,i,j}}$, $i, j \in \{1,2\}$.

The size of population and generation in the MOEA toolbox is set as 400. At the end of the evolution, all the ULTIC controllers satisfy the set of design specifications as listed in Table 10.1.

The tradeoff graph for some of the evolved ULTIC controllers is illustrated in Fig. 10.7, where each line represents a solution found by the evolution. The heavily crossing lines suggest that the solutions are nondominated and tradeoff to each other. As can be seen, all the cost values for the first objective (e.g., stability) are zero, showing that the evolved controllers have stabilized the system with no right-hand-side poles in the closed-loop system. To further illustrate relationship among different specifications, objective 11 (amp_{dcpl}) and objective 12 (e_{ss_dcpl}) are extracted and plotted in Fig. 10.8, which depicts how the steady-state coupling error performance deteriorates as more stringent bound on the coupling magnitude is demanded. The tradeoff graph also unveils that it is possible to reduce e_{ss_dcpl} by almost 100% (which is reduced from 2.2×10^{-3} to 0.2×10^{-3}) without losing too much performance of the system in terms of amp_{dcpl} (which is increased from 0.34 to 0.4). Further investigations between any other two objectives can be performed in a same manner.

Figure 10.9 shows the transient and steady-state responses for tracking and regulating performances of both channels in the system. It can be seen that all the time domain design requirements as specified by the objectives of 8 to 12 in Table 10.1 have been met. The various frequency responses of the optimized system are shown in Fig. 10.10, which indicate that all the frequency responses are satisfactorily bounded under the performance requirements as specified by the objectives of 2 to 7 in Table 10.1.

To illustrate robustness performance of the distillation system in the presence of disturbance, a sinusoidal signal is applied to both channels of the system as the disturbance input. The attenuated sinusoidal signals of the MIMO system for all Pareto optimal ULTIC controllers are illustrated by the solid lines in Fig. 10.11, which show a satisfactory magnitude reduction for both the disturbances. Figure 10.12 shows the system output responses with the state matrix A of the nominal model being perturbed substantially in the range of

$$\frac{A_1}{10} \leq A \leq A_1, \tag{10.13}$$

where $A_1 = 2A$. As shown in Fig. 10.12, the distillation system is able to maintain reasonable good responses and stability performances in the presence of plant uncertainties.

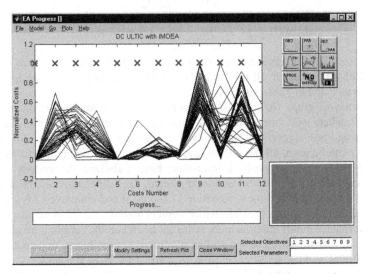

Fig. 10.7. Tradeoff graph for the MIMO ill-conditioned distillation control system.

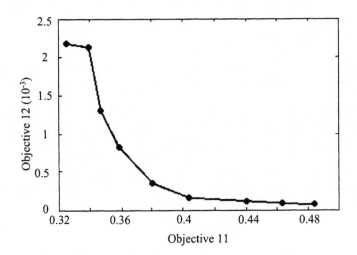

Fig. 10.8. Tradeoff graph between the objectives of amp_{dcpl} and e_{ss_dcpl} .

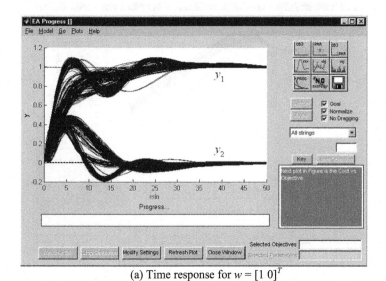

(a) Time response for $w = [1\ 0]^T$

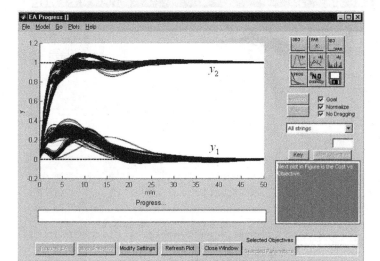

(b) Time response for $w = [0\ 1]^T$

Fig. 10.9. The MOEA optimized output responses of the MIMO distillation system.

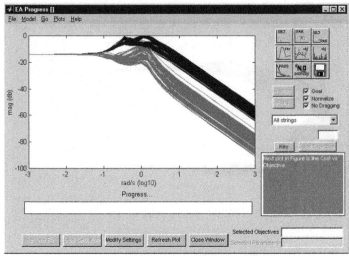

(a)   Frequency responses of W_2T

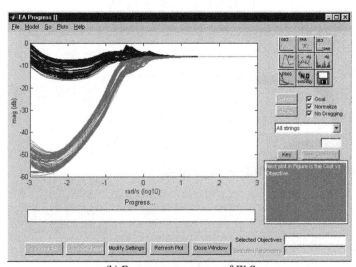

(b) Frequency responses of W_1S

Fig. 10.10. Frequency responses of the MIMO distillation system (continued on next page).

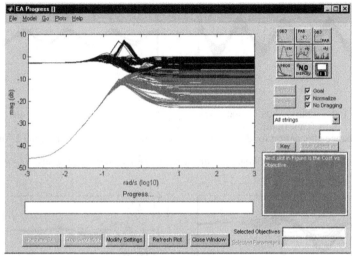

(c) Frequency responses of *HS*

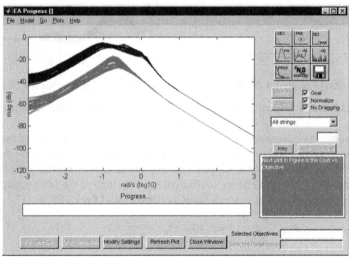

(d) Frequency responses of SG_0^d

Fig. 10.10. (Continued) Frequency responses of the MIMO distillation system.

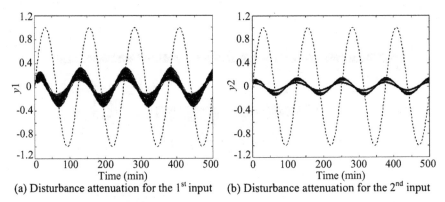

(a) Disturbance attenuation for the 1st input   (b) Disturbance attenuation for the 2nd input

Fig. 10.11. The sinusoidal disturbance and its attenuated signals.

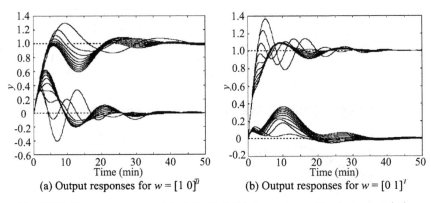

(a) Output responses for $w = [1\ 0]^{T}$ (b) Output responses for $w = [0\ 1]'$

Fig. 10.12. Output responses of the MIMO distillation system with plant uncertainties.

The quantitative assessment of correlation coefficient and the slope of the least-squares line can be used to provide statistical information of the evolving decision variables toward the objective components. For any decision variable x_j and objective component f_k, the correlation coefficient $r_{k,j}$ and slope of the least-squares line $m_{k,j}$ for a population size of N are defined as (Devore and Peck 1997)

$$r_{k,j} = \frac{S_{xf}}{\sqrt{S_{xx}}\sqrt{S_{ff}}} \quad \text{and} \quad m_{k,j} = \frac{S_{xf}}{\sqrt{S_{xx}}}, \tag{10.14}$$

where

$$S_{xx} = \sum_{i=1}^{N} x_{i,j}^2 - \frac{1}{N}\left(\sum_{i=1}^{N} x_{i,j}\right)^2, \tag{10.15}$$

$$S_{ff} = \sum_{i=1}^{N} f_{i,k}^2 - \frac{1}{N}\left(\sum_{i=1}^{N} f_{i,k}\right)^2, \tag{10.16}$$

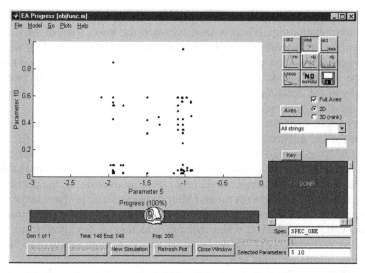

(a) 2-dimension

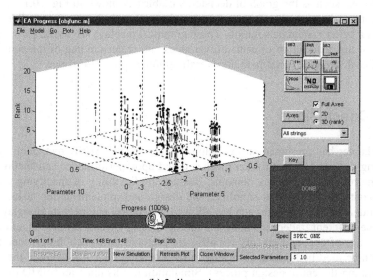

(b) 3-dimension

Fig. 10.13. Distribution of controller parameters.

$$S_{xf} = \sum_{i=1}^{N} x_{i,j} f_{i,k} - \frac{1}{N} \left(\sum_{i=1}^{N} x_{i,j} \right) \left(\sum_{i=1}^{N} f_{i,k} \right). \tag{10.17}$$

The correlation coefficient $r_{k,j}$ gives a quantitative measure of how strongly a decision variable x_j and an objective component f_k is related. The value of $r_{k,j}$ is between -1 and $+1$. A value near the upper limit of $+1$ is an indication of substantial positive relationship, whereas an $r_{k,j}$ close to the lower limit of -1 suggests a prominent negative relationship. In the case where decision variable x_j and objective component f_k are not correlated to each other, the value of $r_{k,j} = 0$ is found. For the slope of the least-squares line $m_{k,j}$, its magnitude represents the measure of sensitivity of the decision variable x_j to the objective component f_k. The larger the magnitude of $m_{k,j}$, the more sensitive is the decision variable.

For example, consider a population distribution of the optimized controller parameters for the distillation control problem, the value of $r_{k,j}$ for $\{x_2, f_9\}$ and $\{x_4, f_9\}$ is -0.6720 ($r_{9,2}$) and -0.1956 ($r_{9,4}$), respectively; and the corresponding magnitude of $m_{k,j}$ is 0.0065 ($m_{9,2}$) and -0.7596 ($m_{9,4}$), respectively. This shows that with respect to the objective component f_9 (e.g., tracking overshoot), the decision variable x_2 is more correlated than x_4; and both decision variables have negative relationship with f_9. Therefore, more concerns should be given for a slight increase of decision variable x_2 than x_4 when manual reduction of f_9 is performed. On the other hand, compared to x_2, the decision variable x_4 is more sensitive to the objective f_9, e.g., a little variation of x_4 will lead to a large change of f_9.

The MOEA toolbox also supports other types of plotting in two or three dimensions, such as the graph of decision variables as shown in Fig. 10.13. In the three-dimension plot, the z-axis represents the rank value, where a smaller rank implies a better candidate solution. These graphical displays are useful for visualization of the distribution of decision variables and understanding of the contribution of each decision variable to the overall optimization performance.

10.4 Conclusions

This chapter has presented an evolutionary automated CACSD methodology by unifying various LTI control approaches based upon performance satisfactions in both the time and frequency domains. Besides the flexibility of specifying a low-order control structure that simplifies the design and implementation tasks, such an evolutionary design approach has allowed the control engineer to interplay and examine different tradeoffs among the multiple design specifications. In addition, the settings of goal and priority for different preference on each design specification can be modified online according to the evolving tradeoffs, without the need of repeating the entire design process. Simulation results upon an MIMO distillation control system have illustrated the practical usefulness of the design methodology. It has been shown that the quantitative assessments of correlation coefficient and slope of the least-squares line are useful for examining the relationship between decision variables and objective components.

11
Evolutionary Design Automation of Multivariable QFT Control System

11.1 Introduction

Quantitative feedback theory (QFT) is a well-known frequency domain controller design methodology that utilizes Nichols chart (NC) to achieve a desired robust design and performance tolerance over specified ranges of structured plant parameter uncertainties with or without control effector failures (Houpis 1993). The basic idea of QFT is to convert design specifications on closed-loop response and plant uncertainty into robust stability and performance bounds on open-loop transmission of the nominal system. A fixed structure controller $H(s)$ and prefilter $F(s)$ are then synthesized using gain-phase loop-shaping technique so that the two-degree-of-freedom output feedback system as shown in Fig. 11.1 is controlled within specification for any member of the plant templates.

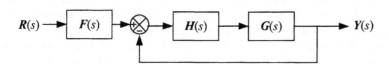

$$R(s) \longrightarrow \boxed{F(s)} \longrightarrow \bigotimes \longrightarrow \boxed{H(s)} \longrightarrow \boxed{G(s)} \longrightarrow Y(s)$$

Fig. 11.1. A typical output feedback system in QFT.

In brief, the step-by-step QFT controller design procedures from (Houpis and Rasmussen 1999) consist of the following:

Step 1. The desired tracking model is synthesized.
Step 2. The desired disturbance model is synthesized.
Step 3. The J linear time-invariant (LTI) plant models or plant templates that define the boundary of the region of plant parameter uncertainty are identified.
Step 4. Plant templates, at specified frequencies, that pictorially describe the region of plant uncertainty on the NC are obtained.
Step 5. The nominal plant transfer function $G_o(s)$ is selected.
Step 6. The stability contour (U-contour) on the NC is determined.

Step 7.   The disturbance, tracking, and optimal bounds on the NC are determined.

Step 8.   The nominal loop transmission function $L_o(s) = G_o(s)H(s)$ that satisfies all the bounds and stability contour is synthesized.

Step 9.   Based upon steps 1 through 8, the prefilter $F(s)$ is synthesized.

Step 10.   The system is simulated in order to obtain the time response data for each of J plants.

For multi-input–multi-output (MIMO) systems, the conventional QFT design method requires the design process to break the MIMO system into a sequence of multi-input–single-output (MISO) problems before the above QFT design procedure is performed for each MISO system (Yaniv and Horowitz 1986; Yaniv and Schwartz 1990; Houpis 1993). In an MIMO system, the transfer functions $F(s)$, $H(s)$, and $G(s)$ as shown in Fig. 11.1 become transfer function matrixes. Given an h-input h-output QFT control problem, the combined solution of controller and prefilter in QFT are $H(s) = diag[h_i(s)]$ and $F(s) = [f_{ij}]$, $\forall\ i, j = 1, 2,..., h$, respectively. In MIMO QFT design procedure, the solution for the first set of MISO problems via the above QFT design procedure, is the first transfer function of the diagonal controller $h_1(s)$ and the first row of prefilter $[f_{11}(s), f_{12}(s), ..., f_{1h}(s)]$. Then a new set of MISO problems is defined based on the plant $h_1(s)$ and $[f_{11}(s), f_{12}(s),..., f_{1h}(s)]$, which results in the solution for the controller $h_2(s)$ and prefilter $[f_{21}(s), f_{22}(s), ..., f_{2h}(s)]$, etc. Hence, this method leads to an overall design of h^2 equivalent loops and its size grows exponentially with the number of inputs/outputs, which makes the design process very tedious and conservative (Houpis 1993). Readers may refer to Yaniv and Horowitz (1986); Yaniv and Schwartz (1990); Houpis (1993) for detailed information regarding the QFT design procedure of MIMO plants.

As pointed out by Snell and Hess (1997), there are no other methods that can be employed to determine these series of loops apart from the manual trial-and-error process. Moreover, this sequential MISO design procedure is conservative since the solution of an SISO problem is dependent and restricted by other loops. The user may thus need to repeat the design procedure from the first loop synthesis whenever any subsequent loop turns out to be unfeasible or is unable to meet the design criteria due to improper or overdesign of the previous loops. Besides, the QFT bounds on Nichols chart for each specification at all frequency points must be acquired a priori, which is often an exhaustive trial-and-error procedure. The reason is that, for every frequency point with sufficiently small frequency interval, the template needs to be manually shifted up or down on the NC until the gain variation of the template is equal to the gain variation allowed for any particular robust specification at that frequency. In addition, only the controller can be synthesized via the QFT bound computation using conventional loop-shaping methods. Another independent design task has to be accomplished in order to obtain the prefilter within a two-stage design framework for each loop.

The acquisition of an optimal QFT controller is an MO design optimization problem that involves simultaneously determining multiple controller and prefilter parameters to satisfy different competing performance requirements, such as sensitivity bounds, cross-coupling bounds, and robust margin. A few analytical or automatic design techniques have been proposed for QFT (Thompson and Nwo-kah 1994; Bryant and Halikias 1995; Chait 1997). However, these convex-based design approaches often impose certain assumptions that may lead to a conservative design. With the view of tackling these drawbacks and automating the QFT design procedure, various "intelligent" trial-and-error design methodologies based upon evolutionary computation have been proposed (Chen and Balance 1998; Chen et al. 1998; Chen et al. 1999; Tan et al. 1999a, 2001b).

This chapter presents an evolutionary-based methodology for design automation of MIMO QFT control systems. The approach is capable of evolving the controller and prefilter concurrently for the entire set of MISO subsystems in order to meet the performance requirements in QFT, without going through the sequential design stages for each of the MISO subsystems. It also avoids the conventional QFT bound computation and manual loop-shaping design procedure, without violating the QFT design specifications. Moreover, it is capable of evolving a set of noncommensurable solutions that allows engineers to examine the tradeoffs among different design specifications. The chapter is organized as follows: A number of general QFT design specifications are formulated in Section 11.2, which include an overview of robust tracking and cross-coupling that is useful for formulating the time domain design specifications in QFT. Implementation of the evolutionary design methodology for a benchmark MIMO QFT control problem is illustrated in Section 11.3. Conclusions are drawn in Section 11.4.

11.2 Problem Formulation

11.2.1 Overview of Tracking and Cross-Coupling Specifications

In QFT, tracking thumbprint specification is often used to determine the robust tracking performance of an SISO system and the diagonal transfer functions of an MIMO system. It is based upon the satisfaction of an upper and lower bound in the time-domain response as shown in Fig. 11.2 (Snell and Hess 1997), where the region within the upper and lower bounds represents the bounded step response. For each ith diagonal element of the closed-loop system, $y_{(i,i)}(t)_U$ is the upper bound, which is usually an underdamped $(m_{(i,i)p}, t_{(i,i)p}, t_{(i,i)s}, t_{(i,i)r}, K_{(i,i)m})_U$ step response, while $y_{(i,i)}(t)_L$ is the lower bound that is often represented by an overdamped step response $(t_{(i,i)s}, t_{(i,i)r}, K_{(i,i)m})_L$. $m_{(i,i)p}$ denotes the system overshoot, $t_{(i,i)p}$ the peak time, $t_{(i,i)s}$ the settling time, $t_{(i,i)r}$ the rise time, and $K_{(i,i)m}$ the gain margin.

Based on the time-domain specification of $m_{(i,i)p}, t_{(i,i)p}, t_{(i,i)s}, t_{(i,i)r}$ and the required gain margin $K_{(i,i)m}$, the desired control ratio can be modeled in the frequency domain as shown in Fig. 11.3. Here, $T_{(i,i)U}$ is the transformed upper bound and $T_{(i,i)L}$ the transformed lower bound of the ith diagonal element of the closed-loop system, which may be in the form of a second-order transfer function as given by (Horowitz 1982)

$$T_{(i,i)}(s) = \frac{\omega_{n(i,i)}^2}{s^2 + 2\zeta_{(i,i)}\omega_{n(i,i)}s + \omega_{n(i,i)}^2}, \qquad (11.1)$$

where $\omega_{n(i,i)}$ is the natural frequency and $\zeta_{(i,i)}$ the damping ratio. Intuitively, $\omega_{n(i,i)}$ and $\zeta_{(i,i)}$ can be easily determined from the time-domain specifications as given in Fig. 11.2. The specification of tracking thumbprint in QFT is thus to design the controller and prefilter in Fig. 11.1 such that the system frequency responses of all plant templates are inside the region within the specified tracking bounds in the Bode plot as shown in Fig. 11.3. Note that the high-frequency range between $T_{(i,i)U}$ and $T_{(i,i)L}$ can be increased along with the increasing of frequency without violating the desired time-response characteristics (D'Azzo and Houpis 1995). This can be achieved by augmenting $T_{(i,i)L}$ with a negative real pole that is as close to the origin as possible without affecting the time response significantly. This will lower the value of $T_{(i,i)L}$ in the high-frequency range. On the other hand, the curve of $T_{(i,i)L}$ can be raised by augmenting it with a zero as close to the origin as possible without affecting the time response substantially.

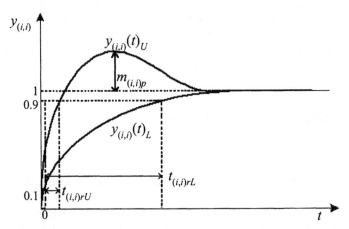

Fig. 11.2. Tracking thumbprint specification for the ith diagonal element.

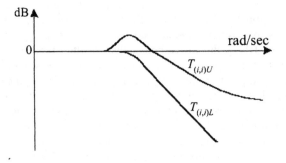

Fig. 11.3. Bode plot of upper and lower bounds.

For MIMO QFT designs, besides the tracking performance of the diagonal elements, it is also essential to reduce the coupling effect from the off-diagonal transfer functions of the closed-loop system for all the plant templates. In contrast to the tracking bounds where both the upper and lower limits are prescribed, only upper bounds are needed (Snell and Hess 1997) to satisfy the objective of reducing the gain and bandwidth of the off-diagonal transfer functions. The upper bound of coupling effect represented by the transfer function $T_{(i,j)U}$ for off-diagonal transfer functions (i,j) where $i \neq j$ can be intuitively defined based on the allowable gain K and bandwidth between w_1 and w_2, which generally takes the form of

$$T_{(i,j)U}(s) = \frac{K(\frac{1}{w_1}s)}{\left(\frac{1}{w_1}s+1\right)\left(\frac{1}{w_2}s+1\right)}. \tag{11.2}$$

The approximated frequency response of the above $T_{(i,j)U}$ is illustrated in Fig. 11.4.

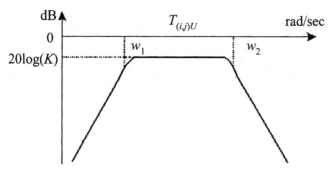

Fig. 11.4. Bode plot of upper cross-coupling bound model.

11.2.2 MO QFT Design Formulation

Apart from the tracking thumbprint specification in QFT, other design objectives such as robust margin performance, robust disturbance sensitivity, and high-frequency gain are also important requirements to be satisfied in the design. In contrast to the conventional two-stage loop-shaping approach, these performance requirements can be formulated as an MO design optimization problem.

i. Stability (*RHSP*)

The cost of stability, *RHSP*, is included to ensure stability of the closed-loop system, which could be evaluated by solving for the roots of the characteristic polynomial. Mathematically, *RHSP* is defined as the total number of unstable closed-loop poles for all the plant templates $\wp$,

$$RHSP = \sum_i Nr([real(pole(\frac{g_i hf}{1+g_i h})]) > 0, \quad \forall g_i \in \wp. \tag{11.3}$$

To obtain a stable closed-loop system for all the plant templates $\wp$, the value of $RHSP$ should be zero. In order to ensure internal stability and to guarantee no unstable pole and nonminimum phase zero cancellations, it is desirable that a minimum phase and stable controller is designed. This implies that the search range for a polynomial coefficient set is limited to either the first or the third "quadrant," i.e., all coefficients in the numerator or denominator must be of the same sign (Chen et al. 1999). The poles and zeros of the controllers can be calculated explicitly to avoid right-hand-side pole (RHP) cancellations or alternatively, the Horowitz method for QFT design of unstable and nonminimum phase plants can be used, i.e., QFT bounds for an unstable/nonminimum phase nominal plant can be translated to those for a stable and minimum phase plant by shifting the robust stability and performance bounds (Horowitz and Sidi 1978; Horowitz 1992) if necessary.

ii. Robust Upper and Lower Tracking Performance ($ERRUT$ & $ERRLT$)

The cost of upper tracking performance for SISO transfer function or the ith diagonal element of the MIMO closed-loop transfer function, given as $ERRUT_{(i,i)}$, is included to address the specification of upper tracking bound as shown in Fig. 11.3. It is computed as the sum of absolute error at each frequency point as given by

$$ERRUT_{(i,i)} = \sum_{k=1}^{n} \left| e_{(i,i)ut}(\omega_k) \right|, \tag{11.4}$$

where n is the total number of interested frequency points; $e_{(i,i)ut}(\omega_k)$ is the difference between the upper bound of the (i,i) element of the closed-loop transfer function $CL_{(i,i)U}$ and the prespecified upper tracking bound $T_{(i,i)U}$ at frequency ω_k, if the upper bound of the closed-loop system is greater than the prespecified upper tracking bound or less than the prespecified lower tracking bound $T_{(i,i)L}$; otherwise, $e_{(i,i)ut}(\omega_k)$ is equal to zero as stated in (11.5). In Fig. 11.5, the length of vertical dotted lines at each frequency ω_k represents the magnitude of $e_{(i,i)ut}(\omega_k)$.

$$e_{(i,i)ut}(\omega_k) = \begin{cases} 0 & T_{(i,i)L}(\omega_k) < CL_{(i,i)U}(\omega_k) < T_{(i,i)U}(\omega_k), \\ CL_{(i,i)U}(\omega_k) - T_{(i,i)U}(\omega_k) & \text{otherwise.} \end{cases} \tag{11.5}$$

The cost of lower tracking performance for SISO transfer function or the ith diagonal element of the closed-loop transfer function, $ERRLT_{(i,i)}$, can be defined as the sum of absolute error at each frequency point,

$$ERRLT_{(i,i)} = \sum_{k=1}^{n} \left| e_{(i,i)lt}(\omega_k) \right|, \tag{11.6}$$

where n is the number of frequency points; $e_{(i,i)lt}$ is the difference between the lower bound of the closed-loop system $CL_{(i,i)L}$ and the prespecified lower tracking bound $T_{(i,i)L}$, if the lower bound of the closed-loop system is greater than the prespecified upper tracking bound $T_{(i,i)U}$ or less than the prespecified lower tracking bound $T_{(i,i)L}$; Otherwise, $e_{(i,i)lt}$ is equal to zero as stated in (11.7) and is illustrated in Fig. 11.6.

$$e_{(i,i)lt}(\omega_k) = \begin{cases} 0 & T_{(i,i)L}(\omega_k) < CL_{(i,i)L}(\omega_k) < T_{(i,i)U}(\omega_k), \\ CL_{(i,i)L}(\omega_k) - T_{(i,i)L}(\omega_k) & \text{otherwise.} \end{cases} \quad (11.7)$$

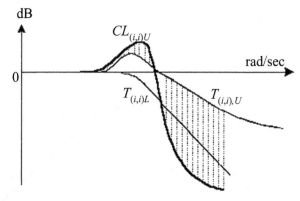

Fig. 11.5. Computation of upper tracking performance for the ith diagonal element.

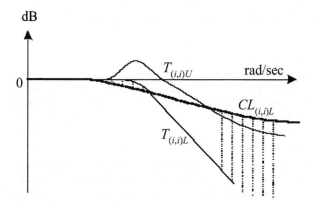

Fig. 11.6. Computation of lower tracking performance for the ith diagonal element.

iii. Cross-Coupling Performance (*ERRUC*)

For an MIMO system, the cost of cross-coupling for off-diagonal elements (i, j) of the closed-loop transfer function, $ERRUC_{(i,j)}$, where $i \neq j$, should be bounded by the upper cross-coupling bound specification as shown in Fig. 11.4. It is computed as the sum of absolute error at each frequency point,

$$ERRUC_{(i,j)} = \sum_{k=1}^{n} \left| e_{(i,j)uc}(\omega_k) \right|, \quad \text{for } i \neq j, \quad (11.8)$$

where n is the number of frequency points; $e_{(i,j)uc}(\omega_k)$ at ω_k is the difference between the upper bound of the closed-loop system $CL_{(i,j)U}$ and the prespecified upper cross-coupling bound $T_{(i,j)U}$, if the upper bound of the closed-loop system is greater than the prespecified upper cross-coupling bound $T_{(i,j)U}$; Otherwise, $e_{(i,j))uc}$ is equal to zero as described in (11.9) and is illustrated in Fig. 11.7 for $i \neq j$.

$$e_{(i,j)uc}(\omega_k) = \begin{cases} CL_{(i,j)U}(\omega_k) - T_{(i,j)U}(\omega_k) & CL_{(i,j)U}(\omega_k) > T_{(i,j)U}(\omega_k), \\ 0 & \text{otherwise.} \end{cases} \quad (11.9)$$

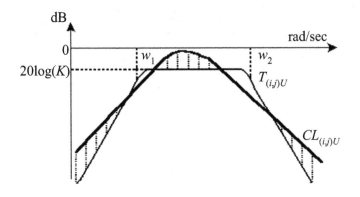

Fig. 11.7. Computation of upper cross-coupling performance for off-diagonal elements.

iv. Robust Margin (*RM*)

Besides the parametric uncertainties as described above, practical control applications may also involve neglected uncertainties or unmodeled dynamics at the high frequencies (Skogestad and Postlethwaite 1996). The unmodeled dynamic uncertainty is different from the parametric uncertainty, where the structure of the model including the order is known but some of the parameters are uncertain and can be represented in a finite set of plant templates. It is of great importance that a control system is designed so that the neglected uncertainty is taken into consideration as well. Two types of robust stability margin for unmodeled uncertainty are considered in the evolutionary QFT design here, e.g., the robust margin with multiplicative uncertainty and the robust margin with inverse multiplicative uncertainty.

Figure 11.8 shows a feedback system with multiplicative plant uncertainty, which can be represented by $G_p(s) = G(s)\{I + W_I \Delta_I\}$ where Δ denotes the unknown but unity-bounded uncertainty. The robust margin that maintains the closed-loop stability for multiplicative plant uncertainty according to the uncertainty weighting function W_I can be defined as (Skogestad and Postlethwaite 1996)

$$RM = \left| \frac{L_i(j\omega)}{I + L_i(j\omega)} \right| < \frac{1}{W_I(j\omega)}, \quad \forall \omega, \tag{11.10}$$

where $L_i(j\omega)$ is the ith open-loop function with jth loop closed in an MIMO system, which is simply the loop transmission $G(j\omega)H(j\omega)$ in an SISO system.

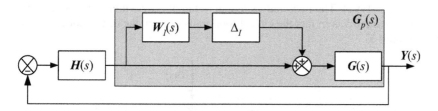

Fig. 11.8. Feedback system with multiplicative uncertainty.

Consequently, consider the robust margin for a feedback system with inverse multiplicative plant uncertainty $G_{ip}(s) = G(s)\{I + W_{il}(s)\Delta_{il}\}^{-1}$, as shown in Fig. 11.9.

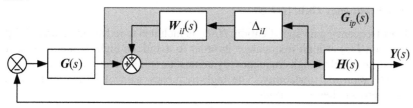

Fig. 11.9. Feedback system with inverse multiplicative uncertainty.

With a similar definition of loop transmission $L_i(j\omega)$, the robust margin is defined as (Skogestad and Postlethwaite, 1996)

$$RM = \left| \frac{1}{I + L_i(j\omega)} \right| < \frac{1}{W_{il}(j\omega)}, \quad \forall \omega. \tag{11.11}$$

The primary requirement for the robust margin with multiplicative uncertainty or inverse multiplicative uncertainty is that the nominal loop transfer function $L_i(s)$ must be stable. Since the QFT design involves parametric uncertainties as well, which is represented by plant templates, the above primary requirements should be extended so that the loop transfer function $L_i(s)$ of any plant template $G \in \wp$ is stable as formulated in the first design specification (*RHSP*).

v. Robust Sensitivity Rejection (*RS*)

The robust sensitivity rejection is to find a QFT controller that minimizes the maximum amplitude of the regulated output over all possible disturbances of bounded magnitude. A general structure to represent the disturbance rejection is given in Fig. 11.10, which depicts a particular case where the disturbance enters the system at the plant output. The mathematical representation is given as

$$S = \{I + G(s)H(s)\}^{-1}.$$ (11.12)

The matrix S is known as the *sensitivity* or *disturbance rejection* function (Doyle et al. 1992). The maximum singular value of S determines the disturbance attenuation since S is in fact the closed-loop transfer from the disturbance D to the plant output Y.

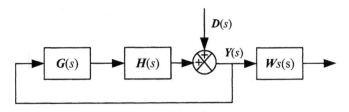

Fig. 11.10. A sensitivity rejection problem.

vi. High-Frequency Gain (*HFG*)

The high-frequency gain specification, *HFG*, is included to reduce the gain of loop transmission $L(s)$ at high frequencies in order to avoid the high-frequency sensor noise and unmodeled high-frequency dynamics/harmonics that may result in actuator saturation and instability. The high-frequency gain of loop transmission $L(s)$ is given as (Chen et al. 1998)

$$\lim_{s \to \infty} s^r L(s),$$ (11.13)

where r is the relative order of $L(s)$. Since only controller in the loop transmission is to be optimized, this performance requirement is equivalent to the minimization of high-frequency gain of the controller or the magnitude of b_n/a_m for a controller structure given as

$$H_{(i,i)}(s) = \frac{b_{(i,i)n}s^n + b_{(i,i)n-1}s^{n-1} + \cdots b_{(i,i)0}}{a_{(i,i)m}s^m + a_{(i,i)m-1}s^{m-1} + \cdots a_{(i,i)0}},$$ (11.14)

where n and m are the order of the numerator and denominator in the (i,i) element of diagonal controller $H(s)$, respectively; b and a denote the coefficients of the numerator and denominator, respectively.

vii. Controller Order (*CO*)

It is often desirable that the controller is designed as simple as possible, since a simple controller often requires less computation and implementation efforts as compared to a higher-order controller. Here, the order of the controller can be included as one of the QFT design specifications in order to find the smallest-order controller that satisfies all the design specifications.

As described, there are a number of usually conflicting design objectives to be satisfied concurrently in an multivariable QFT control problem. In contrast to the conventional two-stage loop-shaping approach, these performance requirements can be formulated as an MO design optimization problem (Tan et al. 1999a, 2001b). The aim is then to design the nominal controller $H(s)$ and prefilter $F(s)$ simultaneously in order to satisfy all the required specifications in the QFT control system.

11.3 MIMO QFT Control Problem

The benchmark MIMO QFT control problem based on the model of Borghesani et al. (1995) is studied in this section. Here, additional robust tracking and cross-coupling specifications as well as full-matrix prefilters are included for a wider consideration of the design specifications. Besides, the specification of high-frequency gain (Tan et al. 1999a; Chen et al. 1998) is also included in the design as a soft optimization objective, in order to avoid high-frequency sensor noise or unmodeled high-frequency dynamics/harmonics. As shown in Fig. 11.1, the QFT control system with an MIMO uncertainty plant set of $G(s) = [g_{i,j}(s)]$ for $\forall\, i, j = 1, 2$, is given as

$$
G(s) = \begin{bmatrix} \dfrac{l}{\Lambda(s)} & \dfrac{3+0.5l}{\Lambda(s)} \\[2mm] \dfrac{1}{\Lambda(s)} & \dfrac{8}{\Lambda(s)} \end{bmatrix},
\tag{11.15}
$$

where $\Lambda(s) = s^2 + 0.03ls + 10$ and $l \in [6,8]$. The various closed-loop performance requirements for the QFT control system design are formulated as follows:

i. Robust tracking bounds for diagonal transfer functions:

$$
T_{(i,i)L}(\omega) \le \left| CL_{(i,i)}(j\omega) \right| \le T_{(i,i)U}(\omega), \quad \text{for } i = 1,2,
\tag{11.16}
$$

where the upper tracking model is

$$
T_{(1,1)U}(\omega) = \left| \frac{1.9 \times 10^4 (j\omega) + 6.4 \times 10^5}{(j\omega)^3 + 2.3 \times 10^2 (j\omega)^2 + 1.9 \times 10^4 (j\omega) + 6.4 \times 10^5} \right|,
\tag{11.17a}
$$

$$
T_{(2,2)U}(\omega) = \left| \frac{6.4 \times 10^3 (j\omega) + 3.4 \times 10^5}{(j\omega)^3 + 1.5 \times 10^2 (j\omega)^2 + 8 \times 10^3 (j\omega) + 3.4 \times 10^5} \right|,
\tag{11.17b}
$$

and the lower tracking model is

$$
T_{(1,1)L}(\omega) = \left| \frac{1 \times 10^6}{(j\omega)^3 + 3 \times 10^2 (j\omega)^2 + 3 \times 10^4 (j\omega) + 1 \times 10^6} \right|,
\tag{11.18a}
$$

$$
T_{(2,2)L}(\omega) = \left| \frac{2.5 \times 10^5}{(j\omega)^3 + 2.3 \times 10^2 (j\omega)^2 + 1.5 \times 10^4 (j\omega) + 2.5 \times 10^5} \right|.
\tag{11.18b}
$$

ii. Robust cross-coupling bounds for off-diagonal transfer functions:

$$\left| CL_{(i,j)}(j\omega) \right| \leq T_{(i,j)U}(\omega), \quad \text{for } i \neq j, \text{ and } i,j = 1,2,$$

where

$$T_{(1,2)U}(\omega) = \left| \frac{0.0032(j\omega)}{[0.016(j\omega)+1]\ [0.016(j\omega)+1]} \right|, \tag{11.19a}$$

$$T_{(2,1)U}(\omega) = \left| \frac{6.3 \times 10^{-3}(j\omega)}{[0.016(j\omega)+1]\ [0.016(j\omega)+1]} \right|. \tag{11.19b}$$

iii. Robust sensitivity rejections for the full-matrix transfer functions:

$$\left| S_{i,j}(j\omega) \right| < d_{i,j}(j\omega), \quad \text{for } \omega < 10, \tag{11.20}$$

where $d_{i,j} = 0.01\omega$, for $i = j$; $d_{i,j} = 0.005\omega$, for $i \neq j$.

iv. Robust margin:

$$\left| \frac{1}{1+L_{i,i}(j\omega)} \right| < 1.8, \quad \text{for } \forall i = 1,2, \text{ and } \omega > 0. \tag{11.21}$$

The performance bounds of QFT are computed within a wide frequency range of 10^{-2} rad/sec to 10^3 rad/sec. The structure of the diagonal controller $H(s)$ is chosen in the form of a general transfer function (Borghesani et al. 1995) as given by

$$H_{i,j}(s) = \begin{cases} \sum_{m=0}^{4} b_m s^m \Big/ \sum_{n=0}^{4} a_n s^n & \text{for } i = j, \forall\ b_m, a_n \in \Re, \text{ for } i,j = 1,2, \\ 0 & \text{otherwise.} \end{cases} \tag{11.22}$$

The population and generation size are 200 and 100, respectively. To guide the evolutionary QFT design optimization process, the goal and priority for each of the performance requirements may be included optionally as shown in Fig. 11.11. At the end of the evolution, all individuals in the final population are nondominated to each other and all the specified goals have been met. Figure 11.12 shows the progress ratio evaluated at each generation of the evolution. As can be seen, the progress ratio is relatively high at the initial stage of evolution and is decreased asymptotically toward zero as the evolution proceeds or as the population gets closer to the global tradeoff surface, as desired.

The merit of the evolutionary QFT design approach is that it allows online examination of different tradeoffs among the multiple conflicting specifications, modification of existing objectives and constraints, or zooming into any region of interest before selecting one final set of controller and prefilter for real-time implementation. The tradeoff graph for some of the evolved QFT controllers is shown in Fig. 11.13, where each line represents a Pareto optimal solution found at the end of the evolution. The x-axis shows the design specifications or objectives, the y-axis shows the normalized cost of controllers and prefilters in each objective domain, and the cross-marks show the design goals. The costs for stability

(*RHSP*), robust tracking, and cross-coupling performances as labeled by objectives 1 to 7 (*ERRUT* and *ERRLT*) are all equal to zero. It can be observed that objectives 12 (*RS*21) and 13 (*RS*22) are not competing with each other, whereas objectives 8 (*RM*1) and 9 (*RM*2) appear to compete heavily. The information contained in the tradeoff graph also suggests that a lower goal setting for sensitivity ($S_{i,j}$) is possible, where further optimization can be performed to achieve even better robust performance.

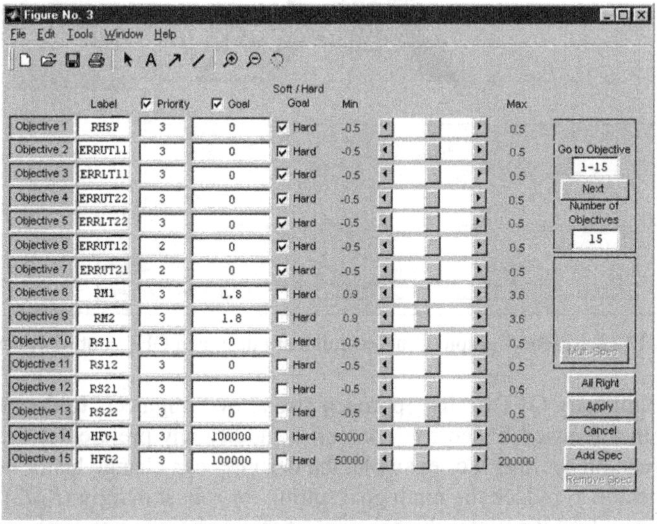

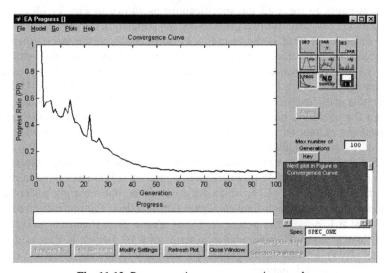

Fig. 11.11. Settings of the MOEA toolbox for the MIMO QFT design problem.

Fig. 11.12. Progress ratio versus generation number.

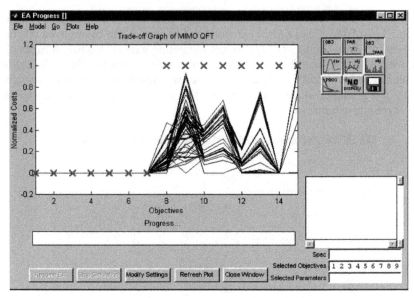

Fig. 11.13. Tradeoff graph of the evolutionary designed QFT control system.

The evolutionary QFT design approach also allows engineers to divert the evolution to other focused tradeoff regions or to modify any preferences on the current specification settings. For example, the designer can change his or her preference and decide to reduce the ninth goal setting for robust margin ($RM2$) from 1.8 to 1.3. Figure 11.14 illustrates the behavior of the evolution upon such a modification. Due to the sudden change for a tighter goal setting, initially none of the individuals manages to meet all the specifications as shown in Fig. 11.14(a). After continuing the evolution for two generations, the population moves toward satisfying the objective of $RM2$ as shown in Fig. 11.14(b), at the performance expense of other objectives since these specifications are correlated and competing with each other. The evolution then continues and leads to the satisfaction of all the required goal settings, including the stricter setting of $RM2$ as shown in Fig. 11.14(c). Clearly, this man–machine interactive design approach has enabled QFT designers to divert the evolution into any interesting tradeoff regions or to modify certain specifications online, without the need of restarting the entire design process as required by conventional means.

To further illustrate the relationship among different specifications, objectives 9 (robust margin, $RM2$) and 15 (high-frequency gain, $HFG2$) are extracted from Fig. 11.13 and plotted in Fig. 11.15, which depicts how the robust margin performance deteriorates as a lower high-frequency gain is demanded. The tradeoff graph also reveals that it is possible to reduce $HFG2$ by almost 50% (from 10^6 to 0.5×10^6) without losing too much performance in terms of $RM2$ (which is increased from -0.55 to -0.45). Further investigations between any other two objectives can be performed in a similar manner.

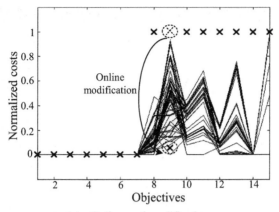

(a)   Online goal modification.

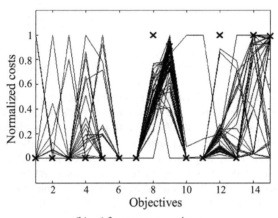

(b)   After two generations.

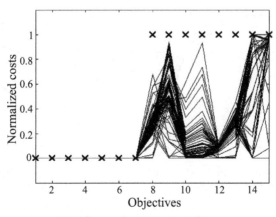

(c) After another two generations.

Fig. 11.14. Effect of evolution upon the tighter goal setting of *RM2*.

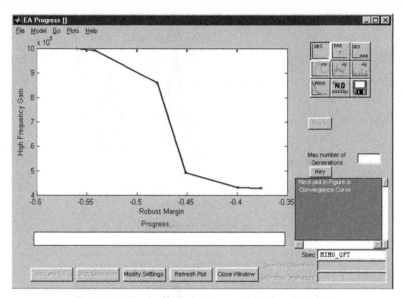

Fig. 11.15. Tradeoff graph between objectives 9 and 15.

Figure 11.16 shows the robust tracking performance in the frequency domain for the two diagonal elements of the closed-loop system. It can be seen that all the frequency responses of CL_U and CL_L for both diagonal channels are located successfully within their respective prespecified tracking bounds of T_U and T_L as stated in (11.4) and (11.6), respectively. Besides, the coupling effects from the off-diagonal elements of the closed-loop system for all the plant templates have also been reduced and successfully bounded by the upper coupling bound with minimal gain and bandwidth of the off-diagonal transfer functions, as shown in Fig. 11.17.

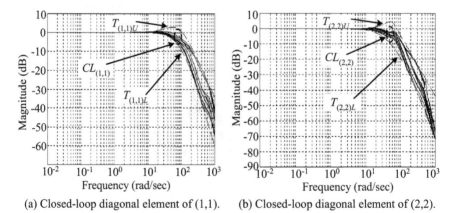

(a) Closed-loop diagonal element of (1,1).   (b) Closed-loop diagonal element of (2,2).

Fig. 11.16. The tracking performance in the frequency domain.

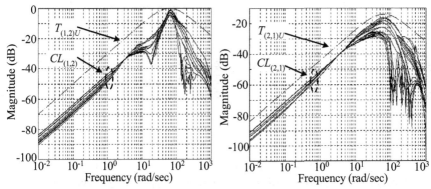

(a) Closed-loop off-diagonal element of (1,2). (b) Closed-loop off-diagonal element of (2,1).

Fig. 11.17. The cross-coupling performance in the frequency domain.

Figures 11.18 and 11.19 show the unit step tracking and coupling performance, respectively, in the time domain for all the plant templates. Clearly, all the time-domain tracking and coupling performances are satisfied and within the required prescribed tracking bounds, as desired.

The frequency responses for all the optimized robust sensitivity transfer functions in the frequency domain are shown in Fig. 11.20. As can be seen, all the frequency responses are satisfactorily bounded under the norm constraints as specified by objectives 10 to 13 in Fig. 11.11. Figure 11.21 shows the robust margin performance in the frequency domain, where all the peak responses within the specified range of frequency (e.g., 10^{-2}–10^3 rad/sec) are less than 1.8 as required by (11.21).

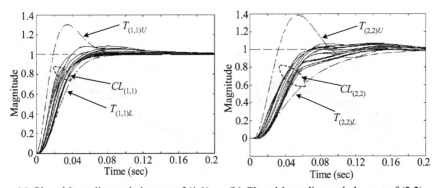

(a) Closed-loop diagonal element of (1,1).   (b) Closed-loop diagonal element of (2,2).

Fig. 11.18. The tracking responses of closed-loop diagonal elements.

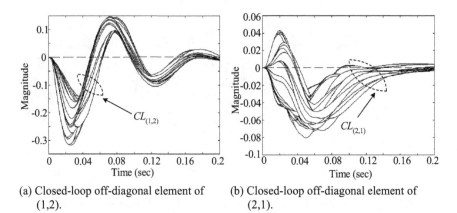

(a) Closed-loop off-diagonal element of (1,2).

(b) Closed-loop off-diagonal element of (2,1).

Fig. 11.19. The coupling responses of closed-loop off-diagonal elements.

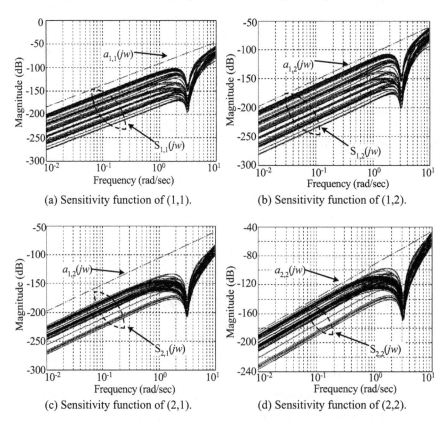

(a) Sensitivity function of (1,1).

(b) Sensitivity function of (1,2).

(c) Sensitivity function of (2,1).

(d) Sensitivity function of (2,2).

Fig. 11.20. Frequency responses of robust sensitivity transfer functions.

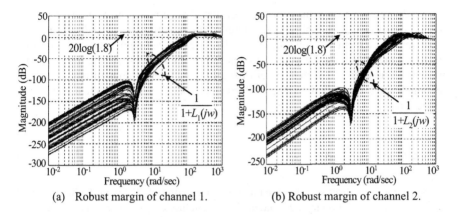

(a) Robust margin of channel 1.   (b) Robust margin of channel 2.

Fig. 11.21. Robust margin performance in the frequency domain.

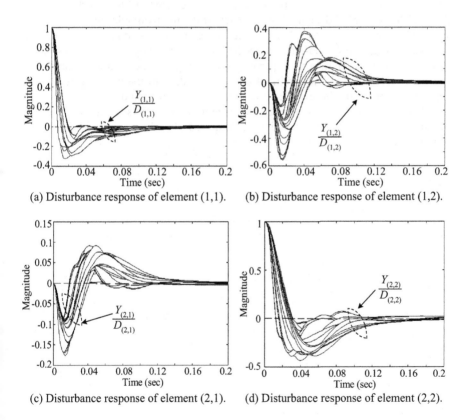

(a) Disturbance response of element (1,1).   (b) Disturbance response of element (1,2).

(c) Disturbance response of element (2,1).   (d) Disturbance response of element (2,2).

Fig. 11.22. Output responses for the unit step disturbance in the time domain.

To illustrate the robustness in terms of disturbance rejection, a unit step disturbance signal $D(s)$ was applied to the input of the sensitivity transfer function S for each matrix element as shown in Fig. 11.10. The resulted output responses for disturbance are illustrated by the solid lines in Fig. 11.22. Clearly, the unit step disturbance has been attenuated to zero for all the different values of parameter uncertainties, as quantified by the performance specification of robust sensitivity rejection.

11.4 Conclusions

This chapter has discussed the weaknesses of existing QFT design techniques and presented an evolutionary automated design methodology for multivariable QFT control systems. Unlike existing design methods, the evolutionary design approach is capable of automatically evolving both the nominal controller and prefilter simultaneously to meet all performance requirements in QFT, without going through the sequential design stages for each of the multivariable subsystems. Besides, the approach has avoided the need of conventional manual QFT bound computation and trial-and-error loop-shaping design procedures. It has been shown that control engineers' expertise as well as goal and priority information can be easily included and modified online according to the evolving tradeoffs. The effectiveness of the evolutionary QFT design methodology has been illustrated upon a benchmark multivariable system, which offers a set of low-order Pareto optimal controllers satisfying the required closed-loop specifications and constraints.

12
Evolutionary Design of HDD Servo Control System

12.1 Introduction

Magnetic hard disk drives (HDDs) are the primary permanent storage devices used in computers today. Over the years, the storage capacity in HDDs has been increasing at a steady rate while the form factor has been decreasing. Such a phenomenal growth rate of capacities and track densities in HDDs implies that the track width has to be smaller, leading to a lower error tolerance in positioning the magnetic head. In most hard disk drives, a rotating disk coated with a thin magnetic layer or recording medium is written with data arranged in concentric circles or tracks. Data are then read or written with a read/write (R/W) head that consists of a small horseshoe-shaped electromagnet. The aim of the servo system in HDDs is to achieve fast transition or to move the R/W head from one track to another target track in minimum time using a bounded control effort (track seeking) as well as to maintain precise positioning of the R/W head on the destination track center while information is being read or written onto the disk (track following) (Franklin et al. 1998).

One of the factors contributing to the rapid development in disk storage is the advanced track following control that achieves tighter regulation of closed-loop servomechanism in hard disk drives. Currently, many available HDD servo systems are designed using conventional PID controllers operated in the track following mode (Franklin et al. 1998; Hoagland 1991). Due to the tradeoffs between track following speed and overshoot performances, problems such as huge peak overshoots in step response may occur when the track following speed is pushed up for drives with a single voice coil motor (VCM) actuator. Complexity, nonlinearity and constraints in HDDs, such as voltage/current limits, noise, and disturbance, make the conventional PID servo control system difficult to meet the ever-increasing stringent performance requirements in the industry of hard disk drive (Goh 1999).

Goh et al. (1999, 2001) propose the method of robust and perfect tracking (RPT) for servo control systems, which provides a better control performance as compared to conventional PID controllers. While the RPT controller has a simple first-order control structure and is capable of fully utilizing all the available information associated with the actual system, its performance depends on the selection of a parameter ε in a trial-and-error manner. Li and Tomizuka (1999) propose a two-degree-of-freedom (2DOF) control technique for both track seeking and track following operations, which avoids the need of mode switching encountered in many conventional approaches. Although such a 2DOF design approach was claimed to be robust against plant perturbations, it requires a disturbance observer to attenuate runout disturbances. Among other methods, Hanslemann and Engelke (1988) applied the continuous-time optimal LQG/LTR technique to design a tracking controller for a high resonant disk drive actuator, where Chiu et al. (1993) adopted a frequency loop-shaping LQG/LTR approach to improve the runout performance of a disk drive system. These methods were extended by Maciejowski (1989) into discrete-time LQG/LTR, which was applied later to design a tracking controller for compound (dual stage) disk drive actuator system by Yen et al. (1990) and Weerasooriya and Phan (1995). Based upon the frequency domain specifications on bandwidth and stability margins, Hirata et al. (1992) applied the method of modern H_∞ control to synthesis a head positioning servo system in HDDs. Since the system has two poles at the origin, the mixed sensitivity minimization problem in H_∞ controller synthesis cannot be solved directly and has to be dealt with a priori by adjusting the design specifications in order to satisfy the numerical assumptions in the design (Doyle and Stein 1981; Glover and Doyle 1988; Hirata et al. 1992).

This chapter presents the design and real-time implementation of a robust track following HDD servo control system using the MOEA toolbox presented in Chapter 9. Besides the flexibility of specifying a low-order servo controller structure for easy implementation, the evolutionary design approach is capable of optimizing multiple controller parameters simultaneously to satisfy different HDD design specifications and constraints in both the time and frequency domains. Such an evolutionary servo control system optimally moves the magnetic head onto the desired track with minimal control effort and keeps it on the track robustly against different runout disturbances and plant uncertainties. The rest of this chapter is organized as follows: In Section 12.2, the model of an HDD with single VCM actuator is studied and identified according to physical frequency response data. Section 12.3 shows the evolutionary design of an HDD servo controller based upon the model identified in previous section, as well as its robustness validation and real-time implementation for physical 3.5-inch open HDD with a TMS320 digital signal processor. Comparison results of the evolutionary design against conventional PID and RPT approaches are also shown in this section. Conclusions are drawn in Section 12.4.

12.2 The Physical HDD Model

A typical plant model of HDD servo system includes a driver (power amplifier), a VCM, and a rotary actuator that is driven by the VCM (Goh el al. 2001). A magnetic head is supported by a suspension and carriage and is suspended several mi-cro-inches above the disk surface. On the surface of disk are thousands of data tracks for which the VCM actuates the carriage and moves the head on a desired track. The frequency responses of a physical HDD servo system are shown in Fig. 12.1, which indicates that there exist many resonance modes in the system. The original plant model is extremely complex with a model order of 40, which was simplified for analytical purposes such that noises, nonlinearities, and additional dynamics are left out (Franklin et al. 1998; Hoagland 1991). Dynamics of this simplified pure inertia model with an ideal VCM actuator is often formulated as a second-order state-space model (Weerasooriya 1996) and has been typically adopted in HDD servo control systems. Without loss of generality, the continuous-time rigid model of the servo system is expressed by the following state-space equation:

$$\begin{pmatrix} \dot{y} \\ \dot{v} \end{pmatrix} = \begin{pmatrix} 0 & K_y \\ 0 & 0 \end{pmatrix} \begin{pmatrix} y \\ v \end{pmatrix} + \begin{pmatrix} 0 \\ K_v \end{pmatrix} u , \tag{12.1}$$

where u is the actuator input (in volts); y and v are the position (in tracks) and ve-locity of the R/W head, respectively; K_v is the acceleration constant and K_y the po-sition measurement gain, where $K_y = K_t/m$ with K_t being the current-force con-version coefficient and m being the mass of the VCM actuator. To derive a mathematical model of the HDD, experimentation on a physical 3.5-inch HDD was carried out and the frequency responses of the system are collected and shown by the solid line in Fig. 12.1. As can be seen from the frequency response charac-teristics, it is sufficiently accurate to model the plant dynamics as a double integra-tor as given by

$$G_{v_1}(s) = \frac{K_v K_y}{s^2}. \tag{12.2}$$

If the high-frequency resonance modes in Fig. 12.1 are to be considered, a more realistic model for the ideal VCM actuator can be modeled by the following fourth-order model:

$$G_v(s) = G_{v_1}(s) \cdot \frac{K_d s + \omega_n^2}{s^2 + 2\zeta\omega_n s + \omega_n^2}, \tag{12.3}$$

where ζ is the damping ratio, ω_n the resonant frequency, and K_d the constant gain to be identified in the model. From the measured frequency response data of the physical system as shown in Fig. 12.1, a fourth-order model of the VCM actuator was obtained using the "worst-case" system identification technique in the fre-quency domain (Tan and Li 2000),

$$G_v(s) = \frac{4.4 \times 10^{10} s + 4.87 \times 10^{15}}{s^2(s^2 + 1.45 \times 10^3 s + 1.1 \times 10^8)}. \tag{12.4}$$

As shown by the dashed line in Fig. 12.1, frequency responses of the identified fourth-order model accurately matches the physical measured data up to the range of 10^4 rad/s, which has far exceeded the working frequency range of a practical VCM actuator. With a sampling frequency of 4 kHz, the continuous-time second-order plant model (12.2) is transformed into a discrete-time model for the servo controller design studied in this chapter,

$$x(k+1) = \begin{pmatrix} 1 & 1.664 \\ 0 & 1 \end{pmatrix} x(k) + \begin{pmatrix} 1.384 \\ 1.664 \end{pmatrix} u \cdot \quad (12.5)$$

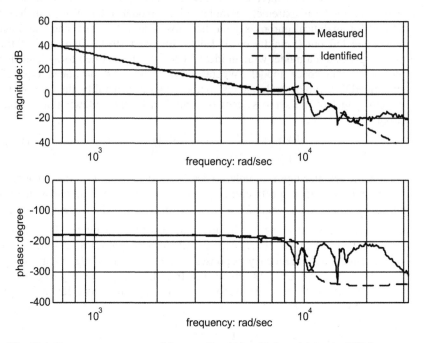

Fig. 12.1. Frequency responses of the actual and identified model for the VCM actuator.

12.3 Design of HDD Servo Control System

12.3.1 The HDD Design Specifications

The position control of the HDD read/write head is a unique example of high-performance, bandwidth-limited, and robust digital servo control problem. It requires high-performance control because the R/W head needs to maintain its position over a given track of typical width of 4–6 μm with an accuracy of ±3% in the presence of runout and external disturbances (Weerasooriya and Phan 1995). Practical design specifications for such a head servo control system include a number of performance requirements in both the time and frequency domains as given by (Franklin et al. 1998):

1. The control input should not exceed ±2 volts due to physical constraints on the actual VCM actuator;
2. The overshoots and undershoots of the step response should be kept less than 5% as the R/W head can start to read or write within ±5% of the target;
3. The 5% settling time in the step response should be less than 2 ms;
4. An excellent steady-state accuracy in terms of small steady-state errors;
5. Robustness in terms of disturbance rejection;
6. Robustness in terms of parameter uncertainty or sensitivity attenuation.

All the above specifications and its respective design objectives are listed in Table 12.1. It is obvious that spec. 4 could be quantified by setting a hard constraint of ±2 volts on the control input, while specs. 5 to 8 could be measured based upon the performance of closed-loop step responses in the time domain such as rise time, overshoots and undershoots, settling time, and steady-state errors (Tan et al. 2003b). To formulate specs. 2 and 3, the following weighted mixed-sensitivity function is adopted (Doyle and Stein 1981; Hirata et al. 1999):

$$J_{mix\_sen} = \left\| \begin{array}{c} \dfrac{W_1}{1+PC} \\[2mm] \dfrac{W_2 PC}{1+PC} \end{array} \right\|_{\infty} = \left\| \begin{array}{c} W_1 S \\ W_2 T \end{array} \right\|_{\infty}, \tag{12.6}$$

where P denotes the nominal model of the plant and C the servo controller; S represents the *sensitivity function* and T the *complementary sensitivity function* of the system. The sensitivity function determines the disturbance attenuation since S is in the closed-loop transfer function from the disturbance to the plant output. T is used to measure the stability margins of the system in the presence of multiplicative plant uncertainties. W_1 and W_2 are the weighting functions, which are described respectively by two different filters as shown in Fig. 12.2 (Hirata et al. 1999). These weights reflect the design philosophy of making the output immune to disturbances in the low frequencies and guaranteeing high-frequency robustness for uncertainty perturbations.

Table 12.1. The HDD Servo Control System Design Specifications

		Design specifications	Objective	Goal
Freq. Domain	1.	Stability (closed-loop poles)	$Nr\{Re(eig)>0\}$	0
	2.	Closed-loop sensitivity/ disturbance rejection	$\| W_1 S \|_{\infty}$	1
	3.	Plant uncertainty	$\| W_2 T \|_{\infty}$	1
Time Domain	4.	Actuator saturation	$Max(u)$	2 volts
	5.	Rise time	T_{rise}	2 ms
	6.	Overshoots	O_{shoot}	0.05
	7.	Settling time	5% $T_{settling}$	2 ms
	8.	Steady-state error	SS_{error}	0.0001

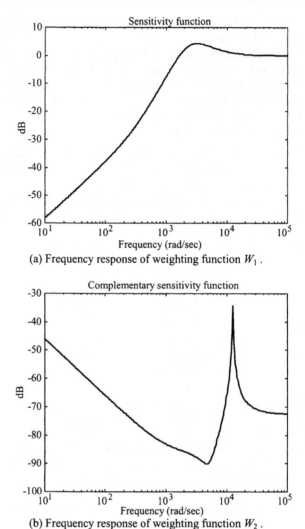

(a) Frequency response of weighting function W_1 .

(b) Frequency response of weighting function W_2 .

Fig. 12.2. Frequency responses of the weighting functions.

12.3.2 Evolutionary Design

As shown by the Simulink block diagram in Fig. 12.3, a 2DOF controller is designed and implemented on the physical read/write head servo control system in HDDs. The 2DOF control system has the striking feature that one can design the command input response and the closed-loop characteristics independently (Man et al. 1998). The philosophy here is to use the feedback controller K_s to meet the requirements of internal stability, disturbance rejection, measurement noise attenuation, or sensitivity minimization. The feedforward controller K_p is then applied to the reference signal, which optimizes the responses of the overall system to the command input. Since the design of feedforward controller K_p depends on the closed-loop performance requirements, it can be synthesized together with the feedback controller K_s. For simplicity in real-time implementation, a first-order discrete-time controller with a sampling frequency of 4kHz is adopted here for the design of both feedforward and feedback controllers, which is given in the form of

$$K_p = K_f\left(\frac{z + ff_1}{z + ff_2}\right), \quad K_s = K_b\left(\frac{z + fb_1}{z + fb_2}\right). \quad (12.7)$$

Obviously, the HDD control system design needs to search for multiple optimized controller parameters in order to satisfy the set of noncommensurable and often competing design specifications concurrently as listed in Table 12.1. Such an optimization problem is often semi-infinite and generally not everywhere differentiable (Tan et al. 2001e). It is thus hard to solve the problem via traditional numerical approaches that often rely on a differentiable performance index, which forms the major obstacle for the development of a generalized numerical optimization package for HDD servo control applications.

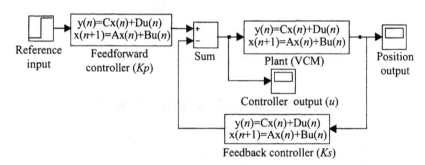

Fig. 12.3. The 2DOF servo control system in Simulink block diagram.

An evolutionary automated design methodology for the HDD servo control optimization problem is presented in this chapter. Figure 12.4 shows the architecture of the evolutionary HDD servo control system design. As can be seen, the overall HDD controller design environment is supervised and monitored effectively, which helps control engineers in making appropriate actions such as examining the competing design tradeoffs altering the design specifications, or even modifying the HDD controller structure if necessary. The process may continue until the control engineer is satisfied with the required performance or after all the design specifications have been met.

The MOEA toolbox was applied to search for a set of controller parameters $\{K_f, K_b, ff_1, ff_2, fb_1, fb_2\}$ such that the HDD servo control system meets the eight design specifications as listed in Table 12.1. The parameter settings of the MOEA toolbox are shown in Fig. 12.5. Note that only the double-integrator model of (12.5) is used during the evolutionary HDD servo control system design. However, all the step responses and robustness tests are performed based upon the fourth-order model of (12.4) that includes also the high-frequency resonance modes, in order to better evaluate the robustness of the evolutionary 2DOF HDD servo control system.

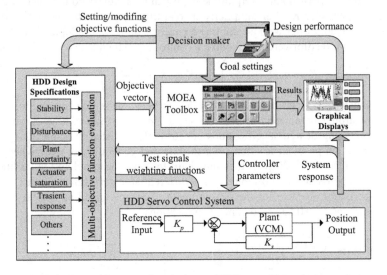

Fig. 12.4. The architecture of evolutionary HDD servo control system design.

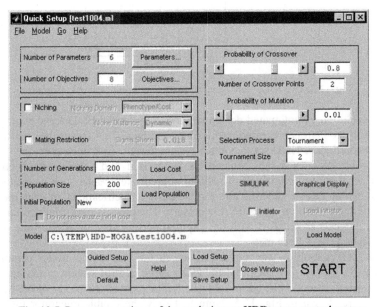

Fig. 12.5. Parameter settings of the evolutionary HDD servo control system.

All the design specifications as listed in Table 12.1 have been satisfied at the end of the evolution, and the final design tradeoff graph is shown in Fig. 12.6, where each line represents a solution found. Clearly, tradeoffs between adjacent specifications results in the crossing of the lines between them (e.g., steady-state error and control effort), whereas concurrent lines that do not cross each other indicate the specifications do not compete with one another (e.g., overshoots and settling time). The discretized 2DOF evolutionary controller is validated upon the fourth-order model of the VCM actuator, and the step response of the overall system with a final nondominated parameters set of $\{K_f, K_b, ff_1, ff_2, fb_1, fb_2\} = \{0.038597, -0.212, 0.63841, 0.39488, -0.783, 0.014001\}$ is shown by the solid line in Fig. 12.7. It can be seen that the response meets all the design specifications listed in Table 12.1, with an excellent transient performance and a destination track crossover of approximately 1.8 ms.

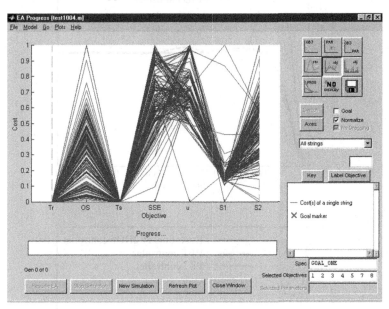

Fig. 12.6. Tradeoff graph of the evolutionary HDD servo control system.

12.3.3 Conventional Controllers

i. PID Controller
The step response of the discrete-time PID controller with a sampling frequency of 4 kHz is shown by the dotted line in Fig. 12.7. The PID controller was manually tuned to achieve a good compromised performance as given by (Goh 1999)

$$u = \frac{0.13z^2 - 0.23z + 0.1}{z^2 - 1.25z + 0.25}(r - y), \tag{12.8}$$

where r is the reference input and y the servo system output. It can be seen that even though the PID controller has a second-order control structure, it is not as robust and has a significantly large overshoot of approximately 50% in the step response when tested upon the fourth-order servo model. To achieve a settling time of 4–5 ms, it is necessary to tune the PID controller such that the overshoot becomes smaller but at the expense of a longer rise time. Such performance deficiency could be mainly due to its limiting control structure, i.e., it only feeds in the error signal of $(r - y)$ instead of both the y and r independently (Goh 1999).

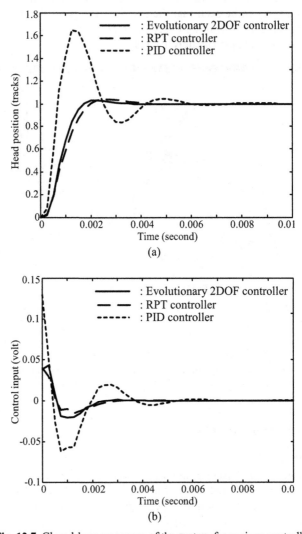

Fig. 12.7. Closed-loop responses of the system for various controllers.

ii. RPT Controller

For comparison, the robust and perfect tracking (RPT) controller proposed by Goh et al. (1999) is included and the closed-loop step response is shown by the dashed line in Fig. 12.7. As mentioned in the Introduction, the parameter ε plays a vital role in determining the RPT control performance and has to be tuned manually in a trial-and-error process. ε is set as 0.9 here for good performance. The discrete-time RPT controller with a sampling frequency of 4 kHz is given as

$$x(k+1) = -0.04x(k) + 15179r(k) - 453681y(k),$$

$$u(k) = -3.43 \times 10^{-7} x(k) + 0.04r(k) - 0.18y(k).$$

(12.9)

It can be seen from Fig. 12.7 that the evolutionary 2DOF controller has outperformed both the PID and RPT controllers in the step response, with a relatively fast rise time, smaller overshoots, and shorter settling time, while maintaining the stability margins imposed by the design specifications. In Table 12.2, the performance characteristics of the various control systems in both the frequency and time domains are compared. As can be seen, although the PID closed-loop system has a bandwidth higher than RPT and evolutionary design, it gives a large overshoot of 50% in the step response and a longer settling time of 4.25 ms. The closed-loop bandwidth of evolutionary 2DOF based servo system is also observed to be larger than that of the RPT system.

Table 12.2. Performance Comparisons Among PID, RPT, and Evolutionary 2DOF Controllers

Performance specifications		PID	RPT	Evolutionary 2 DOF
Freq. domain	Bandwidth	3340 Hz	1250 Hz	1690 Hz
	Gain margin	9 dB	14.45 dB	10.28 dB
	Phase crossover frequency	4570 Hz	3648 Hz	3397.2 Hz
Time domain	Rise time	1 ms	2 ms	1.75 ms
	Overshoots	> 50%	4.7%	3.98%
	Settling time	4.25 ms	1.75 ms	1.75 ms

12.3.4 Robustness Validation

i. Plant Uncertainties and Perturbations

In actual HDD manufacturing, the resonant frequency of ω_n in the VCM actuator might vary from one to another for the same batch of drives. During drive operations, there may also exist parameter drifts due to the changing temperature, humidity, or zone effects. The servo controller that is designed for the nominal model should thus be capable of maintaining its optimal performance under these changes and uncertainties. For this, a common practice in the disk drive industry is to add some notch filters in the servo system in order to attenuate these unpredicted resonant peaks (Goh et al. 1999). Since the evolutionary servo system incorporates the specification of plant uncertainties as given by spec. 3 in Table

12.1, it should be capable of withstanding any major variations of resonance frequencies in the HDDs without the need of adding notch filters. Figures 12.8(a) and 12.8(b) show the step responses of evolutionary 2DOF, RPT, and PID-based servo system, with a variation of 150% (ω_n = 15.73k rad/s) and 75% (ω_n = 7.86k rad/s) of the nominal resonant frequency, respectively. From the figures, it can be observed that the evolutionary 2DOF servo system is robust with only minor variations in the step response despite significant changes of the resonant frequencies.

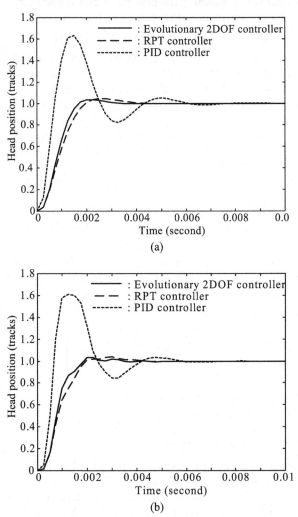

Fig. 12.8. Step responses of closed-loop system for evolutionary 2DOF, RPT, and PID controllers with different resonant frequencies. (a) VCM model with resonant frequency ω_n = 15.73k rad/s (variation of 150% of the nominal resonant frequency). (b) VCM model with resonant frequency ω_n = 7.86k rad/s (variation of 75% of the nominal resonant frequency).

ii. Runout Disturbance Rejection

Runout refers to the eccentricity of tracks on the disk surfaces, which results in the failure of the head to follow the track on the disk surface faithfully as the disk spins. This could result in serious consequences, especially during the writing process when data from adjacent tracks could have been written over. There are generally two types of runout, namely the repeatable runout (RRO) and nonrepeatable runout (NRRO). Repeatable runout is locked to the spindle rotation both in amplitude and phase. It occurs during servo-writing when irregularities and defects of many types cause the position reference on the disk surface to appear as though it was not written on a circular path. Another possible cause could be due to slips of the disk from its center point after being servo-written. Nonrepeatable runout could come from many sources. It could be due to disk drive vibrations caused by spindle ball bearings, air turbulence, electronic and thermal noises, pivot hysteresis, transient vibrations, or external disturbances.

In order to simulate the effect of runout disturbances in the HDD servo system, a sinusoidal signal was applied to the measurement output, i.e., the new measurement output is now the sum of the actuator output and the runout disturbance. Figure 12.9 shows the output responses of the evolutionary 2DOF, RPT, and PID-based servo systems comprising a fictitious runout disturbance injection of $w(t) = 0.5 + 0.1\cos(110\pi t) + 0.05\sin(220\pi t)$. It can be observed that the evolutionary 2DOF servo system has attenuated the first few modes of the runout disturbances successfully.

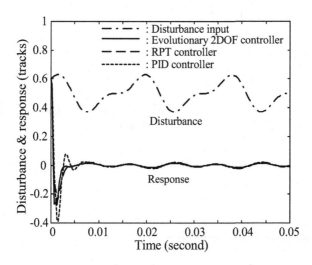

Fig. 12.9. The runout disturbance and its attenuated responses for the evolutionary 2DOF, RPT, and PID controllers.

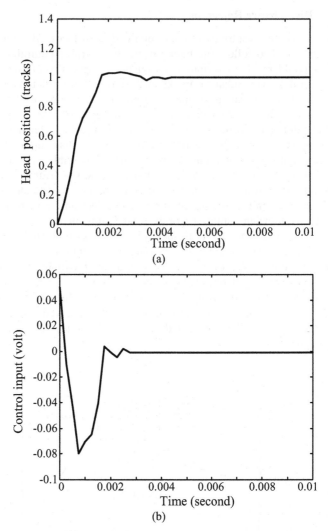

Fig. 12.10. Responses of real-time implementation for the evolutionary 2DOF servo system.

12.3.5 Real-Time Implementation

The performance of the evolutionary 2DOF servo control system is further verified and experimented on a typical disk drive servo system consisting of the physical 3.5-inch HDD, power amplifier, VCM actuator, servo demodulator, DAC, ADC associated logic circuitry with a TMS320 digital signal processor (DSP), and a sampling rate of 4 kHz. The only measurement variable is position, which includes the position error signal (PES) and track address. The PES represents the relative error between track center and the read/write head. The R/W head position was measured using a laser doppler vibrometer (LDV) and the resolution used was 1 μm/volt. The structure of Kp and Ks used in the real-time implementation are given as

$$K_p = (0.038597)\left(\frac{z+0.63841}{z+0.39488}\right), \quad K_s = (-0.212)\left(\frac{z-0.783}{z+0.014001}\right). \quad (12.10)$$

The real-time implementation results of the evolutionary HDD servo control system are shown in Fig. 12.10, which is fully consistent with the simulated step response of Fig. 12.7 and shows an excellent closed-loop performance in the face of unseen plant uncertainties or disturbances.

12.4 Conclusions

This chapter has designed and implemented a practical 2DOF HDD servo control system using an MOEA toolbox. It has been shown that the evolutionary designed HDD servo control system optimally moves the magnetic head onto the desired track with minimal control effort and keeps it on the track robustly against plant uncertainties and runout disturbances. In addition, the evolutionary design approach is capable of specifying a low-order control structure for easy execution of the DSP codes during real-time implementation. Simulation results of the evolutionary 2DOF servo control system have been compared with conventional PID and RPT controllers, which show an excellent closed-loop response with good robustness in the face of practical perturbations in the system.

13
Evolutionary Scheduling – VRPTW

13.1 Introduction

"Vehicle routing problem" (VRP) is a generic name referred to a class of combinatorial problem in which customers are to be served by a number of vehicles. In particular, vehicle routing problem with time window (VRPTW) is an example of the popular extension from VRP. In VRPTW, a set of vehicles with limited capacity is to be routed from a central depot to a set of geographically dispersed customers with known demands and predefined time window. The time window can be specified in terms of a single-sided or double-sided window. In the single-sided time window, the pickup points usually specify the deadlines by which they must be serviced. In the double-sided time window, however, both the earliest and the latest service times are imposed by the nodes. A vehicle arriving earlier than the earliest service time of a node will incur waiting time. This penalizes the transport management in either the direct waiting cost or the increased number of vehicles, since a vehicle can only service fewer nodes when the waiting time is longer. Due to its inherent complexities and usefulness in real life, the VRPTW continues to draw attentions from researchers and has become a well-known problem in network optimization. Surveys about VRPTW can be found in Desrochers et al. (1992), Desrosier et al. (1995), Golden and Assad (1988), Solomon (1987), Laporte et al. (2000), Kilby et al. (2000), Toth and Vigo (2002), Bräysy and Gendreau (2001a, 2001b), and so on.

A number of heuristic approaches, exact methods, and local searches have been applied to solve the VRPTW, which is an NP-hard problem (Beasley and Christofides 1997; Bräysy 2003; Breedam 2001; Chiang and Russel 1996, 1997; Christofides et al. 1981; Desrosier et al. 1995; Golden and Assad 1998; Laporte 1992; Lee et al. 2003; Potvin et al. 1993, 1996; Savelsbergh 1985; Yellow 1970; Caseau and Laburthe 1999; Dullaert et al. 2002; Rego 2001; Bard et al. 2002; Gezdur and Türkay 2002; Ioannou et al. 2001; Shaw 1998; Kilby et al. 1999; Tan et al. 2001f; Li and Lim 2002; Chavalitwongse et al. 2003). While optimal solutions for VRPTW may be obtained using the exact methods, the computation time required to obtain such solutions may be unfeasible when the problem size becomes very large (Desrochers et al. 1992). Conventional local searches and heuristic algorithms are commonly devised to find the optimal or near-optimal solutions for

VRPTW within a reasonable computation time (Cordeau et al. 2002). However, these methods may be sensitive to the datasets given and some heuristic methods may even require a set of training data during the learning process, i.e., the accuracy of training data and the coverage of data distribution can significantly affect the performance (Bertsimas and Simchi-Levi 1993).

Categorized by Fisher (1995) as the third-generation approach for solving vehicle routing problems, evolutionary algorithms have been applied to solve the VRPTW with optimal or near-optimal solutions (Gehring and Homberger 2001, 2002; Grefenstette et al. 1985; Homberger and Gehring 1999; Louis et al. 1999; Tan et al. 2001g; Thangiah et al. 1994; Jung and Moon 2002). For instance, Thangiah (1995) proposed a genetic algorithm-based approach named GIDEON, which follows the cluster-first route-second method where adaptive clustering and geometric shapes are applied to solve the VRPTW. This approach devised a special genetic representation called genetic sectoring heuristic that keeps the polar angle offset in the genes, and it solved the 100-customer Solomon problems to near-optimal.

The VRPTW involves the minimization of multiple conflicting cost functions concurrently, such as traveling distance and number of vehicles, which should be best solved by means of MO optimization. Many existing VRPTW techniques, however, are single-objective-based heuristic methods that incorporate penalty functions or combine the different criteria via a weighting function (Berger et al. 2001; Desrosier et al. 1995; Golden and Assad 1988; Toth and Vigo 2002). Although MOEAs have been applied to solve combinatorial optimization problems, such as flowshop/jobshop scheduling, nurse scheduling, and timetabling (Ben et al. 1998; Burke and Newall 1999; Chen et al. 1996; Murata and Ishibuchi 1996; Jaszkiewicz 2001), these algorithms are designed with specific representation or genetic operators that could only be used in a particular application domain.

This chapter presents a hybrid multiobjective evolutionary algorithm (HMOEA), which incorporates various heuristics for local exploitation in the evolutionary search and the concept of Pareto's optimality for solving the MO VRPTW optimization. Unlike conventional MOEAs that are designed for parameterized optimization problems (Alexandre et al. 2002; Cvetkovic and Parmee 2002; Knowles and Corne 2000a; Tan et al. 2001c), the HMOEA is featured with specialized genetic operators and variable-length chromosome representation to accommodate the sequence-oriented optimization in VRPTW. The design of the algorithm is focused on the need of VRPTW by integrating the vehicle routing sequence with the consideration of timings, costs, and vehicle numbers. Without aggregating multiple criteria into a compromise function, the HMOEA optimizes all routing constraints and objectives concurrently, which improves the routing solutions in many aspects, such as lower routing cost, wider scattering area, and better convergence trace.

The chapter is organized as follows: Section 13.2 gives the problem formulation of VRPTW, which includes the mathematical modeling and the description of Solomon's 56 benchmark problems for VRPTW. Section 13.3 describes the applications of MOEAs for a number of domain-specific combinatorial optimization problems. The program flowchart of HMOEA and each of its features including variable-length chromosome representation, specialized genetic operators, Pareto fitness ranking, and local search heuristics are also described in this section. Section 13.4 presents the extensive simulation and comparison results of HMOEA based upon the famous Solomon's 56 datasets. The advantages of HMOEA for MO optimization in VRPTW are also discussed in this section. Conclusions are drawn in Section 13.5.

13.2 The Problem Formulation

13.2.1 Problem Modeling of VRPTW

This section presents the mathematical model of VRPTW, including the frequently used notations such as route, depot, customer, and vehicles. Figure 13.1 shows the graphical model of a simple VRPTW and its solutions. This example has two routes, R_1 and R_2, and every customer is given a number as its identity. The arrows connecting the customers show the sequences of visits by the vehicles, where every route must start and end at the depot.

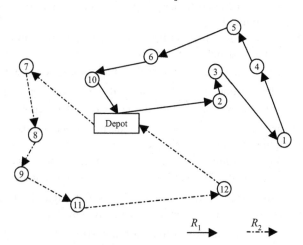

Fig. 13.1. Graphical representation of a simple vehicle routing problem.

The definition of the terms and constraints for the VRPTW is given as follows:
- *Depot:* The depot is denoted by v_0, which is a node where every vehicle must start and end its route. It does not have load, but it has a specified time window to be followed.
- *Customers:* There are N customers and the set $\{0, 1,..., N\}$ represents the sites of these N customers. The number 0 represents the depot. Every customer i has a demand, $k_i \geq 0$ and a service time, $s_i \geq 0$. Formally, $\Omega = \{0, 1, 2,..., N\}$

is the customer set and $\Omega(r)$ represents the set of customers served by a route r.

- *Vertex*: A vertex is denoted by $v_i(r)$, which represents the customer that is served at the ith sequence in a particular route r. It must be an element in the customer set defined as $v_i(r) \in \Omega$.

- *Vehicles*: There are m identical vehicles and each vehicle has a capacity limit of K. The number of customers that a vehicle can serve is unlimited given that the total load does not exceed the capacity limit K. The vehicles may arrive before the earliest service time and thus may need to wait before servicing customers.

- *Traveling cost*: The traveling cost between customers i and j is denoted by c_{ij}, which satisfies the triangular inequality where $c_{ij} + c_{jk} \geq c_{ik}$. The cost is calculated with the following equation:

$$c_{ij} = \sqrt{\left(i_x - j_x\right)^2 + \left(i_y - j_y\right)^2}, \qquad (13.1)$$

where i_x is the coordinate x for customer i and i_y is the coordinate y for customer i. Clearly, the routing cost is calculated as the Euclidean distance between two customers. An important assumption is made here: One unit distance corresponds to one unit traveling time, i.e., every unit distance may take exactly a unit of time to travel. Therefore, c_{ij} not only defines the traveling cost (distance) from customer i to customer j, but also specifies the traveling time from customer i to customer j.

- *Routes*: A vehicle's route starts at the depot, visits a number of customers, and returns to the depot. A route is commonly represented as $r = \langle v_0, v_1(r), v_2(r), ..., v_r(r), v_0 \rangle$. Since all vehicles must depart and return to the depot v_0, the depot can be omitted in the representation, i.e., $r = \langle v_1(r), v_2(r), ..., v_r(r) \rangle$. However, the costs from the depot to the first customer node and from the last customer node to the depot must be included in the computation of the total traveling cost.

- *Customers in a route*: The customers in a route are denoted by $\Omega(r) = \{v_1(r), ..., v_n(r)\}$. The size of a route, n, is the number of customers served by the route. Since every route must start and end at the depot implicitly, there is no need to include the depot in the notation of $\Omega(r)$.

- *Capacity*: The total demands served by a route, $k(r)$, is the sum of the demands of the customers in the route r, i.e., $k(r) = \sum_{i \in \Omega(r)} k_i$. A route satisfies its capacity constraint if $k(r) \leq K$.

- *Traveling cost*: The traveling cost of a route $r = \langle v_1, ..., v_n \rangle$, denoted by $t(r)$, is the cost of visiting all customers in the route, i.e.,

$$t(r) = \sum_{i=1}^{n-1} c_{v_i(r), v_{i-1}(r)} + c_{v_0, v_1(r)} + c_{v_n(r), v_0}.$$

- *Routing plan*: The routing plan, G, consists of a set of routes $\{r_1, ..., r_m\}$. The number of routes should not exceed the maximum number of vehicles M allowed, i.e., $m \leq M$. The following condition that all customers must be routed and no customers can be routed more than once must be satisfied:

$$\bigcup_{i=1}^{m} \Omega(r_i) = \Omega, \tag{13.2}$$

$$\Omega(r_i) \cap \Omega(r_j) = \varnothing, \quad i \neq j.$$

- *Time windows*: The customers and depot have time windows. The time window of a site, i, is specified by an interval $[e_{v_i(r)}, l_{v_i(r)}]$, where $e_{v_i(r)}$ and $l_{v_i(r)}$ represent the earliest and the latest arrival time, respectively. All vehicles must arrive at a site before the end of the time window $l_{v_i(r)}$. The vehicles may arrive earlier but must wait until the earliest time of $e_{v_i(r)}$ before serving any customers. The notation of e_{v_0} represents the time that all vehicles in the routing plan leave the depot, while l_{v_0} corresponds to the time that all vehicles must return to the depot. In fact, the interval $[e_{v_0}, l_{v_0}]$ is the largest time window for which all the customers' time windows must be within that range.

The earliest service time of vertex $v_i(r)$ is generally represented as $a_{v_i(r)}$ and the departure time from the vertex $v_i(r)$ is denoted by $d_{v_i(r)}$. The definitions of the earliest service time and the departure time are given as

$$d_{v_0} = 0,$$

$$a_{v_i(r)} = \max(d_{v_{i-1}(r)} + c_{v_{i-1}(r),v_i(r)}, \; e_{v_i(r)}) \qquad \text{for } \forall r \text{ and } 1 \leq i \leq n,$$

$$d_{v_i(r)} = a_{v_i(r)} + s_{v_i(r)} \qquad \text{for } \forall r \text{ and } 1 \leq i \leq n,$$

$$d_{v_{n+1}(r)} = d_{v_n(r)} + c_{v_n(r),v_0} \qquad \text{for } \forall r.$$

$d_{v_{n+1}(r)}$ is the completion time of a route or the time that a vehicle completes all its jobs. v_{i-1} refers to the information of the previous customer in a route. The time window constraints in the VRPTW model are given as

$$d_{v_{n+1}(r)} \leq l_{v_0} \qquad \text{for } \forall r \in G,$$

$$a_{v_i(r)} \geq e_{v_i(r)} \qquad \text{for } \forall r \in G \text{ and } 1 \leq i \leq n,$$

$$a_{v_i(r)} \leq l_{v_i(r)} \qquad \text{for } \forall r \in G \text{ and } 1 \leq i \leq n.$$

A solution to the VRPTW is a routing plan $G = \{r_1, \ldots, r_m\}$ satisfying both the capacity and time window constraints, i.e., for all routes,

$$k(r_j) \leq K, \tag{13.3}$$

where $1 \leq j \leq m$. The VRPTW consists of finding a solution G that minimizes the number of vehicles and the total traveling cost as given below:

$$f(G)_1 = |G| = m, \tag{13.4}$$

$$f(G)_2 = \sum_{r \in G} t(r).$$

Both the capacity and time windows are specified as hard constraints in VRPTW. As illustrated in Fig. 13.2, there are two possible scenarios based on the time window constraints in the model. As shown in Fig. 13.2a, when a vehicle leaves the current customer and travels to the next customer, it may arrive before the earliest arrival time, $e_{v_i(r)}$, and therefore has to wait until the $e_{v_i(r)}$ starts. The vehicle will thus complete its service for this customer at the time of $e_{v_i(r)} + s_{v_i(r)}$. Figure 13.2b shows the situation where a vehicle arrives at a customer node after the time window starts. In this case, the arrival time is $d_{v_{i-1}(r)} + c_{v_{i-1}(r),v_i(r)}$ and the vehicle will complete its service for the customer i at the time of $d_{v_{i-1}(r)} + c_{v_{i-1}(r),v_i(r)} + s_{v_i(r)}$.

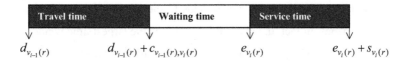

$$d_{v_{i-1}(r)} \qquad d_{v_{i-1}(r)} + c_{v_{i-1}(r),v_i(r)} \qquad e_{v_i(r)} \qquad e_{v_i(r)} + s_{v_i(r)}$$

(a)   Vehicle arrives before the earliest service time.

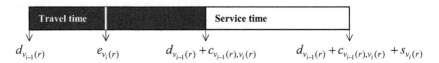

$$d_{v_{i-1}(r)} \qquad e_{v_i(r)} \qquad d_{v_{i-1}(r)} + c_{v_{i-1}(r),v_i(r)} \qquad d_{v_{i-1}(r)} + c_{v_{i-1}(r),v_i(r)} + s_{v_i(r)}$$

(b) Vehicle arrives after the earliest service time.

Fig. 13.2. Examples of the time windows in VRPTW.

13.2.2 Solomon's 56 Benchmark Problems for VRPTW

The six benchmark problems (Solomon 1987) designed specifically for the vehicle routing problem with time window constraints (VRPTW) are studied in this chapter. Solomon's problems consist of 56 datasets, which have been extensively used for benchmarking different heuristics in literature. The problems vary in fleet size, vehicle capacity, traveling time of vehicles, spatial and temporal distribution of customers. In addition to that, the time windows allocated for every customer and the percentage of customers with tight time-windows constraint vary for different test cases. The customers' details are given in the sequence of customer index, location in x- and y- coordinates, the demand for load, the ready time, due date, and the service time required. All the test problems consist of 100 customers, which are generally adopted as the problem size for performance comparisons in VRPTW. The traveling time between customers is equal to the corresponding Euclidean distance. The 56 problems are divided into six categories based on the pattern of customers' locations and time windows. These six categories are named as C_1, C_2, R_1, R_2, RC_1, and RC_2.

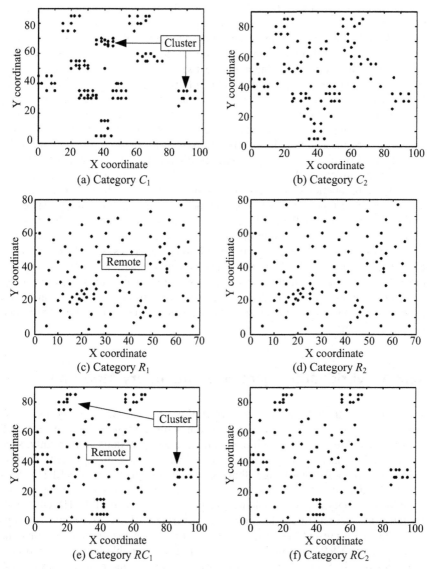

Fig. 13.3. Customers' distribution for the problem categories of C_1, C_2, R_1, R_2, RC_1, and RC_2.

The problem category R has all customers located remotely and the problem category C refers to clustered type of customers. The RC is a category of problems having a mixed of remote and clustered customers. The geographical distribution determines the traveling distances between customers (Desrochers et al. 1992). In the cluster type of distribution, customers' locations are closer to each other and thus the traveling distances are shorter. In the remote type of distribution, customers' locations are remotely placed. Therefore, the traveling distance is relatively longer in the R category as compared to the C category problems. Generally, the C category problems are easier to be solved because their solutions are less sensitive to the usually small distances among customers. In contrast, the R category problems require more efforts to obtain a correct sequence of customers in each route, and different sequences may result in large differences in terms of the routing cost.

The datasets are further categorized according to the time windows constraints. The problems in category 1, e.g., C_1, R_1, RC_1, generally come with a smaller time window, and the problems in category 2, e.g., C_2, R_2, and RC_2, are often allocated with a longer time window. In the problem sets of R_1 and RC_1, the time windows are generated randomly. In the problem set of C_1, however, the variations of time windows are small. A shorter time window indicates that many candidate solutions after reproduction can become unfeasible easily due to the tight constraint. In contrast, a larger time window means that more feasible solutions are possible and subsequently encourage the existence of longer routes, i.e., each vehicle can serve a larger number of customers. In Fig. 13.3, the x–y-coordinate depicts the distribution of customers' locations for the six different categories, C_1, C_2, R_1, R_2, RC_1, and RC_2. Figures 13(a), 13(c), and 13(e) are labeled with "cluster" or/and "remote" to show the distribution of customers corresponding to its problem category. For example, in Fig. 13.3(e), there exist two types of customer distribution patterns, i.e., cluster and remote, since the RC category consists of both the R- and C- type problems.

13.3 A Hybrid Multiobjective Evolutionary Algorithm

As described in the Introduction, the VRPTW can be best solved by means of MO optimization, i.e., it involves optimizing routes for multiple vehicles to meet all constraints and to minimize multiple conflicting cost functions concurrently, such as the traveling distance and the number of vehicles. This section presents a hybrid multiobjective evolutionary algorithm specifically designed for the VRPTW. Section 13.3.1 describes the applications of MOEAs for a number of domain-specific combinatorial optimization problems. The program flowchart of the HMOEA is illustrated in Section 13.3.2 to provide an overview of the algorithm. Sections 13.3.3 to 13.3.6 present the various features of HMOEA incorporated to solve the multiobjective VRPTW optimization, including the variable-length chromosome representation in Section 13.3.3, specialized genetic operators in Section 13.3.4, and Pareto fitness ranking in Section 13.3.5. Following the concept of hybridizing local optimizers with MOEAs (Tan et al. 2001c), Section 13.3.6 describes the various heuristics that are incorporated in HMOEA to improve its local search exploitation capability for VRPTW.

13.3.1 Multiobjective Evolutionary Algorithms in Combinatorial Applications

Although MOEAs have been applied to solve a number of domain-specific combinatorial optimization problems, such as flowshop/jobshop scheduling, nurse scheduling, and timetabling, these algorithms are designed with specific representation or genetic operators that can only be used in a particular application domain. For example, Murata and Ishibuchi (1996) presented two hybrid genetic algorithms (GAs) to solve a flowshop scheduling problem that is characterized by unidirectional flow of work with a variety of jobs being process sequentially in a one-pass manner. Jaszkiewicz (2001) proposed the algorithm of Pareto simulated annealing (PSA) to solve a multiobjective nurse scheduling problem. Chen et al. (1996) provided a GA-based approach to tackle continuous flowshop problem in which the intermediate storage is required for partially finished jobs. Dorndorf and Pesch (1995) proposed two different implementations of GA using priority-rule-based-representation and machine-based representation to solve a jobshop scheduling problem (JSP). The JSP concerns the processing on several machines with mutable sequence of operations, i.e., the flow of work may not be unidirectional as encountered in the flowshop problem. Ben et al. (1998) later devised a specific representation with two partitions in a chromosome to deal with the priority of events (in permutation) and to encode the list of possible time slots for events respectively. Jozefowiez et al. (2002) solve a multiobjective capacitated vehicle routing problem using a parallel genetic algorithm with hybrid Tabu search to increase the performance of the algorithm. Paquete and Fonseca (2001) propose an algorithm with modified mutation operator (and without recombination) to solve a multiobjective examination timetabling problem. It should be noted that although the methods described above shared a common objective of finding the optimal sequences in combinatorial problems, they are unique with different mathematical models, representations, genetic operators, and performance evaluation functions in their respective problem domains, which are different from that of the VRPTW problem.

13.3.2 Program Flowchart of HMOEA

Unlike many conventional optimization problems, the VRPTW does not have a clear neighborhood structure, e.g., it is often difficult to trace or predict good solutions in VRPTW since feasible solutions may not be located at the neighborhood of any candidate solutions in the search space. To design an evolutionary algorithm that is capable of solving such a combinatorial and ordered-based MO optimization problem, a few features such as variable-length chromosome representation, specialized genetic operators, Pareto fitness ranking, and efficient local search heuristics are incorporated in HMOEA. The program flowchart of HMOEA is shown in Fig. 13.4. The simulation begins by reading in customers' data and constructing a list of customers' information. The preprocessing process builds a database for customers' information, including all relevant coordinates (position), customers' load, time windows, service times required, and so on. An initial population is then built such that each individual must at least be a feasible candidate solution, i.e., every individual and route in the initial population must be feasible. The initialization process is random and starts by inserting customers one by one into an empty route in a random order. Any customer that violates any constraints is deleted from the current route. The route is then accepted as part of the solution. A new empty route is added to serve the deleted customer and other remaining customers. This process continues until all customers are routed and a feasible initial population is built, as depicted in Fig. 13.5.

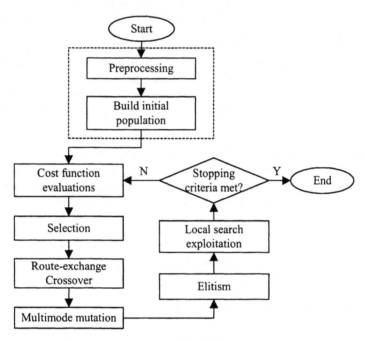

Fig. 13.4. The program flowchart of HMOEA.

After the initial population is formed, all individuals will be evaluated based on the objective functions as given in Eq. (13.4) and ranked according to their respective Pareto dominance in the population. After the ranking process, tournament selection scheme (Tan et al. 2001c) with a tournament size of 2 is performed, where all individuals in the population are randomly grouped into pairs and those individuals with a lower rank will be selected for reproduction. The procedure is performed twice to preserve the original population size. A simple elitism mechanism is employed in the HMOEA for faster convergence and better routing solutions. The elitism strategy keeps a small number of good individuals (0.5% of the population size) and replaces the worst individuals in the next generation, without going through the usual genetic operations. The specialized genetic operators in HMOEA consist of route-exchange crossover and multimode mutation. To further improve the internal routings of individuals, heuristic searches are incorporated in the HMOEA at every 50 generations (considering the tradeoff between optimization performance and simulation time) for better local exploitation in the evolutionary search. Note that the feasibility of all new individuals reproduced after the process of specialized genetic operations and local search heuristics is retained, which avoids the need of any repairing mechanisms. The evolution process repeats until the stopping criterion is met or no significant performance improvement is observed over a period of 10 generations.

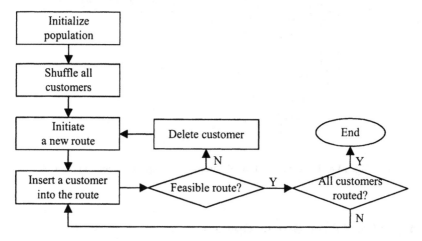

Fig. 13.5. The procedure of building an initial population of HMOEA.

13.3.3 Variable-Length Chromosome Representation

The chromosomes in evolutionary algorithms, such as genetic algorithms, are often represented as a fixed-structure bit string, for which the bit positions are assumed to be independent and context-insensitive. Such a representation is not suitable for VRPTW, which is an order-oriented NP-hard optimization problem where sequences among customers are essential. In HMOEA, a variable-length chromosome representation is applied such that each chromosome encodes a complete solution including the number of routes/vehicles and the customers served by these vehicles. Depending on how the customers are routed and distributed, every chromosome can have a different number of routes for the same dataset. As shown in Fig. 13.6, a chromosome may consist of several routes and each route or gene is not a constant but a sequence of customers to be served. Such a variable-length representation is efficient and allows the number of vehicles to be manipulated and minimized directly for MO optimization in VRPTW. Note that most existing routing approaches only consider a single objective or cost of traveling distance, since the number of vehicles is often uncontrollable in these representations.

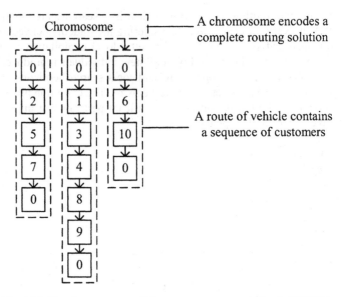

Fig. 13.6. The data structure of chromosome representation in HMOEA.

13.3.4 Specialized Genetic Operators

Since standard genetic operators may generate individuals with unfeasible routing solutions for VRPTW, specialized genetic operators of route-exchange crossover and multimode mutation are incorporated in HMOEA, which are described in the following subsections.

13.3.4.1 Route-Exchange Crossover

The classical one-point crossover may produce unfeasible route sequence because of the duplication and omission of vertices after reproduction. Goldberg and Lingle (1985) proposed a PMX crossover operator suitable for sequencing optimization problems. The operator cuts out a section of the chromosome and puts it in the offspring. It maps the remaining sites to the same absolute position or the corresponding bit in the mate's absolute position to avoid any redundancy. Whitley et al. (1989) proposed a genetic edge recombination operator to solve a TSP problem. For each node, an edge-list containing all nodes is created. The crossover parents shared the edge-lists where several manipulations on the edge-list are repeated until all edge-lists are processed. Ishibashi et al. (2000) propose a two-point ordered crossover that randomly selects two crossing points from the parents and decides which segment should be inherited to the offspring.

A simple crossover operator is used in HMOEA, which allows the good sequence of routes or genes in a chromosome to be shared with other individuals in the population. The operation is designed such that infeasibility after the change can be eradicated easily. The good routes in VRPTW are those with customers/nodes arranged in sequence where the cost of routing (distance) is small and the time window fits perfectly one after another. In a crossover operation, the chromosomes would share their best route to each other as shown in Fig. 13.7. The best route is chosen according to the criteria of averaged cost over nodes, which can be computed easily based on the variable-length chromosome representation in HMOEA. To ensure the feasibility of chromosomes after the crossover, each customer can only appear once in a chromosome, i.e., any customer in a chromosome will be deleted during the insertion of new routes if the customer is also found in the newly inserted route. The crossover operation will not cause any violation in time windows or capacity constraints. Deleting a customer from a route will only incur some waiting time before the next customer is serviced and thus will not cause any conflicts for the time windows. Meanwhile, the total load in a route will only be decreased when a customer is deleted from the route and thus will not violate any capacity constraints. Therefore, all chromosomes will remain feasible routing solutions after the crossover in HMOEA.

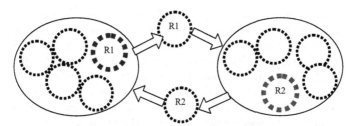

Fig. 13.7. The route-exchange crossover in HMOEA.

13.3.4.2 Multimode Mutation

Gendreau et al. (1999) proposed an RAR (remove and reinsert) mutation operator, which extracts a node and inserts it into a random point of the routing sequence in order to retain the feasibility of solutions. Ishibashi et al. (2000) extend the approach to a shift mutation operator that extracts a segment or a number of nodes (instead of a node) and inserts it into a new random point for generating the offspring. During the crossover by HMOEA, routes' sequence is exchanged in a whole chunk and no direct manipulation is made to the internal ordering of the nodes in VRPTW. The sequence in a route is modified only when any redundant nodes in the chromosome are deleted. A multimode mutation operator is presented in HMOEA, which serves to complement the crossover by optimizing the local route information of a chromosome. As shown in Fig. 13.8, three parameters are related to the multimode mutation, i.e., mutation rate (PM), elastic rate (PE), and squeeze rate (PS). In HMOEA, random numbers will be generated and compared to these parameter values in order to determine if the mutation operations (for each mutation type) should be performed.

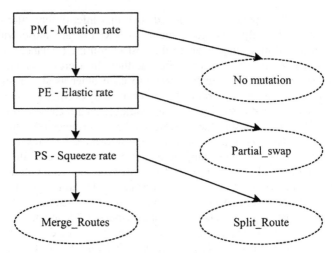

Fig. 13.8. The multimode mutation in HMOEA.

The mutation rate is considerably small since it could be destructive to the chromosome structure and information of routes. In order to trigger more moves with better routing solutions, a few operations including Partial_Swap (Bagchi 1999), Split_Route, and Merge_Routes (Pinaki and Elizabeth 1999) are implemented. In this case, only one operation is chosen if the mutation is performed. The elastic rate determines the operation of Partial_Swap, which picks two routes in a chromosome and swaps the two routes at a random point that has a value smaller or equal to the shortest size of the two chosen routes. The swapping must be feasible or else the original routes will be restored. The squeeze rate determines the operation of splitting or merging a route. The Split_Route operation breaks a route at a random point and generates two new feasible routes. The operation has an always-true condition, unless the number of vehicles exceeds the maximum vehicles allowed. A number of constraints should be satisfied in the operation of Merge_Routes, e.g., it should avoid any violation against the hard constraints, such as time windows and vehicle capacity. During the Merge_Routes operation, the two routes with the smallest number of customers are chosen, and these routes must have the capacity to accommodate additional customers. Let the two selected routes be route A and route B, the operation first inserts all customers, one by one, from route B into route A. If there is any violation against the capacity or time window constraints in route A, the remaining nodes will be kept at the route B. If all the customers in route B are shifted to route A, then route B will be deleted.

13.3.5 Pareto Fitness Ranking

The VRPTW is a MO optimization problem where a number of objectives such as the number of vehicles (NV) and the cost of routing (CR) as given in Eq. (13.4) need to be minimized concurrently, subject to a number of constraints like time window and vehicle capacity. Figure 13.9 illustrates the concept of MO optimization in VRPTW, for which the small boxes represent the solutions resulting from the optimization. Point "*d*" is the minimum for both the objectives of *NV* and *CR*, which is sometimes unfeasible or cannot be obtained. Point "*b*" is a compromised solution between the cost of routing (*CR*) and the number of vehicles (*NV*). If a single-objective routing method is employed, its effort to push the solution toward point "*b*" may lead to the solution of point "*a*" (if only the criterion of *CR* is considered) or the solution of point "*c*" (if only the criterion of *NV* is considered). Instead of giving only a particular solution, the HMOEA for MO optimization in VRPTW aims to discover the set of nondominated solutions concurrently, i.e., points "*a*", "*b*," and "*c*" together, for which the designer could select an optimal solution depending on the current situation, as desired.

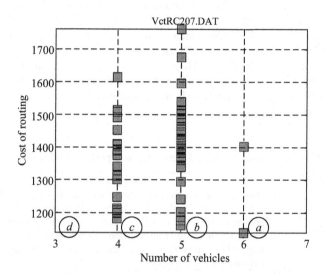

Fig. 13.9. Tradeoff graph for the cost of routing and the number of vehicles.

The Pareto fitness ranking scheme (Fonseca 1995) for evolutionary MO optimization is adopted here to assign the relative strength of individuals in the population. The ranking approach assigns the same smallest rank for all nondominated individuals, while the dominated individuals are inversely ranked according to how many individuals in the population dominating them based on the criteria below:

- A smaller number of vehicles but an equal cost of routing
- A smaller routing cost but an equal number of vehicles
- A smaller routing cost and a smaller number of vehicles

Therefore, the rank of an individual *p* in a population is given by $(1 + q)$, where *q* is the number of individuals that dominate the individual *p* based on the above criteria.

13.3.6 Local Search Exploitation

As stated by Tan et al. (2001c), the role of local search is vital in MO evolutionary optimization in order to encourage better convergence and to discover any missing tradeoff regions. The local search approach can contribute to the intensification of the optimization results, which is usually regarded as a complement to evolutionary operators that mainly focus on global exploration. Jaszkiewicz (1998) proposed a multobjective metaheuristic based on the approach of local search to generate a set of solutions approximate to the whole nondominated set of a traveling salesman problem. For the VRPTW as addressed in this chapter, the local search exploitation is particularly useful for solving the problem of R category, where the customers are far away from each other and the swapping of two nodes in a route implemented by the local optimizers could improve the cost of routing significantly. Three local heuristics are incorporated in the HMOEA to search for better routing solutions in VRPTW, which include the Intra_Route, Lambda_Interchange (Osman and Christofides 1989), and Shortest_pf (Lin 1965). Descriptions of these heuristics are given in Table 13.1. There is no preference made among the local heuristics in HMOEA, and one of them will be randomly executed at the end of every 50 generations for all individuals in a population to search for better local routing solutions.

Table 13.1. The Three Local Heuristics Incorporated in HMOEA

Local heuristic	Description
Intra_Route	This heuristic picks two routes randomly and swaps two nodes from each route. The nodes are chosen based on randomly generated numbers. After the swapping is done, feasibility is checked for the newly generated routes. If the two new routes are acceptable, they will be updated as part of the solutions; otherwise the original routes will be restored.
Lambda_ Interchange	This heuristic is cost-oriented where a number of nodes will be moved from one route into another route. Assume two routes A and B are chosen; the heuristic starts by scanning through nodes in route A and moves the feasible node into route B. The procedure repeats until a predefined number of nodes are shifted or the scanning ends at the last node of route A.
Shortest_pf	This heuristic is modified from the "shortest path first" method. It attempts to rearrange the order of nodes in a particular route such that nodes with the shortest distance are given the priority. For example, given a route A that contains 5 customers, the first node is chosen based on its distance from the depot and the second node is chosen based on its distance from the first customer node. The process repeats until all nodes in the original route are rerouted. The original route will be restored if the new route obtained is unfeasible.

13.4 Simulation Results and Comparisons

Section 13.4.1 presents the system specification of HMOEA. The advantages of HMOEA for MO optimization in VRPTW, such as lower routing cost, wider scattering area, and better convergence trace as compared with conventional single-objective approaches are described in Section 13.4.2. Section 13.4.3 includes some performance comparisons for the features incorporated in HMOEA, such as genetic operators and local search heuristics. Section 13.4.4 presents the extensive simulation results of HMOEA based upon Solomon's 56 datasets. The performance of the HMOEA is compared with the best-known VRPTW results.

13.4.1 System Specification

The HMOEA was programmed in C++ based on a Pentium III 933 MHz processor with 256 MB RAM under the Microsoft Windows 2000 operating system. The vehicle, customer, route sequence, and set of solutions are modeled as classes of objects. The class of node is the fundamental information unit concerning a customer. The class of route is a vector of nodes, which describes a continuous sequence of customers by a particular vehicle. The class of chromosome consists of a number of routes that carries the solution of the routing problem. Constraints and objectives are modeled as behaviors in the classes, e.g., a predefined number limits the maximum capacity of a vehicle which is included as one of the behaviors in the route. In all simulations, the following parameter settings were chosen after some preliminary observations:

Crossover rate	= 0.7
Mutation rate	= 0.1
Elastic rate	= 0.5
Squeeze rate	= 0.7
Elitism rate	= 0.5% of the population size
Population size	= 1000
Generation size	= 1500 or no improvement over the last 10 generations

13.4.2 MO Optimization Performance

This section presents the routing performance of HMOEA, particularly on the MO optimization that offers the advantages of improved routing solutions, wider scattering area and better convergence trace over conventional single-objective routing approaches.

In vehicle routing problems, the logistic manager is often not only interested in getting the minimal routing cost, but also the smallest number of vehicles required to service the plan. Ironically, many literatures especially the classical models are often formulated and solved with respect to a particular cost or by linearly combining the multiple objectives into a scalar objective via a predetermined aggregating function to reflect the search for a particular solution. The drawback of such an objective reduction approach is that the weights are difficult to determine pre-cisely, particularly when there is often insufficient information or knowledge con-cerning the large real-world vehicle routing problem. Clearly, these issues could be addressed via HMOEA that optimizes both objectives concurrently without the need of any calibration of weighting coefficients.

In the VRPTW model as formulated in Section 13.2, there are two objectives including the number of vehicles and the total traveling cost to be optimized con-currently. Although both the objectives are quantitatively measurable, the relation-ship between these two values in a routing problem is unknown until the problem has been solved. These two objectives may be positively correlated with each other, or they may be conflicting to each other. For example, a fewer number of vehicles employed in service do not necessarily increase the routing cost. On the other hand, a higher routing cost may be incurred if more vehicles are involved. From the computational results of Solomon's 56 datasets, an analysis is carried out to count the number of problem instances with conflicting objectives as well as the number of instances having positively correlating objectives. As shown in Fig. 13.10, although all instances in the categories of C_1 and C_2 are having posi-tively correlating objectives (the routing cost of a solution is increased as the number of vehicles is increased), there are many instances in R_1, R_2, RC_1, and RC_2 categories that have conflicting objectives (the routing cost of a solution is re-duced as the number of vehicles is increased). Obviously, such a relationship (con-flicting or positively correlating) between the two objectives in a routing problem could be effectively discovered using the approach of HMOEA.

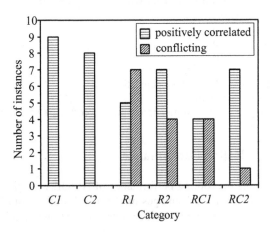

Fig. 13.10. Number of instances with conflicting or positively correlating objectives.

To illustrate the performance of HMOEA, three types of simulations with simi-lar settings but different set of optimization criteria (for evolutionary selection op-eration) in VRPTW have been performed, i.e., each type of simulation concerns the optimization criterion of routing cost (*CR*), vehicle numbers (*NV*), and multiple objectives (*MO*) including *CR* and *NV*, respectively. Figure 13.11 shows the comparison results for the evolutionary optimization based upon the criterion of *CR*, *NV*, and *MO*, respectively. The comparison was performed using the multiplicative aggregation method (Van Veldhuizen and Lamont 1998b) of average cost and average number of routes for the different categories of datasets. The results of C_1 category is omitted in the figure since no significant performance difference is observed for this dataset. As can be seen, the *MO* produces the best performance with the smallest value of *CR×NV* for all the categories.

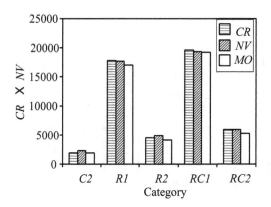

Fig. 13.11. Performance comparisons for different optimization criteria of *CR*, *NV*, and *MO*

In general, the MO optimization tends to evolve a family of points that are widely distributed or scattered in the objective domain such that a broader coverage of solutions is possible. Figure 13.12 illustrates the distribution of individuals in the objective domain (*CR vs. NV*) for one randomly selected instance in each of the five categories of datasets. In the figure, each individual in a population is plotted as a small box based on its performance of *CR* and *NV*. A portion appears darker than others when its solution points are congested in the graph. In contrast, a portion looks lighter if its solution points are fairly distributed in the objective domain. As can be seen, all graphs in Fig. 13.12 using the optimization criteria of *MO* appear to be fairly distributed over a large area in the objective domain. This can also be illustrated from the measure of scattering points by dividing the entire interested region in the objective domain into grids. If any individual exists in a grid, one scattering point is counted regardless of the number of individuals in that particular grid. Table 13.2 shows the percentage of area covered by the scattering points. As shown in the table, *MO* outperforms the *CR* and *NV* by scoring the highest percentage for all the 5 categories of datasets. For example, in category RC_{1-07}, *MO* scored 40% area while *CR* and *NV* scored only 24% and 23%, respectively.

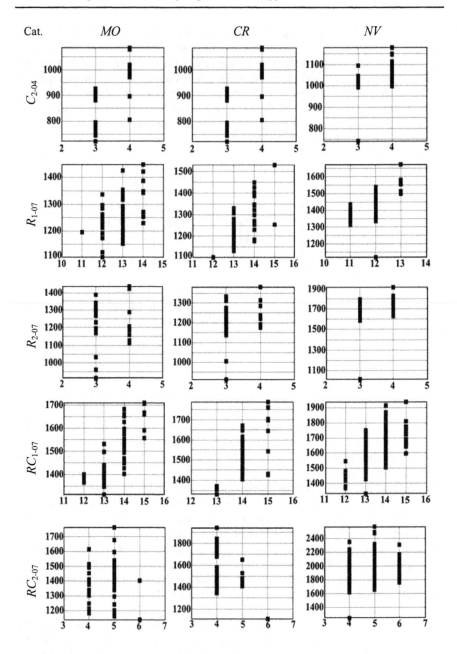

Fig. 13.12. Comparison of population distribution in the objective domain (*CR* along *y*-axis *vs. NV* along *x*-axis) for different optimization criteria of *CR*, *NV*, and *MO*.

Table 13.2. Comparison of Scattering Points for Optimization Criteria *CR*, *NV*, and *MO*

Category	Objective space covered by scattering points (%)		
	CR	*NV*	*MO*
$C_{2\text{-}04}$	17.00	16.00	23.00
$R_{1\text{-}07}$	19.05	15.71	25.71
$R_{2\text{-}07}$	11.11	8.89	12.22
$RC_{1\text{-}07}$	24.00	22.67	40.00
$RC_{2\text{-}07}$	14.76	20.00	23.33

13.4.3 Specialized Operators and Hybrid Local Search Performance

In this section, the performance of HMOEA is compared with two variants of evolutionary algorithms, i.e., MOEA with standard genetic operators as well as MOEA without hybridization of local search. This examines the effectiveness of the features, such as specialized genetic operators and local search heuristic, in the HMOEA.

i. Specialized Genetic Operators

Two standard genetic operators are devised here to solve the VRPTW. The MOEA with standard genetic operators (STD_MOEA) devised the commonly known cycle crossover and RAR mutation. The cycle crossover is a general crossover operator that preserves the order of sequence in the parent partially and was applied to solve the traveling salesman problems by Oliver et al. (1987). The remove and reinsert (RAR) mutation operator removes a task from the sequence and reinserts it to a random position (Gendreau et al. 1999). The experiment setups and parameters for STD_MOEA are similar to the settings for HMOEA. Figure 13.13 shows the normalized values for the two objectives in VRPTW for all 56 simulation results. As shown in the figure, the STD_MOEA (the lines with larger markers) tend to incur a higher cost and a larger number of vehicles. The specialized operators in HMOEA have performed better with lower objective values in general, by exploiting important information from the problem domain. The preservation of feasible routes in the next generation is easier with the specialized operators in HMOEA as compared to the standard genetic operators that do not exploit knowledge from the problem representation.

ii. Hybrid Local Search Performance

The HMOEA incorporates local search heuristics in order to exploit local routing solutions in parallel. To demonstrate the effectiveness of local exploitations in HMOEA, the convergence trace of the best and average routing costs in a population for six randomly selected instances (one from each category) with and without local search are plotted in Fig. 13.14. In the figure, *NV* indicates the number of vehicles for the convergence with the best routing cost in the instances. As shown in Fig. 13.14, the HMOEA with local search performs better by having a lower routing cost (*CR*) and a smaller number of vehicles (*NV*) for almost all instances as compared with the one without any local exploitation. It has also been observed that other instances in Solomon's 56 datasets exhibit similar convergence performances as those shown in Fig. 13.14, which confirmed the importance of incorporating local search exploitation in HMOEA.

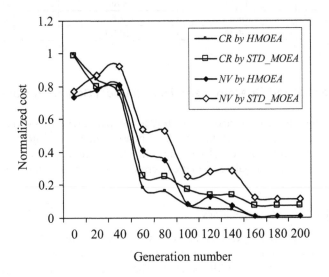

Fig. 13.13. Comparison of performance for different genetic operators.

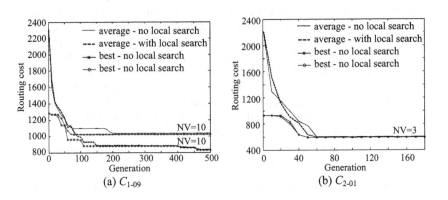

Fig. 13.14. Comparison of simulations with and without local search exploitation in HMOEA (continued on next page).

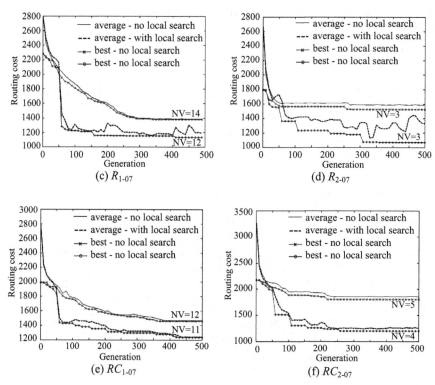

Fig. 13.14. (Continued) Comparison of simulations with and without local search exploitation in HMOEA.

13.4.4 Performance Comparisons

In this section, the results obtained from HMOEA are compared with the best-known routing solutions obtained from different heuristics in the literature. Table 13.3 shows the comparison results between HMOEA and the best-known results in the literature, for which instances with significant results or improvements are bolded. It can be observed that the HMOEA gives excellent routing results with 23 datasets achieving a lower routing cost with slightly higher vehicle numbers as compared to the best-known solutions obtained from various heuristics in the literature. Besides, the HMOEA also produces competitive routing solutions for 18 instances with similar or smaller number of vehicles and slightly higher routing cost (1%–2% in average) as compared to the best-known VRPTW solutions.

Table 13.3. Comparison Results Between HMOEA and the Best-Known Routing Solutions (Continued on Next Page)

Dataset	Best-known result		Source*	HMOEA	
	NV	CR		NV	CR
C_{1-01}	10	827	Desrochers et al. (1992)	**10**	**824.62**
C_{1-02}	10	827	Desrochers et al. (1992)	10	828.19
C_{1-03}	10	826.3	Taveres et al. (2003)	10	828.06
C_{1-04}	10	824	Rochat and Tailard (1995)	10	825.54
C_{1-05}	10	827.3	Taveres et al. (2003)	**10**	**826.01**
C_{1-06}	10	827	Desrochers et al. (1992)	10	828.17
C_{1-07}	10	827.3	Taveres et al. (2003)	10	829.34
C_{1-08}	10	827.3	Taveres et al. (2003)	10	832.28
C_{1-09}	10	827.3	Taveres et al. (2003)	10	829.22
C_{2-01}	3	589.1	Cook and Rich (1999)	**3**	**588.62**
C_{2-02}	3	589.1	Cook and Rich (1999)	3	591.56
C_{2-03}	3	591.17	Li and Lim (2002)	3	593.25
C_{2-04}	3	590.6	Potvin and Bengio (1996)	3	595.55
C_{2-05}	3	588.88	De Backer et al. (2002)	**3**	**588.16**
C_{2-06}	3	588.49	Lau et al. (2001)	3	588.49
C_{2-07}	3	588.29	Rochat and Tailard (1995)	3	588.88
C_{2-08}	3	588.32	Rochat and Tailard (1995)	**3**	**588.03**
R_{1-01}	18	1607.7	Desrochers et al. (1992)	18	1613.59
R_{1-02}	17	1434	Desrochers et al. (1992)	18	1454.68
R_{1-03}	13	1175.67	Lau et al. (2001)	14	1235.68
R_{1-04}	10	982.01	Rochat and Tailard (1995)	**10**	**974.24**
R_{1-05}	15	1346.12	Kallehauge et al. (2001)	15	1375.23
R_{1-06}	13	1234.6	Cook and Rich (1999)	13	1260.20
R_{1-07}	11	1051.84	Kallehauge et al. (2001)	11	1085.75
R_{1-08}	9	960.88	Berger et al. (2001)	**10**	**954.03**
R_{1-09}	12	1013.2	Chiang and Russel (1997)	12	1157.74
R_{1-10}	12	1068	Cook and Rich (1999)	12	1104.56
R_{1-11}	12	1048.7	Cook and Rich (1999)	12	1057.80
R_{1-12}	10	953.63	Rochat and Tailard (1995)	10	974.73
R_{2-01}	4	1252.37	Homberger and Gehring (1999)	**5**	**1206.42**
R_{2-02}	3	1158.98	Lau et al. (2003)	**4**	**1091.21**
R_{2-03}	3	942.64	Homberger and Gehring (1999)	**4**	**935.04**
R_{2-04}	2	825.52	Bent and Van (2001)	**3**	**789.72**
R_{2-05}	3	994.42	Rousseau et al. (2002)	3	1094.65

Table 13.3. (Continued) Comparison Results Between HMOEA and the Best-Known Routing Solutions

Dataset	Best-known result		Source*	HMOEA	
	NV	CR		NV	CR
$R_{2\text{-}06}$	3	833	Thangiah et al. (1994)	3	940.12
$R_{2\text{-}07}$	3	814.78	Rochat and Tailard (1995)	3	852.62
$R_{2\text{-}08}$	2	731.23	Homberger and Gehring (1999)	2	790.60
$R_{2\text{-}09}$	3	855	Thangiah et al. (1994)	3	974.88
$R_{2\text{-}10}$	3	954.12	Berger et al. (2001)	5	982.31
$R_{2\text{-}11}$	2	892.71	Bent and Van (2001)	**4**	**811.59**
$RC_{1\text{-}01}$	15	1619.8	Kohl et al. (1999)	16	1641.65
$RC_{1\text{-}02}$	13	1530.86	Cordone and Wolfler-Calvo (2001)	**13**	**1470.26**
$RC_{1\text{-}03}$	11	1261.67	Shaw (1998)	11	1267.86
$RC_{1\text{-}04}$	10	1135.48	Cordeau et al. (2001)	10	1145.49
$RC_{1\text{-}05}$	13	1632.34	Bräysy (2003)	**14**	**1589.91**
$RC_{1\text{-}06}$	12	1395.4	Chiang and Russel (1997)	**13**	**1371.69**
$RC_{1\text{-}07}$	11	1230.5	Taillard et al. (1997)	**11**	**1222.16**
$RC_{1\text{-}08}$	10	1139.8	Taillard et al. (1997)	**11**	**1133.90**
$RC_{2\text{-}01}$	4	1249	Thangiah et al. (1994)	**6**	**1134.91**
$RC_{2\text{-}02}$	4	1164.3	Taillard et al. (1997)	**5**	**1130.53**
$RC_{2\text{-}03}$	3	1049.62	Czech and Czarnas (2002)	**4**	**1026.61**
$RC_{2\text{-}04}$	3	799.12	Homberger and Gehring (1999)	3	879.82
$RC_{2\text{-}05}$	4	1300.25	Zbigniew and Piotr (2001)	**5**	**1295.46**
$RC_{2\text{-}06}$	3	1152.03	Zbigniew and Piotr (2001)	**4**	**1139.55**
$RC_{2\text{-}07}$	3	1061.14	Zbigniew and Piotr (2001)	**4**	**1040.67**
$RC_{2\text{-}08}$	3	829.69	Rousseau et al. (2002)	3	898.49

* Refer to the references for complete corresponding source entries

Table 13.4 compares the routing performance between nine popular heuristics and HMOEA based on the average number of vehicles and average cost of routing in each category. In each grid, there are two numbers representing the average vehicle numbers (upper) and average cost of routing (lower), respectively. For example, in category C_1, the number pair (10.00, 838.00) means that over the 9 instances in C_1, the average vehicle numbers deployed is 10 and the average traveling distance is 838.00. The last row gives the total accumulated sum indicating the total number of vehicles and the total traveling distance for all 56 instances. As can be seen, the HMOEA has led to new best average results with the smallest CR and NV for category C_1. It also produces the smallest average routing cost for the categories of R_1, RC_1, and RC_2. The average number of vehicles for category R_1 is 2.7% higher as compared to the heuristics giving the second best average routing costs. Although the average routing cost of HMOEA is not the smallest for categories C_2 and R_2, the HMOEA only requires an average of 3.51 vehicles to serve all customers in the category of R_2, which is much smaller than the 5 vehicles that are required by the heuristic giving the best average routing cost in R_2. As shown in the last row of Table 13.4, the HMOEA also provided the best total accumulated routing cost for Solomon's 56 datasets.

Table 13.4. Performance Comparison Between Different Heuristics and HMOEA

Problem class	Potvin and Bengio (1996)	Taillard et al. (1997)	Chiang and Russel (1997)	Schulze and Fahle (1999)	Bräysy and Gendreu (2001b)
C_1	10.00 838.00	10.00 828.45	10.00 828.38	10.00 828.94	10.00 828.38
C_2	3.00 589.90	3.00 590.30	3.00 591.42	3.00 589.93	3.00 589.86
R_1	12.60 1296.83	12.25 1216.70	12.17 1204.19	12.50 1268.42	11.92 1222.12
R_2	3.00 1117.70	3.00 995.38	2.73 986.32	3.09 1055.90	2.73 975.12
RC_1	12.10 1446.20	11.88 1367.51	11.88 1397.44	12.25 1396.07	11.5 1389.58
RC_2	3.40 1360.60	3.38 1165.62	3.25 1229.54	3.38 1308.31	3.25 1128.38
All	422 62572	416 57993	411 58502	423 60651	405 57710

Problem class	Ho et al. (2001)	Tan et al. (2001h)	Tan et al. (2001i)	Lau et al. (2003)	HMOEA
C_1	10.00 833.32	10.00 851.96	10.00 841.96	10.00 832.13	10.00 **827.00**
C_2	3.00 593.00	3.20 620.12	3.00 611.2	3.00 589.86	3.00 590.00
R_1	12.58 1203.32	13.20 1220.0	12.91 1205.0	12.16 1211.55	12.92 **1187.0**
R_2	3.18 951.17	4.40 985.69	5.00 929.6	3.00 1001.12	3.51 951.0
RC_1	12.75 1382.06	13.30 1366.62	12.60 1392.3	12.25 1418.77	12.74 **1355.0**
RC_2	3.75 1132.79	5.20 1108.50	5.80 1080.10	3.37 1170.93	4.25 **1067.00**
All	432 57265	470 57903	471 56931	418 58476	441 **56262**

Figure 13.15 shows the average simulation time (in seconds) for each category of datasets. The difference in computation time among the categories can be attributed to the flexibility of routing problem scenarios. From the statistics in Fig. 13.15, it is observed that all instances with longer time windows (i.e., category C_2, R_2, and RC_2) require a larger computation time. The reason is that these instances allow a more flexible arrangement in the routing plan since their time windows

constraints are larger than other categories. Besides, a vehicle with longer route also takes up more computation time during the cost and feasibility evaluation process. Although the HMOEA is capable of producing good routing solutions, it may require more computationl time as compared to conventional approaches, in order to perform the search in parallel as well as to obtain the optimized routing solutions (Tan et al. 2002b). Similar to most existing vehicle routing heuristics, the computation time should not be viewed as a major obstacle in solving the VRPTW problems, since the HMOEA is developed for offline simulation where the training time (computation time) is less important than the routing solutions. To reduce the computation time significantly, the HMOEA can be integrated into the "Paladin-DEC" distributed evolutionary computing framework (Tan et al. 2002b), where multiple intercommunicating subpopulations are implemented to share and distribute the routing workload among multiple computers over the Internet.

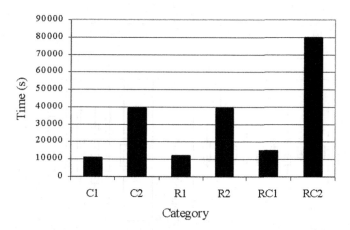

Fig. 13.15. The average simulation time for each category of data sets.

To study the consistency and reliability of the results obtained by HMOEA, 10 repeated simulations with randomly generated initial populations have been performed for Solomon's 56 datasets. The simulation results are represented in box plot format (Chambers et al. 1983) to visualize the distribution of simulation data efficiently. Note that all the routing costs have been normalized to their mean values for easy comparisons among the different test cases. Each box plot represents the distribution of a sample population where a thick horizontal line within the box encodes the median, while the upper and lower ends of the box are the upper and lower quartiles. The dashed appendages illustrate the spread and shape of distribution, while the dots represent the outside values. As shown in Fig. 13.16, the results obtained by HMOEA for the 10 simulation runs are rather consistent and all variances are found to be within 5%–20% from the mean values. It is observed that the category of type 1 (C_1, R_1, RC_1) gives a smaller variance as compared to the category of type 2 (C_2, R_2, RC_2), since the number of customers per route (length of route) is shorter for the category of type 1, e.g., the possibility of variation in simulations is often larger for longer routes. Among all the categories, R_2 gives the largest variance, since the customers' locations are remotely located in this dataset, i.e., a small difference in the routing sequence may result in a significant change to the solutions.

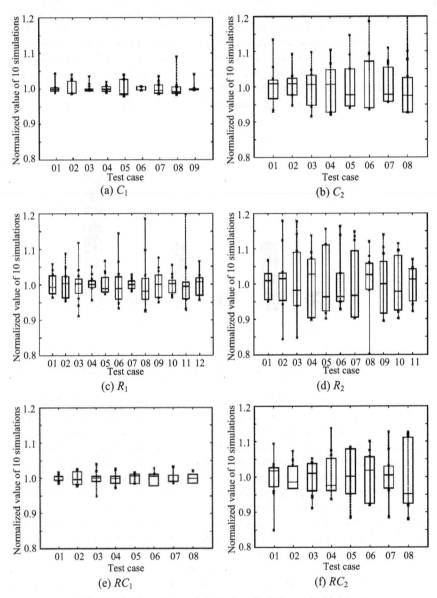

Fig. 13.16. The variance in box plots for Solomon's 56 datasets.

13.5 Conclusions

The vehicle routing problem with time windows involves routing a set of vehicles with limited capacity from a central depot to a set of geographically dispersed customers with known demands and predefined time windows. Thjs problem can be solved by optimizing routes for the vehicles so as to meet all given constraints as well as to minimize the objectives of traveling distance and vehicles numbers. This chapter has presented a hybrid multiobjective evolutionary algorithm for VRPTW, which incorporates various heuristics for local exploitations and the concept of Pareto's optimality for MO optimization. The HMOEA has been featured with specialized genetic operators and variable-length chromosome representation to accommodate the sequence-oriented optimization in VRPTW. Without the need of aggregating multiple criteria or constraints of VRPTW into a compromise function, it has been shown that the HMOEA is capable of optimizing multiple routing constraints and objectives concurrently, which improved the routing solutions in many aspects, such as lower routing cost, wider scattering area, and better convergence trace. Extensive simulations for the HMOEA have been performed upon the benchmark Solomon's 56 VRPTW 100-customer instances, which yielded many competitive results as compared to the best solutions in the literature.

12.5 Conclusions

14
Evolutionary Scheduling – TTVRP

14.1 Introduction

In order to support the port activities in lieu with the extremely high throughput at the port, container-related logistic services are very prosperous in Singapore. A general model for vehicle capacity planning system (VCPS) consisting of a number of job orders to be served by trucks and trailers daily was constructed for a logistic company that provides transportation services for container movements within the country (Lee et al. 2003). Due to the limited capacity of vehicles owned by the company, engineers in the company have to decide whether to assign the job orders of container movements to its internal fleet of vehicles or to outsource the jobs to other companies daily. The Tabu search meta-heuristic was applied to find a solution for the VCPS problem, where some new rules on how to assign jobs for outsourcing were derived and shown to be about 8% better than existing rules adopted by the company (Lee et al. 2003).

By analyzing different kinds of job orders received from the company, this chapter presents a transportation solution for trucks and trailers vehicle routing problem (TTVRP) containing multiple objectives and constraints, which is extended from the VCPS model with detailed maneuver of trailers in a routing plan. In TTVRP, the trailers are resources with certain limitations similar to real-world scenarios, and the allocation of trailers in different locations could affect the routing plans. The TTVRP is a difficult problem that involves many intricate factors, such as time window constraints and availability of trailers. The number of trucks in a fleet regulates the maximum number of jobs that can be handled internally within a certain period of time and all jobs must be serviced within a given time window. Instead of handling jobs by the internal fleet of trucks, the jobs can also be considered for outsourcing, if necessary. The routing plans in TTVRP also need to determine the number of trailer exchange points (TEPs) distributed in the region and to cater different types of trailers that are available at the trailer exchange points. Besides, there are a wide variety of job orders that may have diverse requirements for the types of the trailers, time window constraints, as well as locations of the source and destination.

The transportation solution to TTVRP contains useful decision-making information, such as the best fleet size to accommodate a variety of job orders and the trend for different number of trailers available at TEPs, which could be utilized by the management to visualize the complex correlations among different variables in the routing problem. In this chapter, various test cases for the TTVRP model are generated with random variables simulating the long-term operation of business activities. The management can thus formulate the planning for certain variables, such as the number of trucks (longterm capital cost) so that the day-to-day operational cost could be kept at the minimum. The TTVRP is NP-hard, which involves the optimization of routes for multiple trucks in order to meet all given constraints and to minimize multiple objectives of routing distance and number of trucks concurrently. Existing routing approaches that strive to minimize a single criterion of routing cost or number of trucks is not suitable for solving such a multimodal and multiobjective combinatorial problem. The TTVRP should be best tackled by MO optimization methods, which offer a family of Pareto-optimal routing solutions containing both the minimized routing cost and number of trucks. The hybrid multiobjective evolutionary algorithm (HMOEA) presented in Chapter 13, which incorporates the heuristic search for local exploitation and the concept of Pareto's optimality for finding the tradeoff, is applied to solve the problem of TTVRP in this chapter.

This chapter is organized as follows: Section 14.2 describes the scenario and modeling of the TTVRP with mathematical formulation. Section 14.3 presents the extensive simulation results for the TTVRP problem. Conclusions are drawn in Section 14.4.

14.2 The Problem Scenario

The TTVRP model with detailed maneuver of the trailers in a routing plan is extended from a real-world VCPS system proposed by Lee et al. (2003). The movement of containers among customers, depots, and the port are major transportation job orders considered. A container load is handled like a normal truckload but these loads used containers with a possible chassis instead of trailers only. From the equipment assignment point of view, a correct trailer type is essential for the routing. For an inbound job, a loaded container is taken from a vessel to a customer and returned empty to the depot. For an outbound job, however, an empty container is picked up from the depot and taken to the customer before returning loaded to the vessel. Every job order contains the location of source and destination as well as other customers' information. Other specifications such as load requirement and time windows are specified as hard constraints in the model. There are a total of 6 types of job orders, which are varied according to the source and destination (port, warehouse, depot, or trailer exchange), time windows (tight or loose), loaded trip (or empty), and type of trailers (20 or 40) as follows:

1. Import with trailer type 20
2. Import with trailer type 40
3. Export with trailer type 20
4. Export with trailer type 40
5. Empty container movement with trailer type 20

6. Empty container movement with trailer type 40

The logistic company owns a maximum of 40 trucks and more trailers than trucks. A truck must be accompanied with a trailer when servicing a customer, i.e., the routing needs to consider both the locations of truck and trailer. An "export" job order works as follows: A truck first picks up a correct trailer at a trailer exchange point and a container at the depot. It then proceeds to the warehouse and leaves the trailer and container there for about 2 days where the container is filled. A truck (which may not be the same truck as earlier) will later be allocated to move the loaded container using the earlier assigned trailer and leaves the container at the port before departing with the trailer. In contrast, an "import" job order works as follows: A truck picks up a correct trailer at a TEP before it proceeds to the port. The trailer is used to carry loaded container at the port. The truck then moves the container to the warehouse and leaves it there for about 2 days. A truck (which may not be the same truck as earlier) will later move this empty container from the warehouse to the depot (using a trailer) and leaves the depot with its trailer unloaded. Intuitively, there are times when a truck has a correct trailer type and thus can serve a job without going to a trailer exchange point. Otherwise, a truck is required to pick up a trailer (from the nearest TEP where the trailer is available to be picked up or exchanged) when it has a mismatched trailer type or does not carry a trailer. The number of trailers available at an exchange point depends on how many trailers were picked up and returned to the TEP. The constraint imposed on the model is the time windows at the source and destination of job orders. An assumption is made such that all trailer exchange points have similar operating hours as the truck drivers' working hours, i.e., from 8:00 am to 8:00 pm.

14.2.1 Modeling the Problem Scenarios

Table 14.1. The Task Type and Its Description

Task type	Task description	Source	Destination	Trailer type
1	Subtrip of import job	Port	Warehouse	20
2	Subtrip of import job	Port	Warehouse	40
3	Subtrip of import job	Warehouse	Depot	20
4	Subtrip of import job	Warehouse	Depot	40
5	Subtrip of export job	Depot	Warehouse	20
6	Subtrip of export job	Depot	Warehouse	40
7	Subtrip of export job	Warehouse	Port	20
8	Subtrip of export job	Warehouse	Port	40
9	Empty container movement	Port	Depot	20
10	Empty container movement	Depot	Port/Depot	20
11	Empty container movement	Port	Depot	40
12	Empty container movement	Depot	Port/Depot	40

Based on the scenarios described, some refinements have been made to the model proposed by Lee et al. (2003). The problem is modeled here on a daily basis where the planning horizon spans only one day. All import and export jobs consist of two subtrips and a two-day interval at the customer warehouses. Therefore, the two-day interval at customer warehouses divides a job nicely into two separate planning horizons (one day each). The import and export jobs can be broken into two independent tasks, where each of them falls into a different planning horizon. In this way, job orders are broken into subjob type precisely (hereinafter this is referred as a subjob or a task). Generally a task involves traveling from one point (source) to another point (destination) as listed in Table 14.1.

The number of trailers at TEPs depends on the trailers that are left over from the previous planning horizon. All the pickup, return, and exchange activities can also change the number of trailers available. Besides, a number of trailers could also be parked at the customer warehouses instead of the TEPs. All these undetermined factors suggest that the resource of trailers available at each TEP at the initial of planning horizon is random. Therefore, the daily number of trailers at each trailer exchange point is randomly generated in our model. A truck has to pick up a correct trailer from the nearest TEP if it serves task type 1, 2, 5, 6, 9, 10, 11, or 12 and does not have a trailer or has an incorrect trailer type. For task type 3, 4, 7, or 8, the truck does not need to visit a TEP before servicing the task since the correct trailer has been brought to the place in advance. In contrast, trucks that serve subjob type 3, 4, 7, or 8 must not have any trailers. In this case, if a trailer is attached to the truck, it must be returned to a trailer exchange point before servicing the task. For example, a truck that serves subjob type 7 leaves the destination (port) of a previous task with a trailer. If the same truck is to serve another task type 3, 4, 7, or 8, it must travel to a TEP to drop the trailer obtained previously. In brief, a truck is required to visit a trailer exchange point under the following conditions:

- It needs a trailer for task type 1, 2, 5, 6, 9, 10, 11, or 12 and it does not have a trailer.
- It needs a trailer for task type 1, 2, 5, 6, 9, 10, 11, or 12 and it has an incorrect trailer type.
- It has a trailer but it has to service subjob type 3, 4, 7, or 8, e.g., the truck needs to travel to a TEP for dropping the trailer before servicing the task.

Obviously, the availability of trailers at TEPs should be updated frequently since the number of trailers changes with the pickup and return activities, e.g., a trailer that is returned earlier in a day will be available for pickup later in the same day. To model these activities, the approach of time segmentation for trailer resources is used as follows:

- Working hours per day: 12 hours × 60 min = 720 min
- Time per segment: 10 min
- Number of time slots available: 720/10 slots = 72 slots

Hence the number of trailers available for pickup in a particular time slot is equal to the number of trailers in previous time slot, added by the trailers returned in the previous time slot and deducted by the trailers picked up in the previous time slot. In this approach, different trailer types are managed and updated in separate lists. For example, a TEP has 3 trailers (with type 20) and the following events occurred in the current time slot: 1 trailer (type 20) is returned and 2 trailers (type 20) are picked up. In this case, the trailer exchange point should have 2 trailers (type 20) available for pick up in the next time slot.

14.2.2 Mathematical Model

Decision Variables:

$X_{ik_m} \in \{0,1\}$, where $i = \{1,...,I\}$, $k = \{1,...,K\}$, $m = \{1,...,M\}$. If task i is assigned to truck k as the mth task, $X_{ik_m} = 1$; otherwise $X_{ik_m} = 0$;

$X_{i0} \in \{0,1\}$, $i \in \{1,..,I\}$. If task i is subcontracted to companies, $X_{i0} = 1$; otherwise $X_{i0} = 0$.

Parameters:

I = number of tasks;
K = maximum number of trucks;
M = maximum number of jobs that can be handled by one truck in a planning horizon;
J = number of trailer exchange points;
y = task type, i.e., $y \in \{1,...,12\}$;
$I(y)$ = the set of task with type y;
$\bigcup_y I(y)$ = all tasks = $\{1,...I\}$;
TW = time segment for trailer resources = 10;
MTW = maximum number of time slots = 72.

Symbol
$\lceil x \rceil$: the smallest integer larger or equal to x;
$\lfloor x \rfloor$: the largest integer smaller or equal to x.

Distance of tasks' location
D_{hji} : distance from destination of previous task h to trailer point j followed by source of task i;
D_{hi} : distance from destination of previous task h to source of task i;
D_i : distance source of task i to destination of task i.

Task handling time
H_{i1} : handling time at source of task i;
H_{i2} : handling time at destination of task i.

Task time window
R_{i0} : start time at the source of task i;

R_{i1} : end time at the source of task i;

R_{i2} : start time at the destination of task i;

R_{i3} : end time at the destination of task i;

A_{k0} : start available time for truck k;

A_{kf} : end available time for truck k.

Cost

P_i : routing cost of task i for internal fleet operation;

S_i : routing cost of task i for outsourced.

Number of trailers at trailer exchange point

TP_{40j} : initial number of trailer type 40 at point j;

TP_{20j} : initial number of trailer type 20 at point j.

Minimization Objectives:

The routing solutions should minimize both the criteria of routing cost and the number of trucks concurrently as follows:

$$\text{Routing cost} = \sum_{i=1}^{I}\sum_{k=1}^{K}\sum_{m=1}^{M} X_{ik_m} P_i + \sum_{i=1}^{I}\sum_{k=1}^{K}\sum_{m=1}^{M}(1 - X_{ik_m})S_i ,$$

$$\text{Number of trucks} = \sum_{k=1}^{K}\left\lceil (\sum_{i=1}^{I}\sum_{m=1}^{M} X_{ik_m})/I \right\rceil .$$

subject to the following requirements and constraints:

Task and trailer types requirements

$$pickup20_{k,m}(X_{ik_m}) = \sum_{y=1,2,5,6,4,8,11,12}\;\sum_{y'=1,5,9,10}\;\sum_{j\in I(y)}\sum_{i\in I(y')}(X_{ik_m})(X_{jk_{m-1}})\;\;for\;m > 1;$$

$$pickup20_{k,m}(X_{ik_m}) = \sum_{y=1,5,9,10}\;\sum_{i\in I(y)} X_{ik_m}\;\;\;for\;m = 1;$$

$$pickup40_{k,m}(X_{ik_m}) = \sum_{y=1,2,3,5,6,7,9,10}\;\sum_{y'=2,6,11,12}\;\sum_{j\in I(y)}\sum_{i\in I(y')}(X_{ik_m})(X_{jk_{m-1}})\;\;for\;m > 1;$$

$$pickup40_{k,m}(X_{ik_m}) = \sum_{y=2,6,11,12}\;\sum_{i\in I(y)} X_{ik_m}\;\;\;for\;m = 1;$$

$$return20_{k,m}(X_{ik_m}) = \sum_{y=3,7,9,10}\;\sum_{y'=2,6,11,12,3,4,7,8}\;\sum_{j\in I(y)}\sum_{i\in I(y')}(X_{ik_m})(X_{jk_{m-1}});$$

$$return40_{k,m}(X_{ik_m}) = \sum_{j\in I(y)}\sum_{i\in I(y)}(X_{ik_m})(X_{jk_{m-1}});$$

$for\;y = 4,8,11,12;\;y' = 1,5,9,10,3,4,7,8;$

$visit_{k,m}(X_{ik_m}) \in \{0,1\};$

$$pickup20_{k,m}(X_{ik_m}) + pickup40_{k,m}(X_{ik_m}) + return20_{k,m}(X_{ik_m}) + return40_{k,m}(X_{ik_m})$$
$$\geq visit_{k,m}(X_{ik_m});$$
$$pickup20_{k,m}(X_{ik_m}) + pickup40_{k,m}(X_{ik_m}) + return20_{k,m}(X_{ik_m}) + return40_{k,m}(X_{ik_m})$$
$$\leq visit_{k,m}(X_{ik_m}) \cdot 2.$$

Single assignment
A task is only assigned to one truck k (as the mth task) or outsourced to other companies,

$$\sum_{k=1}^{K}\sum_{m=1}^{M}X_{ik_m} + \sum_{k=1}^{K}\sum_{m=1}^{M}X_{i0} = 1 \quad for\ i \in \{1,...,I\}.$$

Jobs must be assigned sequentially
For $k \in \{1,...,K\}$, $m \in \{1,...,M-1\}$, $\displaystyle\sum_{i=1}^{I}X_{ik_{(m+1)}} \leq \sum_{i=1}^{I}X_{ik_{(m)}}$.

Time sequence for each task
For $k \in \{1,...,K\}$, $m \in \{1,...,M-1\}$, $T_{k_{(m+1)}(0)} = T_{k_{(m)}(2)}$;

For $k \in \{1,...K\}$, $m \in \{1,...M\}$,

$$T_{k_m(1)} \geq T_{k_m(0)} + \sum_{i=1}^{I}X_{ik_{(m)}}\{H_{i1} + [visit_{k,m}(X_{ik_m}) \cdot D_{hji} + (1 - visit_{k,m}(X_{ik_{(m)}})) \cdot D_{hi}]\};$$

$$T_{k_m(2)} \geq T_{k_m(1)} + \sum_{i=1}^{I}X_{ik_m}(D_i + H_{i2}).$$

Time window constraints
For $k \in \{1,...,K\}$, $m \in \{1,...,M-1\}$, $A_{k0} \leq T_{k_m(0)} \leq A_{kf} - (T_{k_m(2)} - T_{k_m(0)})$;

For every particular $i \in \{1,...,I\}$, $\displaystyle R_{i0} \leq \sum_{k=1}^{K}\sum_{m=1}^{M}X_{ik_m}(T_{k_m} - H_{i1}) + X_{i0}R_{i0} \leq R_{i1}$

and $\displaystyle R_{i2} \leq \sum_{k=1}^{K}\sum_{m=1}^{M}X_{ik_m}(T_{k_m(2)} - H_{i2}) + X_{i0}R_{i2} \leq R_{i3}$.

Trailer constraints
$X_{ik_m}(t) \in \{0,1\}$, where $X_{ik_m}(t) = 1$ when the event falls into time window t,

$$X_{ik_m}(t) = 1 - \left\lceil \left| \left(\left\lfloor \frac{T_{k_m(1)}}{TW} \right\rfloor - t \right) \right| / MTW \right\rceil.$$

The number of trailer type 20 at time slot $t = 0$, i.e., $B_{20j}(0) = TP_{20j}$;

For every $t = 0$ to 71, and every j, the number of trailer type 20 available for next time slot, $t + 1$, is

$$B_{20j}(t+1) = B_{20j}(t) + \sum_{i=1}^{I}\sum_{k=1}^{K}\sum_{m=1}^{M}X_{ik_m}(t)\cdot return20_{k,m}(X_{ik_m})$$
$$- \sum_{i=1}^{I}\sum_{k=1}^{K}\sum_{m=1}^{M}X_{ik_m}(t)\cdot pickup_{k,m}20(X_{ik_m}), \text{ where } B_{20j}(t)\geq 0.$$

The number of trailer type 40 at time slot $t=0$, i.e., $B_{40j}(0) = TP_{40j}$.

For every $t=0$ to 71, and every j, the number of trailer type 40 available for next time slot, $t+1$, is,

$$B_{40j}(t+1) = B_{40j}(t) + \sum_{i=1}^{I}\sum_{k=1}^{K}\sum_{m=1}^{M}X_{ik_m}(t)\cdot return40_{k,m}(X_{ik_m})$$
$$- \sum_{i=1}^{I}\sum_{k=1}^{K}\sum_{m=1}^{M}X_{ik_m}(t)\cdot pickup_{k,m}40(X_{ik_m}), \text{ where } B_{40j}(t)\geq 0.$$

14.2.3 Generation of Test Cases

The TTVRP models various factors affecting the routing performance, particularly on the importance of trailer resources, such as the trailer's allocation in multiple trailer exchange sites and the location of trailer exchange points. In order to examine these factors thoroughly, a number of test cases with different combinations of variables are generated according to the following criteria:

- Number of tasks
- Total number of trailers
- Number of trailers and allocation
- Number of trailer exchange points (with trailer resources assigned initially)

The test cases are generated based on the scenario of one-day activity for a logistic company. The jobs schedule starts from 8:00 am to 8:00 pm (12 hours a day). All the tasks must be finished within a day, and the details of every task are generated. The map contains one port, three depots, and five trailer exchange points. The five TEPs are labeled as TEP1, TEP2. TEP3, TEP4, and TEP5, which are located at disperse places and may have different initial number of trailers. The map also defines the location of 80 customer sites spreading across the area randomly. The map of customer sites is created as a 120×120 grid, and the location of customers is given as a pair of (x, y)-coordinates. The distance (traveling time) among any two points is calculated as 0.5×(triangular distance), where the value of 0.5 is merely a scaling factor such that a truck can serve around 3 tasks per day on average. The timing constraint is also specified in the test cases, e.g., the handling time at the source and destination (i.e., port, depot, and customer warehouses) requires 10 minutes, which must be included in calculating the time needed for a complete job handling. The time windows for the source and destination of each job are generated according to the type of jobs. The availability of trailer resources is quantified into 10-minute slots. The return of a trailer is only visible to others after the current time slot, where the retrieval of a trailer gives immediate effect to the current count of trailers. The cost for each task type is based on the way tasks are accomplished, i.e., by self-fleet service or outsourced to external companies. There is no hard rule to specify whether the cost for internal fleet is cheaper than outsource fleet and vice versa, i.e., the cost merely depends on the type of jobs to be served.

There are a total of 28 test cases generated in this study, which differs in terms of the number of task orders, the number of trailers, the allocation of trailers, and the number of trailer exchange points. However, information about customer warehouses and other important locations like port and depots remains unchanged. Table 14.2 lists the test cases for the NORM (Normal) category, where the trailers are allocated "equally" to TEPs. As shown in Table 14.2, the test cases in this category are divided into 4 groups with a different number of tasks in the range of 100 to 132, and all TEPs can contribute to the supply of any demands for trailers. As shown in Table 14.3, the 8 test cases for TEPC (Trailer Exchange Point Case) category contain a constant of 132 tasks, but are assigned with extreme trailer allocation strategies. In some cases, only one TEP is allocated with trailers, while the available number of trailers remains constant at 30 for all test cases in this category. As shown in Table 14.4, the LTTC (Less Trailer Test Case) category comprises 8 test cases with an equal number of trailers. In this category, the available number of trailers is set as 10, e.g., the trailer resources for both TEPC and LTTC test cases share the same distribution ratio but are assigned with different quantity of trailers.

Table 14.2. Test Cases for the Category of NORM

Group	Test case*	Job number	Trailers at each TEP	TEPs allocated with trailers	Distribution
100	test_100_1_2	100	1 or 2	5	uniform
	test_100_3_4	100	2 or 3	5	uniform
	test_100_2_3	100	3 or 4	5	uniform
112	test_112_1_2	112	1 or 2	5	uniform
	test_112_2_3	112	2 or 3	5	uniform
	test_112_3_4	112	3 or 4	5	uniform
120	test_120_1_2	120	1 or 2	5	uniform
	test_120_2_3	120	2 or 3	5	uniform
	test_120_3_4	120	3 or 4	5	uniform
132	test_132_1_2	132	1 or 2	5	uniform
	test_132_2_3	132	2 or 3	5	uniform
	test_132_3_4	132	3 or 4	5	uniform

*The last digit denotes the number of trailers allocated for each TEP.

Table 14.3. Test Cases for the Category of TEPC

Test case	Job number	Number of trailers at TEPs	TEPs allocated with trailers	Distribution*
test_132_tep5	132	30	5	uniform
test_132_tep1a	132	30	1	TEP1
test_132_tep1b	132	30	1	TEP2
test_132_tep1c	132	30	1	TEP3
test_132_tep1d	132	30	1	TEP4
test_132_tep1e	132	30	1	TEP5
test_132_tep3a	132	30	3	Distributed among TEP1, TEP3, and TEP5
test_132_tep3b	132	30	3	Distributed among TEP1, TEP2, and TEP4

* Fixed number of trailers and different distribution of TEPs.

Table 14.4. Test Cases for the Category of LTTC

Test case	Job number	Number of trailers at TEPs	TEPs allocated with trailers	Distribution*
test_132_ltt5	132	10	5	uniform
test_132_ltt1a	132	10	1	TEP1
test_132_ltt1b	132	10	1	TEP2
test_132_ltt1c	132	10	1	TEP3
test_132_ltt1d	132	10	1	TEP4
test_132_ltt1e	132	10	1	TEP5
test_132_ltt3a	132	10	3	Distributed among TEP1, TEP3, and TEP5
test_132_ltt3b	132	10	3	Distributed among TEP1, TEP2, and TEP4

* Less trailers and different distribution of TEPs.

14.3 Computation Results

Table 14.5 shows the simulation parameter settings chosen after some preliminary experiments. These settings should not be regarded as the optimal set of parameter values, but a generalized one for which the HMOEA performs fairly well over the test problems. This section contains the computation results and analysis of optimization performances for all the problem instances. Section 14.3.1 studies the performance of convergence trace and Pareto optimality for MO optimization using the 12 test cases in normal category. Section 14.3.2 analyzes the different trailer allocation scenarios based on the test cases of TEPC and LTTC (each of the TEPC and LTTC categories contains 8 test cases). In Section 14.3.3, the optimization performance of HMOEA is compared with two other MOEAs based upon various performance measures.

Table 14.5. Parameter Settings in the Simulation

Parameter	Value
Crossover rate	0.8
Mutation rate	0.3
Population size	800
Generation size	1000 or no improvement over the last 5 generations
Niche radius	0.04

14.3.1 MO Optimization Performance

14.3.1.1 Convergence Trace

Convergence trace is an important performance indicator to show the effectiveness of an optimization algorithm. The two objectives in TTVRP are the number of trucks and the routing cost. Figure 14.1 shows the normalized average and best routing costs at each generation for the 12 test cases in normal category, where each line represents the convergence trace for each of the test cases. As can be seen, the routing costs decline nicely as the evolution proceeds. The same observation can be found in Fig. 14.2, where the normalized average number of trucks at each generation is plotted.

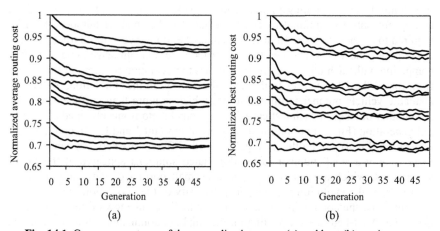

Fig. 14.1. Convergence trace of the normalized average (a) and best (b) routing costs.

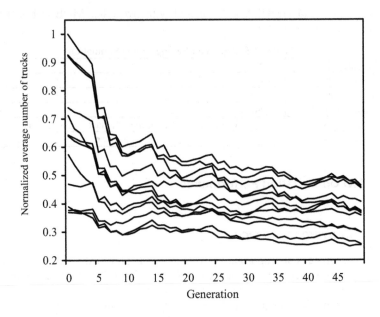

Fig. 14.2. Convergence trace of the normalized average number of trucks.

14.3.1.2 Pareto Front

In solving a vehicle routing problem, the logistic manager is often interested in getting not only the minimal routing cost but also the smallest number of trucks required to service the plan. In order to reduce the routing cost, more trucks are often required and vice versa, i.e., the two criteria are noncommensurable and often competing with each other. Figure 14.3 shows the evolution progress of the Pareto front for all the 12 test cases in the normal category. In the simulation, the largest available vehicle number is limited to 35, which is more than sufficient to cater the number of tasks in each test case. The various Pareto fronts obtained at the initial generation (First), two intermediate generations (Int 1 and Int 2), and the final generation (Final), are plotted in Fig. 14.3 with different markers. As can be seen, there is only a small number of nondominated solutions appeared at the initial generations, which are also congested at a small portion of the solution space. However, as the evolution proceeds, the diversity of the population increases significantly and the nondominated solutions gradually evolve toward the final tradeoff curve. A dashed line connecting all the final nondominated solutions is drawn for each test case in Fig. 14.3, which clearly shows the final tradeoff or routing plan obtained by the HMOEA. It should be noted that the Pareto front includes the plan with zero truck number that subcontracts all tasks to external company, although such a policy is apparently not practical to adopt and is against the will of the logistic management.

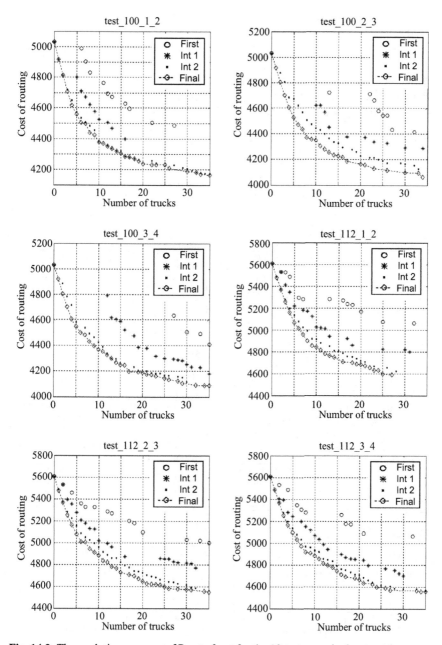

Fig. 14.3. The evolution progress of Pareto front for the 12 test cases in the normal category (continued on next page).

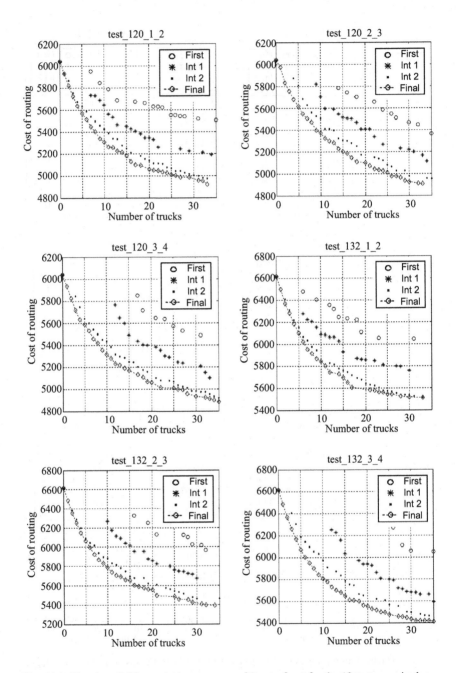

Fig. 14.3. (Continued) The evolution progress of Pareto front for the 12 test cases in the normal category.

14.3.1.3 Routing Plan

The average best routing cost for each truck number of the 12 test cases in the normal category is plotted in Fig. 14.4, which shows an obvious tradeoff between the two objectives of routing cost and truck number in TTVRP. This tradeoff curve is useful for the decision maker to derive an appropriate routing schedule according to the current situation. The information about the number of tasks to be serviced and the number of trailers available at each trailer exchange point is often available. Based on the information, if the number of trucks available in a company is fixed, the logistic manager can estimate the required routing cost from the tradeoff curve in Fig. 14.4. In contrast, if the manager is given a specified budget or routing cost, he or she can then determine the minimum number of internal trucks to be allocated so that the spending can be kept below the budget. For example, if the routing cost is to be kept below 5100, then the company must allocate at least 10 trucks for serving the task orders. However, if only 15 trucks are allocated by the company, then the incurred routing cost would be around 4900 to 5000, including the cost payment for outsourced companies.

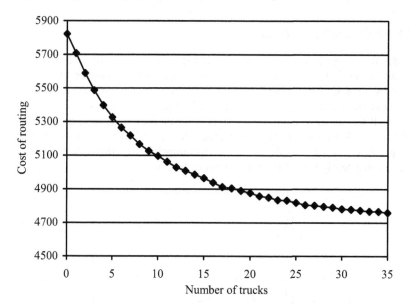

Fig. 14.4. The tradeoff graph between cost of routing and number of trucks.

Figure 14.5 shows the average progress ratio, pr, at each generation for the 12 test cases in the normal category. As shown in Fig. 14.5, the average pr starts from a value close to one, indicating the high probability of improvement to the solutions at the initial stage. As the evolution continues, the pr decreases to a small value, which means that the evolution is nearly converged since the possibility of finding new improved and nondominated solutions is low.

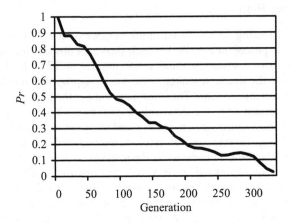

Fig. 14.5. The average *pr* at each generation for the 12 test cases in the normal category.

14.3.1.4 Utilization of Trucks

Besides the tradeoff curve, one interesting aspect to be investigated in TTVRP is the utilization of trucks, which is defined as the average number of tasks completed by a truck. A higher utilization means fewer trucks with smaller associated fixed cost are needed to perform the tasks. Figure 14.6 shows the average utilization of all test cases in the normal category based on the nondominated solutions at the initial (Initial) and final (Final) generation, respectively. Clearly, the utilization performance of TTVRP after the optimization by HMOEA has been improved consistently for a different number of trucks.

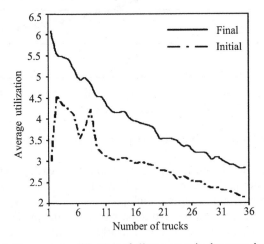

Fig. 14.6. The average utilization of all test cases in the normal category.

Figure 14.7 shows that the utilization of trucks for all the test cases in the normal category increases as the number of trailers is increased, which is plotted by taking the average utilization of every individuals in the final population served by the internal fleets. Besides the number of trucks employed, utilization performance in TTVRP is also correlated to the trailer allocation, e.g., the utilization is higher as the number of trailers increases, since abundant trailer resources help to reduce unnecessary traveling to farther TEPs as well as to eliminate unfeasibility caused by the trailer constraints in TTVRP. Obviously, such information is useful for the management to achieve a high utilization performance in TTVRP before arriving at the final routing plan.

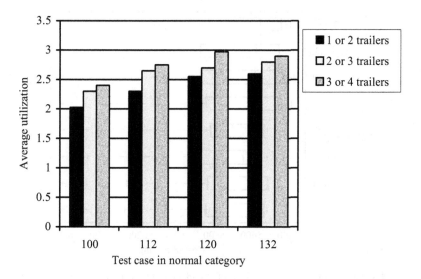

Fig. 14.7. The average utilization of all individuals in the final population.

14.3.2 Computation Results for TEPC and LTTC

The test cases in the TEPC and LTTC categories are designed to examine situations such as excessive or inadequate trailer resources. The following subsections study the extreme trailers allocation policy.

14.3.2.1 Scenario of Extreme Trailer Allocation

The resource of trailers is one of the key elements in TTVRP. In this subsection, the scenario of excessive and limited trailer resources is compared based on the test cases in TEPC (with 30 trailers) and LTTC (with 10 trailers) categories. Figure 14.8 shows the box plots of routing costs for the final nondominated solutions in different test cases of TEPC and LTTC categories. In the figure, 132_tep1 and 132_ltt1 represents the combined result for the test cases with only one TEP for TEPC and LTTC, respectively. As can be seen, the mean routing costs for test cases in TEPC are consistently lower than the cases in LTTC. When the number of trailers is abundant as in TEPC, a feasible solution can be found more easily as compared to LTTC, where resource of trailers is limited and the search for better solutions is restricted by the lack of trailers. The results show that the trailers and their distributions greatly affect the final routing performance. It is thus important to have enough trailers allocation at the initial of planning horizon, and a good routing policy should favor the choice that brings more trailers back to TEPs at the end of each planning horizon.

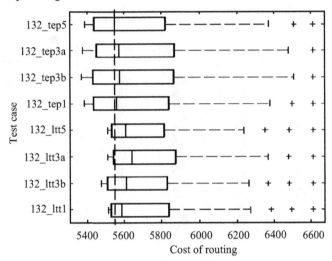

Fig. 14.8. The performance comparison of abundant TEPC with limited trailers in LTTC.

14.3.2.2 The Number and Location of TEPs

This subsection compares the routing performance among different test cases within each category of TEPC and LTTC. Figures 14.9 and 14.10 show the box plots of routing costs for the final nondominated solutions in different test cases of TEPC and LTTC, respectively. In Fig. 14.9, the mean value of test_132_tep5 is extended vertically and chosen as a reference since this test case has its trailer resources distributed uniformly to all the TEPs. It can be seen that the range of routing costs for the various test cases is rather closed to test_132_tep5. In addition, there is only minor difference in terms of the mean routing cost, except for the case of test_132_tep1e, where the trailers are allocated to only one TEP. Hence the location of TEP is not strategic for TTVRP. Similarly, the mean routing cost of test_132_ltt_1e is also inferior as compared to other test cases in the LTTC category, as shown in Fig. 14.10. The results suggest that the final destinations of trailers should be properly planned and allocated at suitable TEPs that support the routing for the next planning horizon.

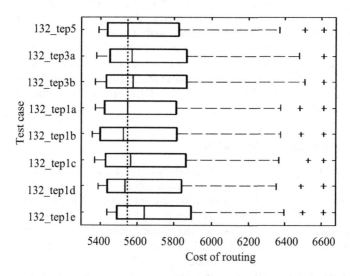

Fig. 14.9. The performance comparison of different test cases in the TEPC category.

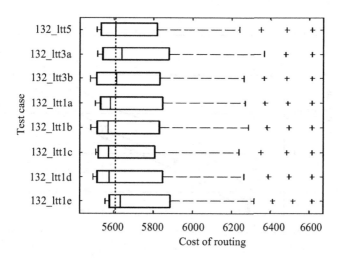

Fig. 14.10. The performance comparison of different test cases in the LTTC category.

14.3.3 Comparison Results

In this section, the performance of HMOEA is compared with two variants of evolutionary algorithms, i.e., MOEA with standard genetic operators as well as MOEA without hybridization of local search. The MOEA with standard genetic operators (STD_MOEA) include the commonly known cycle crossover (Oliver et al. 1987) and RAR mutation (Gendreau et al. 1999). The MOEA without hybridization of local search (NH_MOEA) employs the specialized genetic operators in HMOEA but excludes the local search heuristic. The experimental setups and parameter settings of STD_MOEA and NH_MOEA are similar to that of HMOEA as given in Table 14.5.

14.3.3.1 Average Routing Cost

To compare the quality of solutions produced by the algorithms, the average routing cost (*ARC*) of the nondominated solutions in the final population is calculated for various test cases with a different number of tasks as shown in Fig. 14.11. In the figure, the average value of *ARC* is plotted for each group of the test cases with an equal number of tasks in the normal category. As can be seen, the STD_MOEA that employs standard genetic operators incurs the highest *ARC* since its operators are not tailor-made for the TTVRP problem. According to the no-free-lunch theorem (Wolpert and Macready 1996), any optimization methods should be tailored to the problem domain for best performance. The results in Fig. 14.11 also illustrate that the HMOEA outperforms NH_MOEA and STD_MOEA consistently, which produces the lowest routing cost for all the test cases.

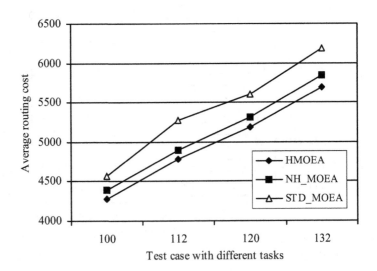

Fig. 14.11. The average routing cost for the normal category.

The average routing cost of the nondominated solutions in the final population for test cases in the categories of TEPC and LTTC is shown in Fig. 14.12 and Fig. 14.13, respectively, where a similar outstanding optimization performance for HMOEA is observed.

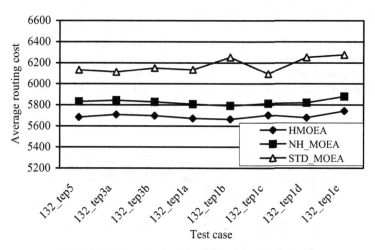

Fig. 14.12. The average routing cost for the TEPC category.

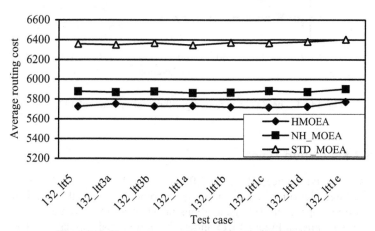

Fig. 14.13. The average routing cost for the LTTC category.

14.3.3.2 Ratio of Nondominated Individuals

In MO optimization, it is often desired to find as many as possible useful candidate solutions that are nondominated in a given population, which could be measured by the ratio of nondominated individuals (*RNI*) (Tan et al. 2001c). For a given population X, the *RNI* in percentage is formulated as

$$RNI(X)\% = \frac{\text{the number of } nondom\_indiv}{N} \times 100\%, \qquad (14.1)$$

where *nondom_indiv* is the nondominated individuals in population *X*, and *N* is the size of the population *X*. Without loss of generality, Fig. 14.14 shows the *RNI* for the three algorithms based on a randomly selected test case of 132_3_4. As can be seen, the *RNI* value of STD_MOEA is the lowest among the three algorithms. The evolution in STD-MOEA stopped at around 90 generations as no improvement was observed for 5 generations continuously. The results also show that the search performance of HMOEA for nondominated solutions is slightly better than that of NH_MOEA. Besides, the HMOEA also has the best average *RNI* of 1.89 as compared to the value of 1.71 and 0.44 for NH_MOEA and STD_MOEA, respectively.

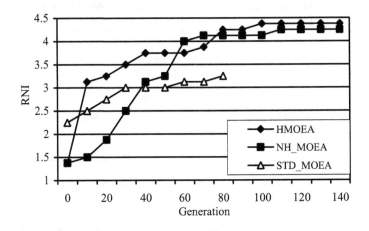

Fig. 14.14. The *RNI* of various algorithms for test case of 132_3_4.

14.3.3.3 Simulation Time

The computation time needed for the different algorithms is studied in this subsection. The three algorithms adopt the same stopping criteria in the simulation, i.e., the evolution stops after 1000 generations or when no improvement is found for the last 5 generations. Figure 14.15 shows the normalized simulation time for the three algorithms based on three randomly selected test cases from each category, e.g., test_132_3_4, test_132_tep5, and test_132_ltt5. As can be seen, the STD_MOEA requires the shortest time to converge or halt the evolution, although the optimization results obtained by the STD_MOEA are much inferior as compared to NH_MOEA and HMOEA. It is believed that the population in STD_MOEA has converged prematurely to a local Pareto front. The results also show that the computation time required by HMOEA is better than NH_MOEA for the normal and TEPC categories (which have abundant trailer resources where more feasible solutions exist) and is comparable to NH_MOEA for the LTTC category (which has fewer trailer resources with a smaller set of feasible solutions).

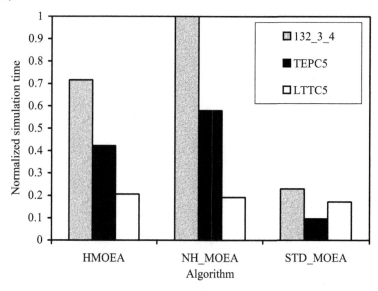

Fig. 14.15. The normalized simulation time for various algorithms.

14.4 Conclusions

A transportation problem for moving empty or laden containers for a logistic company has been studied, and a mathematical model for the truck and trailer vehicle routing problem (TTVRP) has been constructed in this chapter. The objective of the problem is to minimize the routing distance and the number of trucks required, subject to a number of constraints such as time windows and availability of trailers. To solve such a multiobjective and multimodal combinatorial optimization problem, the HMOEA presented in Chapter 13 has been applied here. It has been shown that the HMOEA is effective in finding a set of Pareto optimal routing solutions for TTVRP. Detailed studies have also been performed to extract important decision-making information from the MO optimization results. In particular, the relationships among different variables, such as the number of trucks and trailers, the trailer exchange points, and the utilization of trucks in the routing solutions, have been examined and analyzed.

Bibliography

Abbass HA (2002) The self-adaptive Pareto differential evolution algorithm. In: Proceedings of the 2002 Congress on Evolutionary Computation, vol 1, pp 831–836.

Abbass HA, Sarker R, Newton C (2001) PDE: A Pareto-frontier differential evolution approach for multiobjective optimization problems. In: Proceedings of the 2001 Congress on Evolutionary Computation, vol 2, pp 971–978.

Adeli H, Cheng NT (1994) Augmented Lagrangian genetic algorithm for structural optimization. Journal of Aerospace Engineering 7:104–118.

Alander JT (1992) On optimal population size of genetic algorithms. In: IEEE Proceedings on Computer Systems and Software Engineering, pp 65–70.

Alexandre HFD, Jõao ADV (2002) Multiobjective genetic algorithms applied to solve optimization problems. IEEE Transactions on Magnetic 38(2):1133–1136.

Allenson R (1992) Genetic algorithms with gender for multi-function optimization. Report No. EPCC-SS92-01, Edinburgh Parallel Computing Center, Edinburgh, Scotland.

Andrzej O, Stanislaw K (2000) A new constraint tournament selection method for multicriteria optimization using genetic algorithm. In: Proceedings of the 2000 Congress on Evolutionary Computation, pp 501–507.

Angeline PJ, Pollack JB (1993) Competitive environments evolve better solutions for complex tasks. In: Proceedings of the Fifth International Conference on Genetic Algorithms, pp 264–270.

Arabas J, Michalewicz Z, Mulawka J (1994) GAVaPS-A genetic algorithm with varying population size. In: Proceedings of the First Congress on Evolutionary Computation, vol 1, pp 73–74.

Bäck T (1996) Evolutionary Algorithms in Theory and Practice. Oxford University Press, NY.

Bagchi TP (1999) Multiobjective Scheduling by Genetic Algorithm. Kluwer Academic Publishers, Boston, MA.

Bard JF, Kontoravdis G, Yu G (2002) A branch-and-cut procedure for the vehicle routing problem with time windows. Transportation Science 36(2):250–269.

Beasley D, Bull DR, Martin RR (1993) A sequential niche technique for multimodal function optimization. Journal of Evolutionary Computation 1(2):101–125.

Beasley JE, Christofides N (1997) Vehicle routing with a sparse feasibility graph. European Journal of Operational Research 98(3):499–511.

Ben P, Rankin RC, Cumming A, Fogarty TC (1998) Timetabling the classes of an entire university with an evolutionary algorithm. In: A.E. Eiben, T. Back, M. Schoenauer, and H. Schwefel (eds) Parallel Problem Solving from Nature V, Lecture Notes in Computer Science No. 1498. Springer-Verlag, Amsterdam, Netherlands.

Bent R, Van Hentenryck P (2001) A two-stage hybrid local search for the vehicle routing problem with time windows. Technical Report CS-01-06, Computer Science Department, Brown University, RI.

Bentley PJ, Wakefield JP (1997) Finding acceptable solutions in the Pareto-optimal range using multiobjective genetic algorithms. In: Proceedings of the Second Online World Conference on Soft Computing in Engineering Design and Manufacturing (WSC2).

Berger J, Barkaoui M, Bräysy O (2001) A parallel hybrid genetic algorithm for the vehicle routing problem with time windows. Working Paper, Defense Research Establishment Valcartier, Canada.

Bertsimas D, Simchi-Levi D (1993) A new generation of vehicle routing research: Robust algorithms, addressing uncertainty. Operations Research 44(2):286–304.

Box GE (1998) Scientific learning. In: Abrahem B (ed) Quality Improvement Through Statistical Methods. Birkhäuser, Boston, pp 3–12.

Borges CCH, Barbosa HJC (2000) A non-generational genetic algorithm for multiobjective optimization. In: Proceedings of the 2000 Congress on Evolutionary Computation, pp 172–179.

Borghesani C, Chait Y, Yaniv O (1995) Quantitative feedback theory toolbox user manual. The Math Work Inc.

Branke J (1999) Memory enhanced evolutionary algorithms for changing optimization problems. In: Proceedings of the 1999 Congress on Evolutionary Computation, vol 3, pp 1875–1882.

Bräysy O(2003) A reactive variable neighborhood search algorithm for the vehicle routing problem with time windows. INFORMS Journal on Computing 15(4).

Bräysy O, Gendreau M (2001a) Genetic algorithms for the vehicle routing problem with time windows. SINTEF Applied Mathematics, Internal Report STF42 A01021, Department of Optimisation, Oslo, Norway.

Bräysy O, Gendreau M (2001b) Tabu search heuristics for the vehicle routing problem with time windows. SINTEF Applied Mathematics, Internal Report STF42 A01022, Department of Optimisation, Oslo, Norway.

Breedam AV (2001) Comparing descent heuristic and metaheuristic for the vehicle routing problem. Computer & Operations Research 28(4):289–315.

Bryant GF, Halikias GD (1995) Optimal loop-shaping for systems with large parameter uncertainty via linear programming. International Journal in Control 62(3):557–568.

Burke EK, Newall JP (1999) A multi-stage evolutionary algorithm for the timetable problem. IEEE Transactions on Evolutionary Computation 3(1):63–74.

Cantú-Paz E (1998) A survey of parallel genetic algorithms. Calculateurs Paralleles, Reseaux et Systems Repartis 10(2):141–171.

Caseau Y, Laburthe F (1999) Heuristics for large constrained vehicle routing problems. Journal of Heuristics 5(3):281–303.

Chait Y (1997) QFT loop-shaping and minimization of the high-frequency gain via convex optimization. In: Proceedings of Symposium on Quantitative Feedback Theory and Other Frequency Domain Method and Applications. Glasgow, Scotland, pp 13–28.

Chambers JM, Cleveland WS, Kleiner B, Turkey PA (1983) Graphical Methods for Data Analysis. Wadsworth & Brooks/Cole, Pacific Grover, CA.

Charnes A, Cooper WW (1961) Management Models and Industrial Applications of Linear Programming, vol 1. John Wiley & Sons, NY.

Chavalitwongse W, Kim D, Pardalos PM (2003) GRASP with a new local search scheme for vehicle routing problems with time windows. Journal of Combinatorial Optimization 7(2):179–207.

Chen CL, Neppalli RV, Aljabel N (1996) Genetic algorithms applied to the continuous flowshop problem. Computers and Industrial Engineering 30(4):919–929.

Chen SJ, Hwang CL, Hwang FP (1992) Fuzzy Multiple Attribute Decision Making. Springer-Verlag, p 265.

Chen WH, Balance DJ (1998) QFT design for uncertain nonminimum phase and unstable plants. In: Proceedings of the American Control Conference, vol 4, pp 2486–2590.

Chen WH, Balance DJ, Li Y (1998) Automatic loop-shaping in QFT using genetic algorithms. In: Proceedings of the Third Asia-Pacific Conference on Control & Measurement, pp 63–67.

Chen WH, Ballance DJ, Feng W, Li Y (1999) Genetic algorithm enabled computer-automated design of QFT control systems. In: IEEE International Conference on Control Applications and System Design, pp 492–497.

Chiang RY, Safonov MG (1992) Robust Control Toolbox. The Mathworks, Inc.

Chiang WC, Russel RA (1996) Simulated annealing metaheuristic for the vehicle routing problem with time windows. Annals of Operations Research, 63:3–27.

Chiang WC, Russel RA (1997) A reactive tabu search metaheuristics for the vehicle routing problem with time windows. INFORMS Journal on Computing 9:417–430.

Chipperfield AJ, Fleming PJ (1995) Gas turbine engine controller design using multiobjective genetic algorithms. In: Zalzala AMS (ed) Proceedings of the First IEE/IEEE International Conference on Genetic Algorithms in Engineering Systems: Innovations and Applications, pp 214–219.

Chipperfield AJ, Fleming PJ (1996) Multiobjective gas turbine engine controller design using genetic algorithms. IEEE Transactions on Industrial Electronics 43(5):583–587.

Chiu TC, Kempf C, Yao WH, Tomizuka M (1993) Compensation for repeatable and nonrepeatable tracking errors in disk file systems. In: JSME Conf. on Advanced Mechatronics, Tokyo, Japan.

Christofides N, Mingozzi A, Toth P (1981) Exact algorithms for the vehicle routing problem based on spanning tree and shortest path relaxations. Math. Programming 20(3):255–282.

Cingoski V, Kowata N, Kaneda K, Yamashita H (1997) Inverse shape optimization of a pole of rotating machines using dynamically adjustable genetic algorithms. IEEE Transactions on Magnetics 35:1686–1689.

Coello Coello CA (1996) An empirical study of evolutionary techniques for multiobjective optimization in engineering design. Ph.D. thesis, Department of Computer Science, Tulane University, New Orleans, LA.

Coello Coello CA (1998) An updated survey of GA-based multiobjective optimization techniques. Report No. Lania-RD-98-08, Laboratorio Nacional de Informatica Avanzada (LANIA), Xalapa, Veracruz, Mexico.

Coello Coello CA, Pulido GT (2001) A micro-genetic algorithm for multiobjective optimization. In: Zitzler E, Deb K, Thiele L, Coello Coello CA, Corne D (eds) First International Conference on Evolutionary Multi-Criterion Optimization, Lecture Notes in Computer Science. Springer-Verlag, pp 126–140.

Coello Coello CA, Cortés NC (2002) An approach to solve multiobjective optimization problems based on an artificial immune system. In: Timmis J, Bentley PJ (eds) First International Conference on Artificial Immune Systems (ICARIS'2002). University of Kent at Canterbury, Inglaterra, pp 212–221.

Coello Coello CA, Lechuga MS (2002) MOPSO: A proposal for multiple objective particle swarm optimization. In: Proceedings of the 2002 Congress on Evolutionary Computation, vol 2, pp 1051–1056.

Coello Coello CA, Becerra RL (2003) Evolutionary multiobjective optimization using a cultural algorithm. In: 2003 IEEE Swarm Intelligence Symposium Proceedings. Indianapolis, IN, pp 6–13.

Collard P, Escazut C (1995) Genetic operators in a dual genetic algorithm. In: International Conference on Tools and Artificial Intelligence pp 12–19.

Cook W, Rich JL (1999) A parallel cutting plan algorithm for the vehicle routing problem with time windows. Technical Report, Computational and Applied Mathematics Department, Rice University, Houston, TX.

Cordeau JF, Gendreau M, Laporte G, Potvin JY, Semet F (2002) A guide to vehicle routing heuristics. Journal of the Operational Research Society 53(5):512–522.

Cordeau JF, Laporte G, Mercier A (2001) A unified tabu search heuristic for vehicle routing problems with time windows. Journal of the Operational Research Society 52(8):928–936.

Cordone R, Wolfler-Calvo R (2001) A heuristic for the vehicle routing problem with time windows. Journal of Heuristics 7(2):107–129.

Corne DW, Knowles JD, Oates MJ (2000) The Pareto envelope-based selection algorithm for multiobjective optimization. In: Schoenauer M, Deb K, Rudolph G, Yao X, Lutton E, Merelo JJ, Schwefel HP (eds) Proceedings of the Parallel Problem Solving from Nature VI Conference. Springer, pp 839–848.

Corne DW, Jerram NR, Knowles JD, Oates MJ (2001) PESA-II: Region-based selection in evolutionary multiobjective optimization. In: Spector L, Goodman E, Wu A, Langdon WB, Voigt HM, Gen M, Sen S, Dorigo M, Pezeshk S, Garzon MH, Burke E (eds) Proceedings of the Genetic and Evolutionary Computation Conference (GECCO-2001). Morgan Kaufmann Publishers, pp 283–290.

Corne DW, Deb K, Fleming PJ, Knowles JD (2003) The good of the many outweighs the good of the one: Evolutionary multiobjective optimization. The Newsletter of the IEEE Neural Networks Society 1(1):9–13.

Cvetkovic D, Parmee IC (1998) Evolutionary design and multiobjective optimization. In: The Sixth European Congress on Intelligent Techniques and Soft Computing (EUFIT'98). Aachen, Germany, pp 397–401.

Cvetkovic D, Parmee IC (1999) Genetic algorithm-based multiobjective optimization and conceptual engineering design. In: Proceedings of the 1999 Congress on Evolutionary Computation, vol 1, pp 29–36.

Cvetkovic D, Parmee IC (2002) Preferences and their application in evolutionary multiobjective optimization. IEEE Transactions on Evolutionary Computation 6(1):42–57.

Czech ZJ, Czarnas P (2002) A parallel simulated annealing for the vehicle routing problem with time windows. In: Proceedings of the 10th Euromicro Workshop on Parallel, Distributed and Network-based Processing. Canary Islands, Spain, pp 376–383.

D'Azzo, Houpis H (1995) Linear Control System Analysis and Design: Conventional and Modern, 4th edition. McGraw-Hill, NY.

Dahleh MA, Diaz-Bobillo I (1995) Control of Uncertain Systems: A Linear Programming Approach. Prentice-Hall, Englewood Cliffs, NJ.

David AVV, and Gary BL (2000) Multiobjective evolutionary algorithms: Analyzing state of the art. Journal of Evolutionary Computation 8(2):125–147.

Davidor Y (1991) Epistasis Variance: A Viewpoint on GA-hardness. Morgan Kaufmann, San Mateo, CA, pp 23–35.

De Backer B, Furnon V, Kilby P, Prosser P, Shaw P (2002) Solving vehicle routing problems using constraint programming and metaheuristics. Journal of Heuristics 6(4):501–523.

De Jong KA (1975) Analysis of the behavior of a class of genetic adaptive systems. Ph.D thesis, Department of Computer and Communication Sciences, University of Michigan, Ann Arbor, MI.

Deb K (1999a) Construction of test problems for multiobjective optimization. In: Proceedings of the Genetic and Evolutionary Computation Conference (GECCO-99), vol 1, pp 164–171.

Deb K (1999b) Multiobjective genetic algorithms: Problem difficulties and construction of test problem. Evolutionary Computation 7(3):205–230.

Deb K (2001) Multiobjective Optimization Using Evolutionary Algorithms. John Wiley & Sons, NY.

Deb K, Goldberg DE (1989) An investigation on niche and species formation in genetic function optimization. In: Schaffer JD (ed) Proceedings of the Third International Conference on Genetic Algorithms. Morgan Kaufmann, San Mateo, CA, pp 42–50.

Deb K, Pratap A, Agarwal S, Meyarivan T (2002a) A fast and elitist multiobjective genetic algorithm: NSGA-II. IEEE Transactions on Evolutionary Computation 6(2):182–197.

Deb K, Thiele L, Laumanns M, Zitzler Z (2002b) Scalable multiobjective optimization test problems. In: Proceedings of the 2002 Congress on Evolutionary Computation, pp 825–830.

Dengiz B, Altiparmak F, Smith AE (1997) Local search genetic algorithm for optimal design of reliable networks. IEEE Transactions on Evolutionary Computation 1(3):179–188.

Desrochers M, Desrosiers J, Solomon M (1992) A new optimization algorithm for the vehicle routing problem with time windows. Operational Research 40(2):342–354.

Desrosier J, Dumas Y, Solomon M, Soumis F (1995) Time constraint routing and scheduling. In: Ball M (ed) Handbooks in Operations Research and Management Science 8: Network Routing. Elsevier Science Publishers, Amsterdam, pp 35–139.

Devore J, Peck R (1997) Statistics: The Exploration and Analysis of Data. Duxbury Press, London.

Diggelen F, Glover KA (1992) Hadamard weighted loop shaping design procedure. In: Proceedings of the 31st Conference on Decision and Control, pp 2193–2198.

Dorndorf U, Pesch E (1995) Evaluation based learning in a jobshop scheduling environment. Computers and Operations Research 22:25–40.

Doyle JC, Stein G (1981) Multivariable feedback design: Concepts for a classical/modern synthesis. IEEE Transactions on Automatic Control 26:4–16.

Doyle JC, Francis B, Tannenbaum A (1992) Feedback Control Theory. Macmillan Publishing Company, NY.

Dullaert W, Janssens GK, Sörensen K, Vernimmen B (2002) New heuristics for the fleet size and mix vehicle routing problem with time windows. Journal of the Operational Research Society 53(11):1232–1238.

Esquivel S, Ferrero S, Gallard R, Salto C, Alfonso H, Schütz M (2002) Enhanced evolutionary algorithms for single and multiobjective optimization in the job scheduling problem. Knowledge-Based Systems 15(1–2):13–25.

Everson RM, Fieldsend JE, Singh S (2002) Full elite sets for multiobjective optimization. In: Parmee IC (ed) Proceedings of the Fifth International Conference on Adaptive Computing Design and Manufacture (ACDM 2002). Springer-Verlag, pp 343–354.

Fisher ML (1995) Vehicle routing. In: Ball M (ed) Handbooks in Operations Research and Management Science 8: Network Routing. Elsevier Science Publishers, Amsterdam, pp 1–33.

Fleming PJ, Chipperfield AJ (1998a) Evolutionary algorithms for multiple criteria decision making in control. In: IFAC Workshop on Nonsmooth and Discontinuous Problems of Control and Optimization NDPCO 98, pp 17–20.

Fleming PJ, Chipperfield AJ (1998b) Genetic algorithms and multiobjective optimization in control applications. In: Proceedings Symposium on Intelligent Systems in Control and Measurement. Miskolc, Hungary.

Fonseca CM (1995) Multiobjective genetic algorithms with application to control engineering problems. Ph.D. thesis, Dept. Automatic Control and Systems Eng., University of Sheffield, Sheffield, UK.

Fonseca CM, Fleming PJ (1993) Genetic algorithm for multiobjective optimization: Formulation, discussion and generalization. In: Forrest S (ed) Proceeding of the Fifth International Conference on Genetic Algorithms. Morgan Kaufmann, San Mateo, CA, pp 416–423.

Fonseca CM, Fleming PJ (1994) Multiobjective optimal controller design with genetic algorithms. In: Proceedings on IEE Control, pp 745–749.

Fonseca CM, Fleming PJ (1995a) An overview of evolutionary algorithms in multiobjective optimization. Journal of Evolutionary Computation 3(1):1–16.

Fonseca CM, Fleming PJ (1995b) Multiobjective genetic algorithm made easy: Selection, sharing and mating restriction. In: International Conference on Genetic Algorithm in Engineering Systems: Innovations and Application. UK, pp 12–14.

Fonseca CM, Fleming PJ (1997) Multiobjective optimization. In: Bäck T, Fogel D, Michalewicz Z (eds) Handbook of Evolutionary Computation. Oxford University Press, England, vol 1, pp C4.5:1–C4.5:9.

Fonseca CM, Fleming PJ (1998a) Multiobjective optimization and multiple constraint handling with evolutionary algorithms—part I: A unified formulation. IEEE Transactions on System, Man, and Cybernetics—Part A: Systems and Humans 28(1):26–37.

Fonseca CM, Fleming PJ (1998b) Multiobjective optimization and multiple constraint handling with evolutionary algorithms—part II: Application example. IEEE Transactions on System, Man, and Cybernetics—Part A: Systems and Humans 28(1):38–47.

Forrest S, Javornik B, Smith RE, Perelson AS (1993) Using genetic algorithms to explore pattern recognition in the immune system. Journal of Evolutionary Computation 1(3):191–211.

Fourman MP (1985) Compaction of symbolic layout using genetic algorithms. In: Proceedings of the First International Conference on Genetic Algorithms: Genetic Algorithms and Their Applications. Lawrence Erlbaum, pp 141–153.

Franklin GF, Powell JD, Workman ML (1998) Digital Control of Dynamic Systems, 3rd edition. Addison-Wesley, Reading, MA.

Fujita K, Hirokawa N, Akagi S, Kitamura S, Yokohata H (1998) Multiobjective design automotive engine using genetic algorithm. In: Proceedings of 1998 ASME Design Engineering Technical Conferences. Atlanta, GA, pp 1–11.

Gehring H, Homberger J (2001) A parallel two phase metaheuristic for routing problems with time windows. Asia-Pacific Journal of Operation Research 18(1):35–47.

Gehring H, Homberger J (2002) Parallelization of a two-phase metaheuristic for routing problems with time windows. Journal of Heuristics 3(8):251–276.

Gendreau M, Laporte G, Potvin JY (1999) Metaheuristics for the vehicle routing problem. University of Montreal, Canada, Les Cahiers du GERAD G-98-52.

Gezdur A, Türkay M (2002) MILP solution to the vehicle routing problem with time windows and discrete vehicle capacities. In: XXIII National Operations Research and Industrial Engineering Congress. Istanbul, Turkey.

Glover K, Doyle JC (1988) State-space formulae for all stabilizing controllers that satisfy an H_∞ norm bound and relations to risk sensitivity. Sys. and Contr. Letters 11:169–172.

Goh TB (1999) Development of a dual actuator controller in hard disk drives. Master thesis, Department of Electrical Engineering, National University of Singapore.

Goh TB, Li ZM, Chen BM, Lee TH, Huang T (1999) Design and implementation of a hard disk drive servo system using robust and perfect tracking approach. In: Proc. 31st CDC. Phoenix, AZ, pp 5247–5252.

Goh TB, Li ZM, Chen BM, Lee TH, Huang T (2001) Design and implementation of a hard disk drive servo system using robust and perfect tracking approach. IEEE Trans. on Cont. Syst. Tech 9(2):221–233.

Goldberg DE (1989a) Genetic Algorithms in Search, Optimization, and Machine Learning. Addison-Wesley, Reading, MA.

Goldberg DE (1989b) Sizing populations for serial and parallel genetic algorithms. In Proceedings of the Third International Conference on Genetic Algorithms. Morgan Kaufmann, San Mateo, CA, pp 70–79.

Goldberg DE, Lingle R (1985) Alleles, loci and the traveling salesman problem. In: The First International Conference on Genetic Algorithms. Lawrence Erlbaum, Hillsdale, NJ, pp. 154–159.

Goldberg DE, Richardson J (1987) Genetic algorithms with sharing for multi-modal function optimization. In: Proceedings of the 2nd International Conference on Genetic Algorithms, pp. 41–49.

Golden BL, Assad AA (1988) Vehicle Routing: Methods and Studies. North-Holland, Amsterdam, Netherlands.

Greenwood GW, Hu X, D'Ambrosio JG (1996) Fitness functions for multiple objective optimization problems: Combining preferences with Pareto rankings. In: Foundations of Genetic Algorithms 4 (FOGA-96). Morgan Kaufmann, San Mateo, pp 437–455.

Grefenstette JJ (1984) GENESIS: A system for using genetic search procedures. In: Procddings of the Conference on Intelligent Systems and Machines, pp 161–165.

Grefenstette JJ (1986) Optimization of control parameters for genetic algorithms. IEEE Transactions on Systems, Man and Cybernetics 16(1):122–128.

Grefenstette JJ, Gopal R, Rosmaita B, Van Gucht D (1985) Genetic algorithms for the traveling salesman problem. In: The First International Conference on Genetic Algorithms and Their Applications, pp 160–168.

Guan KX, MacCallum KJ (1996) Adopting a minimum commitment principle for computer aided geometric design systems. In: Gero JS, Sudweeks F (eds) Artificial Intelligence in Design '96. Kluwer Academic Publishers, pp 623–639.

Hagiwara M (1993) Pseudo-hill climbing genetic algorithm (PHGA) for function optimization. In: Proceedings of International Joint Conference on Neural Networks, vol 1, pp 713–716.

Hajela P, Lin CY (1992) Genetic search strategies in multicriterion optimal design. Journal of Structural Optimization 4:99–107.

Hanselmann H, Engelke A (1988) LQG-control of a highly resonant disk drive head positioning actuator. IEEE Trans. on Ind. Elecs. 35(1):100–104.

Harik G (1995) Finding multimodal solutions using restricted tournament selection. In: Eshelman LJ (ed) Proceedings of the 6th International Conference on Genetic Algorithms. Morgan Kaufmann, San Mateo, CA, pp 24–31.

Hirata M, Liu KZ, Mita T, Yamaguchi T (1992) Head positioning control of a hard disk drive using H_∞ theory. In: Proc. 31st CDC, vol 1, pp 2460–2461.

Hirata M, Atsumi T, Murase A, Nonami K (1999) Following control of a hard disk drive by using sampled-data H_∞ control. In: Proc. IEEE Int. Conf. on Cont. Appl., Hawaii, pp 182–186.

Hiroyasu T, Miki M, Watanabe S (1999) Distributed genetic algorithm with a new sharing approach in multiobjective optimization problems. In: Proceedings of the 1999 Congress on Evolutionary Computation, vol 1, pp 69–76.

Ho WK, Chin HJ, Lim A (2001) A hybrid search algorithm for the vehicle routing problem with time windows. International Journal on Artificial Intelligence Tools 10:431–449.

Hoagland AS (1991) Digital Magnetic Recording. Wiley, NY.

Holland JH (1975) Adaptation in Natural and Artificial Systems. University of Michigan Press, Ann Arbor, MI.

Homberger J, Gehring H (1999) Two evolutionary metaheuristic for the vehicle routing problem with time windows. INFOR 37(1):297–318.

Horn J (1997) Multicriterion decision making. In: Bäck T, Fogel D, Michalewicz Z (eds) Handbook of Evolutionary Computation. Oxford University Press, Oxford, vol 1, pp F1.9:1–F1.9:15.

Horn J, Nafpliotis N (1993) Multiobjective optimization using the niched Pareto genetic algorithm. Report No. 930005. Illinois Genetic Algorithms Laboraatory (IlliGAL), University of Illinois at Urbana–Champaign.

Horn J, Nafpliotis N, Goldberg DE (1994) A niched Pareto genetic algorithm for multiobjective optimization. In: Proceedings of the 1994 Congress on Evolutionary Computation, vol 1, pp 82–87.

Horowitz I (1982) Quantitative feedback theory. In: IEE Proceedings, Pt. D, 129(6):215–226.

Horowitz I (1992) Quantitative feedback design theory (QFT). QFT Publications, Colorado, vol 1.

Horowitz I, Sidi M (1978) Optimum synthesis of nonminimum-phase feedback systems with plant uncertainties. International Journal of Control 27:361–386.

Houck CR, Joines JA, Kay MG (1995) A genetic algorithm for function optimization: A Matlab implementation. NCSU-IE Technical Report 9509, North Carolina State University.

Houpis CH (1993) Quantitative feedback theory (QFT) technique. In: Levine WS (ed) The Control Handbook. CRC Press and IEEE Press, pp 701–717.

Houpis CH, Rasmussen SJ (1999) Quantitative Feedback Theory: Fundamentals and Applications. Marcel Dekker, Inc., NY.

Hwang CL, Masud ASM (1979) Multiple Objective Decision Making—Methods and Applications. Springer-Verlag, NY.

Ijiri Y (1965) Management goals and accounting for control. North-Holland, Amsterdan, Netherlands.

Ioannou G, Kritikos M, Prastacos G (2001) A greedy look ahead heuristic for the vehicle routing problem with time windows. Journal of the Operational Research Society 52(5):523–537.

Ishibashi H, Aguirre H, Tanaka K, Sugimura T (2000) Multiobjective optimization with improved genetic algorithm. In: IEEE International Conference on Systems, Man, and Cybernetics (SMC2000). Nashville, TN, pp 3852–3857.

Jakob WM, Gorges-Schleuter, Blume C (1992) Application of genetic algorithms to task planning and learning. In: Männer R, Nanderick B (eds) Parallel Problem Solving from Nature, the 2nd Workshop, Lecture Notes in Computer Science. North-Holland Publishing Company, Amsterdam, pp 291–300.

Jaszkiewicz A (1998) Genetic local search for multiple objective combinatorial optimization. Report No. RA-014/98. Institute of Computing Science, Poznan University of Technology.

Jaszkiewicz A (2001) Multiple objective metaheuristic algorithms for combinatorial optimization. Habilitation thesis 360. Poznań University of Technology, Poznan,

Jin Y, Okabe T, Sendhoff B (2001) Dynamic weighted aggregation for evolutionary multiobjective optimization: Why does it work and how? In: Spector L, Goodman E, Wu A, Langdon WB, Voigt HM, Gen M, Sen S, Dorigo M, Pezeshk S, Garzon MH, Burke E (eds) Proceedings of the Genetic and Evolutionary Computation Conference (GECCO-2001). Morgan Kaufmann Publishers, San Mateo, CA, pp 1042–1049.

Joos HD, Finsterwalder R (1999) Multiobjective design assessment and control law synthesis tuning for flight control development. In: IEEE International Conference on Control Application and System Design. Hawaii, pp 433–438.

Jozefowiez N, Semet F, Talbi E (2002) Parallel and hybrid models for multiobjective optimization: Application to the vehicle routing problem. In: Parallel Problem Solving from Nature, Lecture Notes in Computer Science. Springer-Verlag, NY, pp 271–282.

Jung S, Moon BR (2002) A hybrid genetic algorithm for the vehicle routing problem with time windows. In: The Genetic and Evolutionary Computation Conference. Morgan Kaufmann Publishers, San Mateo, CA, pp 1309–1316.

Jutler H (1967) Liniejnaja modiel z nieskolkimi celevymi funkcjami (linear model with several objective functions). Ekonomika i matematiceckije Metody 3 (in Polish), pp 397–406.

Kadrovach BA, Zydallis JB, Lamont GB (2002) Use of Mendelian pressure in a multiobjective genetic algorithm. In: Proceedings of the 2002 Congress on Evolutionary Computation, vol 1, pp 962–967.

Kallehauge B, Larsen J, Madsen OBG (2001) Lagrangean duality applied on vehicle routing with time windows. Technical Report IMM-TR-2001-9. IMM, Technical University of Denmark.

Keeney RL, Raiffa H (1976) Decisions with Multiple Objectives: Preferences and Value Tradeoffs. Wiley, NY.

Keerativuttiumrong N, Chaiyaratana N, Varavithya V (2002) Multiobjective cooperative coevolutionary genetic algorithm. In: Parallel Problem Solving from Nature—PPSN VII, Lecture Notes in Computer Science No. 2439. Springer-Verlag, NY, pp 288–297.

Khan JA, Sait SM, Minhas MR (2002) Fuzzy bialess simulated evolution for multiobjective VLSI placement. In: Proceedings of the 2002 Congress on Evolutionary Computation, vol 2, pp 1642–1647.

Khan N, Goldberg DE, Pelikan M (2002) Multiobjective Bayesian optimization algorithm. In: Proceedings of the Genetic and Evolutionary Computation Conference (GECCO'2002). Morgan Kaufmann Publishers, San Mateo, CA, pp 684.

Khor EF, Tan KC, Wong ML, Lee TH (2000) Evolutionary algorithm with dynamic population size for multiobjective optimization. In: The Third Asia Conference on Simulated Evolution and Learning (SEAL2000), pp 2768–2772.

Khor EF, Tan KC, Lee TH (2001a) Multiobjective evolutionary optimization with non-stationary search space. In: Proceedings of the 2001 Congress on Evolutionary Computation. Seoul, Korea, pp 527–535.

Khor EF, Tan KC, Lee TH (2001b) Tabu-based exploratory evolutionary algorithm for effective multiobjective optimization. In: The First Conference on Evolutionary Multi-Criterion Optimization (EMO'01), pp 344–358.

Kilby PJ, Prosser P, Shaw P (1999) Guided local search for the vehicle routing problem with time windows. In: Meta Heuristics: Advances and Trends in Local Search Paradigms for Optimization. Kluwer Academic Publishers, pp 473–486.

Kilby PJ, Prosser P, Shaw P (2000) A comparison of traditional and constraint-based heuristic methods on vehicle routing problems with side constraints. Journal of Constraints 5(4):389–414.

Kita H, Yabumoto Y, Mori N, Nishikawa Y (1996) Multiobjective optimization by means of the thermodynamical genetic algorithm. In: Voigt HM (ed) The 4th International Conference on Parallel Problem Solving from Nature. Springer, NY, pp 504–512.

Kiyota T, Tsuji Y, Kondo E (2003) Unsatisfying functions and multiobjective fuzzy satisficing design using genetic algorithms. IEEE Transactions on Systems, Man, and Cybernetics—Part B 33(6):889–897.

Knowles JD, Corne DW (1999) The Pareto archived evolution strategy: A new baseline algorithm for multiobjective optimization. In: Proceedings of the 1999 Congress on Evolutionary Computation, pp 98–105.

Knowles JD, Corne DW (2000a) Approximating the nondominated front using Pareto archived evolutionary strategy. Evolutionary Computation 8(2):149–172.

Knowles JD, Corne DW (2000b) M-PAES: A memetic algorithm for multiobjective optimization. In: Proceedings of the 2000 Congress on Evolutionary Computation, pp 325–333.

Knowles JD, Corne DW (2003) Properties of an adaptive archiving algorithm for storing nondominated vectors. IEEE Transactions on Evolutionary Computation 7(2):100–116.

Kohl N, Desrosiers J, Madsen OBG, Solomon MM, Soumis F (1999) 2 path cuts for the vehicle routing problem with time windows. Transportation Science 33(1):101–116.

Kursawe F (1990) A variant of evolution strategies for vector optimization. In: Proceedings of the First Conference on Parallel Problem Solving from Nature, pp 193–197.

Lahanas M, Baltas D, Zamboglou N (2003) A hybrid evolutionary algorithm for multiobjective anatomy-based dose optimization in high-dose-rate brachytherapy. Physics in Medicine and Biology 48:399–415.

Laporte G (1992) The vehicle routing problem: An overview of exact and approximate algorithms. European Journal of Operational Research 59(3):345–358.

Laporte G, Gendreau M, Potvin JY, Semet F (2000) Classical and modern heuristics for the vehicle routing problem. International Transaction in Operational Research 7:285–300.

Lau HC, Lim YF, Liu QZ (2001) Diversification of search neighborhood via constraint-based local search and its applications to VRPTW. In: The Third International Workshop on Integration of AI and OR Techniques (CP-AI-OR). Kent, UK, pp 1–15.

Lau HC, Sim M, Teo KM (2003) Vehicle routing problem with time windows and a limited number of vehicles. European Journal of Operational Research 148(3):559–569.

Laumanns M, Rudolph G, Schwefel HP (1998) A spatial predator–prey approach to multiobjective optimization: A preliminary study. In: Eiben AE, Schoenauer M, Schewefel HP (eds) Parallel Problem Solving From Nature—PPSN V. Springer-Verlag, Holland, pp 241–249.

Lee LH, Tan KC, Ou K, and Chew YH (2003) Vehicle capacity planning system (VCPS): A case study on vehicle routing problem with time windows. IEEE Transactions on Systems, Man and Cybernetics—Part A (Systems and Humans) 33(2):169–178.

Li H, Lim A (2002) Local search with annealing-like restarts to solve the vehicle routing problem with time windows. In: ACM Symposium on Applied Computing (SAC 2002), pp 560–565.

Li X (2003) A real-coded predator–prey genetic algorithm for multiobjective optimization. In: Fonseca CM, Fleming PJ, Zitzler E, Deb K, Thiele L (eds) Evolutionary Multi-Criterion Optimization: The Second International Conference (EMO2003), Lecture Notes in Computer Science 2632. Springer, pp 207–221.

Li Y, Tomizuka M (1999) Two-degree-of-freedom control with robust feedback control for hard disk servo systems. IEEE/ASME Trans. on Machatronics 4(1):17–24.

Li Y, Tan KC, Ng KC, Murray-Smith DJ (1995) Performance-based linear control system design by genetic algorithm with simulated annealing. In: Proceedings of the 34th Conference on Decision and Control. New Orleans, LA, pp 731–736.

Li Y, Tan KC, Marionneau C (1996) Direct design of linear control systems from plant I/O data using parallel evolutionary algorithms. In: International Conference on Control'96, Special Session on Evolutionary Algorithms for Control Engineering. University of Exeter, UK, pp 680–686.

Limebeer DJN (1991) The specification and purpose of a controller design case study. In: Proceedings of the 30th Conference on Decision and Control. Brighton, England, pp 1579–1580.

Limebeer DJ, Kasenally EM, Perkins JD (1993) On the design of robust two degree of freedom controllers. Automatica: The Journal of IFAC 29(1):157–168.

Lin S (1965) Computer solutions for traveling salesman problem. Bell System Technical Journal 44:2245–2269.

Liong SY, Khu ST, Chan WT (1998) Novel application of genetic algorithm and neural network in water resources: Development of Pareto front. In: The Eleventh Congress of the IAHR-APD, pp 185–194.

Lis J, Eiben AE (1997) A multi-sexual genetic algorithm for multiobjective optimization. In: Proceedings of the 1997 Congress on Evolutionary Computation, pp 59–64.

Liu TH, Mills KJ (1998) Robotic trajectory control system design for multiple simultaneous specifications: Theory and experimentation. Transactions on ASME 120:520–523.

Liu Y, Yao X, et al. (2001) Scaling up fast evolutionary programming with cooperative coevolution. In: Proceedings of the 2001 Congress on Evolutionary Computation, vol 2, pp 1101–1108.

Lohn JD, Kraus WF, Haith GL (2002) Comparing a coevolutionary genetic algorithm for multiobjective optimization. In: Proceedings of the 2002 Congress on Evolutionary Computation, vol 2, pp 1157–1162.

Louis SJ, Yin X, Yuan ZY (1999) Multiple vehicle routing with time windows using genetic algorithms. In: Proceedings of the 1999 Congress on Evolutionary Computation, pp 1804–1808.

Lu H, Yen GG (2002a) Rank-density based multiobjective genetic algorithm. In: Proceedings of the 2002 Congress on Evolutionary Computation, vol 1, pp 944–949.

Lu H, Yen GG (2002b) Dynamic population size in multiobjective evolutionary algorithms. In: Proceedings of the 2002 Congress on Evolutionary Computation, vol 2, pp 1648–1653.

Luh GC, Chueh CH, Liu WW (2003) MOIA: Multiobjective immune algorithm. Engineering Optimization 35(2):143–164.

Luus R, Hartig F, Keil FJ (1995) Optimal drug scheduling of cancer chemotherapy by direct search optimization. Hungarian Journal of Industrial Chemistry Veszprém 23:55–58.

Maciejowski JM (1989) Multivariable Feedback Design. Addison-Wesley, Reading, MA.

Madavan NK (2002) Multiobjective optimization using a Pareto differential evolution approach. In: Proceedings of the 2002 Congress on Evolutionary Computation, vol 2, pp 1145–1150.

Mahfoud SW (1995) Niching methods for genetic algorithms. Ph.D. thesis, University of Illinois, Urbana-Champaign.

Man KF, Tang KS, Kwong S, Halang WA (1998) Evolutionary Algorithms for Control and Signal Processing. Springer, NY.

Mao J, Hirasawa K, Hu J, Murata J (2001) Genetic symbiosis algorithm for multiobjective optimization problems. In: Proceedings of the Genetic and Evolutionary Computation Conference (GECCO-2001). Morgan Kaufmann Publishers, San Mateo, CA, p 771.

Marcu TA (1997) Multiobjective evolutionary approach to pattern recognition for robust diagnosis of process faults. In: International Conference on IFAC Fault Detection, Supervision and Safety for Technical Processes, pp 1183–1188.

Mariano CE, Morales EF (2000) Distributed reinforcement learning for multiple objective optimization problems. In: Proceedings of the 2000 Congress on Evolutionary Computation, vol 1, pp 188–194.

McMullen PR (2001) An ant colony optimization approach to addressing a JIT sequencing problem with multiple objectives. Artificial Intelligence in Engineering 15:309–317.

Merz P, Freisleben B (1998) On the effectiveness of evolutionary search in high-dimensional NK-landscape. In: Proceedings of the 1998 Congress on Evolutionary Computation, vol 1, pp 741–745.

Michalewicz Z, Schoenauer M (1996) Evolutionary algorithms for constrained parameter optimization problems. Evolutionary Computation 4(1):1–32.

Miller BL, Shaw MJ (1996) Genetic algorithms with dynamic niche sharing for multimodal function optimization. In: Proceedings of the 1996 Congress on Evolutionary Computation, pp 786–791.

Molyneaux AK, Leyland GB, Favrat D (2001) A new clustering evolutionary multiobjective optimization technique. In: Proceedings of the Third International Symposium on Adaptive Systems—Evolutionary Computation and Probabilistic Graphical Models. Institute of Cybernetics, Mathematics and Physics, Havana, Cuba, pp 41–47.

Moriarty DE (1997) Symbiotic evolution of neural networks in sequential decision tasks. Ph.D. thesis, The University of Texas at Austin.

Morse JN (1980) Reducing the size of the nondominated set: Pruning by clustering. Comput. Oper. Res. 7(1–2).

Murata T, Ishibuchi H (1995) MOGA: Multiobjective genetic algorithms. In: Proceedings of the 1995 Congress on Evolutionary Computation, vol 1, pp 289–294.

Murata T, Ishibuchi H (1996) Performance evaluation of genetic algorithms for flow shop scheduling problems. Computers and Industrial Engineering 30(4):1061–1071.

Neef M, Thierens D, Arciszewski H (1999) A case study of a multiobjective recombinative genetic algorithm with coevolutionary sharing. In: Proceedings of the 1999 Congress on Evolutionary Computation, pp 796–803.

Ng WY (1989) Interactive multiobjective programming as a framework for computer-aided control system design. Lecture Notes in Control and Information Sciences, Springer-Verlag, NY.

Nye WT, Tits AL (1986) An application-oriented, optimization-based methodology for interactive design of engineering systems. International Journal on Control 43:1693–1721.

Oliver IM, Smith DJ, Holland JRC (1987) A study of permutation crossover operators on the traveling salesman problem. In: Proceedings of the Second ICGA. Lawrence Erlbaum Associates, Hillsdaler, NJ, pp 224–230.

Osman IH, Christofides N (1989) Simulated annealing and descent algorithms for capacitated clustering problem. Research Report, Imperial College, University of London.

Osyczka A (1985) Multicriteria optimization for engineering design. In: , Gero JS (ed) Design Optimization. Academic Press, Cambridge, MA, pp 193–227.

Paquete LF, Fonseca CM (2001) A study of examination timetabling with multiobjective evolutionary algorithms. In: Metaheuristics International Conference. Porto, Portugal,

Pareto V (1896) Cours D'Economie Plitique. vol. 1 and 2, Lausanne:F. Rouge.

Parmee IC, Watson AH (1999) Preliminary airframe design using co-evolutionary multiobjective genetic algorithms. In: Proceedings of the Genetic and Evolutionary Computation Conference (GECCO'99), vol 2, pp 1657–1665.

Pétrowski A (1996) A clearing procedure as a niching method for genetic algorithms. In: Proceedings of the 1996 Congress on Evolutionary Computation. Nagoya, Japan, pp 798–803.

Pinaki M, Elizabeth MR (1999) Genetic algorithms for VLSI design, layout & test automation. Prentice-Hall, Englewood Cliffs, NJ.

Pohlheim H (1998) GEATbx: Genetic and evolutionary algorithm toolbox for use with Matlab—documentation and source. Technical Report.

Poloni C et al. (2000) Hybridization of a multiobjective genetic algorithm: A neural network and a classical optimizer for a complex design problem in fluid dynamics. Computer Methods in Applied Mechanics and Engineering 186(2–4):403–420.

Postlethwaite I, Lin JL, Gu DW (1991) Robust control of a high purity distillation column using Mu-K iteration. In: Proceedings of the 30th Conference on Decision and Control, pp 1586–1590.

Potter MA, De Jong KA (1994) A cooperative coevolutionary approach to function optimization. In: Proceedings of the Parallel Problem Solving from Nature III Conference (PPSN III). Berlin, Germany, pp 249–257.

Potter MA, De Jong KA (2000) Cooperative coevolution: An architecture for evolving coadapted subcomponents. Evolutionary Computation 8(1):1–29.

Potvin JY, Bengio S (1996) The vehicle routing problem with time windows—part II: Genetic search. INFORMS Journal on Computing 8(2):165–172.

Potvin JY, Kervahut T, Garcia B, Rousseau JM (1993) A Tabu search for the vehicle routing problem with time window. Technical Report CRT-855, Centre de Recherche sur les Transports, University de Montreal, Canada.

Potvin JY, Kervahut T, Garcia B, Rousseau JM (1996) The vehicle routing problem with time windows—part I: Tabu search. INFORMS Journal on Computing 8(2):158–164.

Pulido GT, Coello Coello CA (2003) The micro genetic algorithm 2: Towards online adaptation in evolutionary multiobjective optimization. In: Evolutionary Multi-Criterion Optimization: The Second International Conference (EMO2003). Springer, pp 252–266.

Rego C (2001) Node ejection chains for the vehicle routing problem: Sequential and parallel algorithms. Parallel Computing 27(3):201–222.

Rekiek B, Lit PD, Pellichero F, L'Eglise T, Falkenauer E, Delchambre A (2000) Dealing with user's preferences in hybrid assembly lines design. In: Proceedings of the MCPI'2000 Conference.

Richardson JT, Palmer MR, Liepins G, Hilliard M (1989) Some guidelines for genetic algorithms with penalty functions. In: Schaffer JD (ed) Proceedings of the 3rd International Conference on Genetic Algorithms. Morgan Kaufmann, San Mateo, CA, pp 191–197.

Ritzel BJ, Eheart JW, Ranjithan S (1994) Using genetic algorithms to solve a multi objective groundwater pollution containment problem. Water Resources Research 30:1589–1603.

Rivera W (2001) Scalable parallel genetic algorithms. Artificial Intelligence Review 16:153–168.

Rochat Y, Tailard ED (1995) Probabilistic diversification and intensification in local search for vehicle routing problem. Journal of Heuristics 1(1):147–167.

Romero CEM, Manzanares EM (1999) MOAQ and Ant-Q algorithm for multiple objective optimization problems. In: Banzhaf W, Daida J, Eiben AE, Garzon MH, Honavar V, Jakiela M, Smith RE (eds) Genetic and Evolutionary Computing Conference (GECCO 99). Morgan Kaufmann, San Francisco, vol 1, pp 894–901.

Rosin CD, Belew RK (1997) New methods for competitive coevolution. Evolutionary Computation 5(1):1–29.

Rousseau LM, Gendreau M, Pesant G (2002) Using constraint-based operators to solve the vehicle routing with time windows. Journal of Heuristics 8(1):43–58.

Sait SM, Youssef H, Ali H (1999) Fuzzy simulated evolution algorithm or multiobjective optimization of VLSI placement. In: Proceedings of the 1999 Congress on Evolutionary Computation, vol 1, pp 91–97.

Sakawa M, Yauchi K (2001) An interactive fuzzy satisficing method for multiobjective nonconvex programming problems with fuzzy numbers through coevolutionary genetic algorithms. IEEE Transactions on Systems, Man and Cybernetics, Part B 31(3):459–467.

Sakawa M, Kato K, Shibano T (1996) An interactive fuzzy satisfying method for multiobjective multidimensional 0-1 knapsack problems through genetic algorithms. In: Proceedings of the 1996 Congress on Evolutionary Computation, pp 243–246.

Sandgren E (1994) Multicriteria design optimization by goal programming. In: Adeli H (ed) Advances in Design Optimization. Chapman & Hall, London, pp 225–265.

Savelsbergh MWP (1985) Local search for routing problems with time windows. Annals of Operations Research 4:285–305.

Sbalzarini IF, Müller S, Koumoutsakos P (2001) Microchannel optimization using multiobjective evolution strategies. In: First International Conference on Evolutionary Multi-Criterion Optimization. Springer-Verlag, NY, pp 516–530.

Schaffer JD (1985). Multiple objective optimization with vector evaluated genetic algorithms. In: Proceedings of the First International Conference on Genetic Algorithms: Genetic Algorithms and their Applications. Lawrence Erlbaum, pp 93–100.

Schaffer JD, Caruana RA, Eshelman LJ, Das R (1989) A study of control parameters affecting online performance of genetic algorithms for function optimization. In: Proceedings of the 3rd International Conference on Genetic Algorithms, pp 51–60.

Schroder P, Chipperfield AJ, Fleming PJ, Grum N (1997) Multiobjective optimization of distributed active magnetic bearing controllers. In: Conference on Genetic Algorithms in Engineering Systems: Innovations and Applications, pp 13–18.

Schulze J, Fahle T (1999) A parallel algorithm for the vehicle routing problem with time window constraints. Annals of Operations Research 86:585–607.

Schütze O, Mostaghim S, Dellnitz M, Teich J (2003) Covering Pareto sets by multilevel evolutionary subdivision techniques. In: Evolutionary Multicriterion Optimization: The Second International Conference (EMO2003), Lecture Notes in Computer Science 2632. Springer-Verlag, pp 118–132.

Sefrioui M, Periaux J (2000) Nash genetic algorithms: Examples and applications. In: Proceedings of the 2000 Congress on Evolutionary Computation, vol 1, pp 509–516.

Shaw P (1998) Using constraint programming and local search methods to solve vehicle routing problems. In: Maher M, Puget JF (eds) Principles and Practice of Constraint Programming—CP98, Lecture Notes in Computer Science. Springer-Verlag, NY, pp 417–431.

Shaw KJ, Notcliffe AL, Thompson M, Love J, Fonseca CM, Fleming PJ (1999) Assessing the performance of multiobjective genetic algorithms for optimization of batch process scheduling problem. In: Proceedings of the 1999 Congress on Evolutionary Computation, vol 1, pp 37–45.

Silva VVR, Fleming PJ (1998) Multiobjective nonlinear robust control design for gas turbine engines using evolutionary computing. In: Proceedings of Mathematical Theory Networks Systems Conference, pp 1087–1090.

Skogestad S, Postlethwaite I (1996) Multivariable Feedback Control: Analysis and Design. John Wiley & Sons Ltd, West Sussex, England.

Skogestad S, Morari M, Doyle J (1989) Robust control of ill-conditioned plants: High-purity distillation. IEEE Transactions on Automatic Control 33(12):672–681.

Smith RE (1993) Adaptively resizing populations: An algorithm and analysis. In: Forrest S (ed) Proceedings of the Fifth International Conference on Genetic Algorithms. Morgan Kaufmann Publishers, Los Altos, CA, p 653.

Snell SA, Hess RA (1997) Robust, decoupled, flight control design with rate saturating actuators. In: Conference and Exhibition on AIAA Atmospheric Flight Mechanics, pp 733–745.

Socha K, Kisiel-Dorohinicki M (2002) Agent-based evolutionary multiobjective optimization. In: Proceedings of the 2002 Congress on Evolutionary Computation, vol 1, pp 109–114.

Solich R (1969) Zadanie Programowania Liniowego Z Wieloma Funkcjami Celu (Linear Programming Problem with Several Objective Functions). Przeglad Statystyczny 16 (in Polish), pp 24–30.

Solomon MM (1987) Algorithms for vehicle routing and scheduling problem with time window constraints. Operations Research 35(2):254–265.

Srinivas N, Deb K (1994) Multiobjective optimization using nondominated sorting in genetic algorithms. Journal of Evolutionary Computation 2(3):221–248.

Steuer J (1986) Multicriteria Optimization: Theory, Computation, and Application. John Wiley, NY.

Stoorvogel A (1992) Control Problem: A State-Space Approach. Prentice-Hall, Englewood Cliffs, NJ.

Tagami T, Kawabe T (1999) Genetic algorithm based on a Pareto neighbor search for multiobjective optimization. In: Proceedings of the 1999 International Symposium of Nonlinear Theory and Its Applications (NOLTA'99), pp 331–334.

Taillard E, Badeau P, Gendreau M, Guertin F, Potvin JY (1997) A tabu search heuristic for the vehicle routing problem with soft time windows. Transportation Science 31(2):170–186.

Tan KC, Li Y (1997) Multiobjective genetic algorithm based time and frequency domain design unification of control systems. In: IFAC International Symposium on Artificial Intelligence in Real-Time Control, pp 61–66.

Tan KC, Li Y (2000) Evolutionary L-inf identification and model reduction for robust control. Proc. I. Mech. E., Part I, 214:231–237.

Tan, KC, Lee TH, Khor EF (1999a) Control system design automation with robust tracking thumbprint performance using a multiobjective evolutionary algorithm. In: IEEE International Conference on Control Applications and System Design, pp 498–503.

Tan, KC, Lee TH, Khor EF (1999b) Evolutionary algorithms with goal and priority information for multiobjective optimization. In: Proceedings of the 1999 Congress on Evolutionary Computation, vol 1, pp 106–113.

Tan, KC, Khor EF, Lee TH (2001a) Exploratory multiobjective evolutionary algorithm: Performance study and comparisons. In: Genetic and Evolutionary Computation Conference, San Francisco, CA, pp 647–654.

Tan, KC, Lee TH, Khor EF (2001b) Automating design of multivariable QFT control system via evolutionary computation. Proc. I. Mech. E., Part I, 215:245–259.

Tan, KC, Lee TH, Khor EF (2001c) Evolutionary algorithm with dynamic population size and local exploration for multiobjective optimization. IEEE Transactions on Evolutionary Computation 5(6):565–588.

Tan, KC, Lee TH, Khor EF (2001d) Incrementing multiobjective evolutionary algorithms: Performance studies and comparisons. In: International Conference on Evolutionary Multicriteria Optimization (EMO'01), pp 111–125.

Tan, KC, Lee TH, Khoo D, Khor EF (2001e) A multiobjective evolutionary algorithm toolbox for computer-aided multiobjective optimization. IEEE Transactions on System, Man and Cybernetics Part B, 31(4):537–556.

Tan KC, Lee TH, Zhu QL, Ou K (2001f) Heuristic methods for vehicle routing problem with time windows. Artificial Intelligence in Engineering 15(3):281–295.

Tan KC, Lee TH, Ou K (2001g) Hybrid genetic algorithms in solving vehicle routing problems with time window constraints. Asia-Pacific Journal of Operational Research, 18(1):121–130.

Tan KC, Lee LH, Ou K (2001h) Artificial intelligence techniques in solving vehicle routing problems with time window constraints. Engineering Applications of Artificial Intelligence 14:825–837.

Tan KC, Lee TH, Ou K, Lee LH (2001i) A messy genetic algorithm for the vehicle routing problem with time window constraints. In: Proceedings of the 2001 Congress on Evolutionary Computation, pp 679–686.

Tan KC, Lee TH, Khor EF (2002a) Evolutionary algorithms for multiobjective optimization: Performance assessments and comparisons. Artificial Intelligence Review 17(4):251–290.

Tan KC, Khor EF, Cai J, Heng CM, Lee TH (2002b) Automating the drug scheduling of cancer chemotherapy via evolutionary computation. Artificial Intelligence in Medicine 25:169–185.

Tan KC, Tay A, Cai J (2003a) Design and implementation of a distributed evolutionary computing software. IEEE Transactions on Systems, Man and Cybernetics—Part C 33(3):325–338.

Tan KC, Khor EF, Lee TH, Sathikannan R (2003b) An evolutionary algorithm with advanced goal and priority specification for multiobjective optimization. Journal of Artificial Intelligence Research 18:183–215.

Tavares J, Pereira FB, Machado P, Costa E (2003) On the influence of GVR in vehicle routing. In: ACM Symposium on Applied Computing (SAC 2003). Florida.

Thangiah SR, Osman IH, Sun T (1994) Hybrid genetic algorithm, simulated annealing and Tabu search methods for vehicle routing problems with time windows. Technical Report SRU CpSc-TR-94-27, Computer Science Department, Slippery Rock University.

Thangiah SR (1995) An adaptive clustering method using a geometric shape for vehicle routing problems with time windows. In: The Sixth International Conference on Genetics Algorithm, vol 1, pp 452–459.

The Math Works, Inc. (1998) Using MATLAB, version 5.

The Math Works, Inc. (1999) Simulink: User's Guide, version 3.

Thierens D, Bosman PAN (2001) Multiobjective mixture-based iterated density estimation evolutionary algorithms. In: Proceedings of the Genetic and Evolutionary Computation Conference (GECCO'2001). Morgan Kaufmann Publishers, San Mateo, CA, pp 663–670.

Thompson DF, Nwokah ODI (1994) Analytical loop-shaping methods in quantitative feedback theory. Journal of Dynamic Systems, Measurement and Control 116:169–177.

Thompson HA, Fleming PJ (1999) An integrated multidisciplinary optimisation environment for distributed aero-engine control system architectures. In: Proceedings 14th World Congress of International Federation of Automatic Control, pp 407–412.

Toth P, Vigo D (2002) The Vehicle Routing Problem. SIAM, Philadelphia.

Valenzuela-Rendón M, Uresti-Charre E (1997) A non-generational genetic algorithm for multiobjective optimization. In: Proceedings of the Seventh International Conference on Genetic Algorithms. Morgan Kauffmann, San Francisco, CA, pp 658–665.

Van Veldhuizen DA, Lamont GB (1998a) Evolutionary computation and convergence to a Pareto front. In: Koza JR (ed) Late Breaking Papers at the Genetic Programming 1998 Conference. Stanford University Bookstore, CA, pp 221–228.

Van Veldhuizen DA, Lamont GB (1998b) Multiobjective evolutionary algorithm research: A history and analysis. Technical Report TR-98-03, Department of Electrical and Computer Engineering, Air Force Institute of Technology, Ohio.

Van Veldhuizen DA, Lamont GB (1999) Multiobjective evolutionary algorithm test suites. In: Symposium on Applied Computing, San Antonio, TX, pp 351–357.

Van Veldhuizen DA, Lamont GB (2000) Multiobjective evolutionary algorithms: Analyzing the state-of-the-art. Journal of Evolutionary Computation 8(2):125–147.

Vavak F, Jukes K, Fogarty TC (1997) Learning the local search range for genetic optimization in nonstationary environments. In: Proceedings of the 1997 Congress on Evolutionary Computation, pp 355–360.

Vemuri VR, Cedeino W (1995) A new genetic algorithm for multiobjective optimization in water resource management. In: Proceedings of the 1995 Congress on Evolutionary Computation, vol 1, pp 495–500.

Venkat R, Mandava J, Fitzpatrick M, Pickens DR (1989) Adaptive search space scaling in digital image registration. IEEE Transactions on Medical Imaging 8(3):251–262.

Viennet R, Fonteix C, Marc I (1996) Multicriteria optimization using a genetic algorithm for determining a Pareto set. International Journal of Systems Science 27(2):255–260.

Voget S, Kolonko M (1998) Multidimensional optimization with a fuzzy genetic algorithm. Journal of Heuristics 4(3):221–244.

Weerasooriya S, Phan DT (1995) Discrete time LQG/LTR design and modeling of a disk drive actuator tracking servo system. IEEE Trans. on Ind. Elecs. 42(3):240–247.

Weerasooriya S (1996) The Basic Servo Problem Technical Report. Data Storage Institute, National University of Singapore, Singapore.

Whitley D, Starkweather T, Fuquay D (1989) Scheduling problems and traveling salesmen: The genetic edge recombination operator. In: Third International Conference on Genetic Algorithms. Morgan Kaufmann, San Mateo, CA, pp 133–140.

Wilson PB, Macleod MD (1993) Low implementation cost IIR digital filter design using genetic algorithms. In: IEE/IEEE Workshop on Natural Algorithms in Signal Processing. Chelmsford, UK, pp 4/1–4/8.

Wolpert D, Macready G (1996) No free lunch theorems for optimization. IEEE Transactions on Evolutionary Computation 1(1):67–82.

Yaniv O, Schwartz B (1990) A criterion for loop stability in the horowitz synthesis of MIMO feedback systems. International Journal of Control 53(3):527–539.

Yaniv O, Horowitz I (1986) A quantitative design method for MIMO linear feedback system having uncertain plants. International Journal of Control 43(2):401–421.

Yellow P (1970) A computational modification to the saving method of vehicle scheduling. Operational Research Quart. 21(2):281–283.

Yen JY, Hallamasek K, Horowitz R (1990) Track-following controller designs of a compound disk drive actuator. J. Dyn. Syst. Meas. and Contr. 112:391–402.

Yokose Y, Cingoski V, Kaneda K, Yamashita H (1999) Shape optimization of magnetic devices using genetic algorithms with dynamically adjustable parameters. IEEE Transactions on Magnetics 35(3):1686–1689.

Zames G (1966) On the input–output stability of time-varying non-linear feedback systems, parts I and II. IEEE Transactions on Automatic Control, AC-11, 2 & 3, pp. 228-238 & 465–476.

Zbigniew CJ, Piotr C (2001) Parallel simulated annealing for the vehicle routing problem with time windows. Technical report, Silesia University of Technology.

Zhao C, Brizuela A, Sannomiya N (2001) Application of the partial enumeration selection method in genetic algorithms to solving a multiobjective flowshop problem. In: IEEE International Conference on Systems, Man, and Cybernetics, vol 4, pp 2365–2370.

Zhou T, Kimura H (1991) Controller design of ill-conditioned plant using robust stability degree assignment. In: Proceedings of the 30th Conference on Decision and Control, pp 1591–1595.

Zhuang N, Benten MS, Cheung PY (1996) Improved variable ordering of BDDS with novel genetic algorithm. In: IEEE International Symposium on Circuits and Systems, vol 3, pp 414–417.

Zitzler E, Thiele L (1999) Multiobjective evolutionary algorithms: A comparative case study and the strength Pareto approach. IEEE Transactions on Evolutionary Computation 3(4):257–271.

Zitzler E, Deb K, Thiele L (2000) Comparison of multiobjective evolutionary algorithms: Empirical results. Evolutionary Computation 8(2):173–195.

Zitzler E, Laumanns M, Thiele L (2001) SPEA2: Improving the strength Pareto evolutionary algorithm. Technical Report 103, Computer Engineering and Networks Laboratory (TIK), Swiss Federal Institute of Technology (ETH), Zurich, Switzerland.

Index